Experiencing
CORRECTIONS

Experiencing
CORRECTIONS

FROM PRACTITIONER
TO PROFESSOR

Edited by
LEE MICHAEL JOHNSON
University of West Georgia

Los Angeles | London | New Delhi
Singapore | Washington DC

Los Angeles | London | New Delhi
Singapore | Washington DC

FOR INFORMATION:

SAGE Publications, Inc.
2455 Teller Road
Thousand Oaks, California 91320
E-mail: order@sagepub.com

SAGE Publications Ltd.
1 Oliver's Yard
55 City Road
London EC1Y 1SP
United Kingdom

SAGE Publications India Pvt. Ltd.
B 1/I 1 Mohan Cooperative Industrial Area
Mathura Road, New Delhi 110 044
India

SAGE Publications Asia-Pacific Pte. Ltd.
33 Pekin Street #02-01
Far East Square
Singapore 048763

Acquisitions Editor: Jerry Westby
Editorial Assistant: Erim Sarbuland
Production Editor: Karen Wiley
Copy Editor: Patricia Sutton
Typesetter: C&M Digitals (P) Ltd.
Proofreader: Gail Fay
Indexer: Jeanne Busemeyer
Cover Designer: Candice Harman
Marketing Manager: Erica DeLuca

Printed in the United States of America

Library of Congress Cataloging-in-Publication Data

Experiencing corrections: From practitioner to professor / edited by Lee Michael Johnson.

p. cm.

Includes bibliographical references and index.

ISBN 978-1-4129-8847-6 (pbk.)

1. Corrections. 2. Educational sociology. I. Johnson, Lee Michael.

HV8665.E975 2012 364.6—dc22 2010046431

This book is printed on acid-free paper.

11 12 13 14 15 10 9 8 7 6 5 4 3 2 1

Brief Contents

Detailed Contents

Preface

This book is a collection of essays written by professors with practical experience in corrections. It was written to help bridge the gap between academia and practice. Its main purpose is to support teaching and learning activities that integrate vicarious and experiential learning in corrections. Few outlets are offered to social scientists desiring to publish scholarly works using their personal experiences. This is unfortunate given that personal employment experiences of scholars constitute a valuable resource for making concrete connections between academics and practice. Directly experiencing "each world" increases the scholar's ability to identify these connections. Creating this book served as an opportunity for professors to conduct scholarly analyses using personal experiences and to counter the impression that academic scholars are "out of touch" with the real world. It is offered to help readers develop their abilities to connect scholarship and practice and, by doing so, increase their power to improve practice and make corrections work more rewarding.

Getting students to make meaningful connections between course work and "the real world" is important to most teachers, but finding materials that help students make these connections can be difficult. As most students understand, applying academics and practice to one another is a complicated task; the connections are often not readily apparent. Like other important abilities that students are expected to acquire, such as writing and data analysis skills, conceptualizing connections between academics and practice is an ability that teachers must develop in students. One method frequently used by instructors is drawing from past experiences to help explain lecture material, which is attractive because the concreteness and familiarity of personal examples make concepts clearer to students. This book employs the same general strategy but in a more involved and structured way; it gives readers written detailed descriptions that they can carefully analyze.

This book is intended primarily for adoption in college level general corrections courses. Since the essays are narratives written in first person, the book is highly "readable"—comprehendible at all college levels. It is complementary to a number of corrections books, including most introductory texts. The book is useful for students in criminology and criminal justice and social work programs, especially those aspiring to work in a corrections field, along with current practitioners. Because authors demonstrate how to connect academics with practice, the book could also be used in internship, practicum, and some social work courses. Also, while the essays are elegantly written, they are the personal reflections of accomplished scholars and thus contain insights appropriate for advanced study. On the graduate level, the book would work well alone or with another book in courses on correctional treatment and counseling, professional applications, and special topics. Finally, the essays contain useful and citable information, such as anecdotal evidence, that may be of interest to other scholars and current practitioners.

This book has unique features intended to make it an important contribution to criminal justice literature. Few books focus on the use of personal experience in studying and teaching corrections. This book reviews academic and practice knowledge garnered by individuals who have been correctional practitioners and are now academic scholars. The essays contain authors' valuable and insightful reflections on their efforts to achieve important objectives while they were employed in the field. Authors use their real world experiences to explain and illustrate theoretical and methodological concepts and to demonstrate approaches to practice. In retrospectively applying concepts and perspectives to corrections, the authors contribute significantly to the development of a marriage between academics and practice.

While the essays are diverse with regard to topics, writing style, and specific organization, each author includes pertinent background information, an overview of the workplace, a narrative of experiences, and conclusions or implications based on the experiences. Spanning the three general types of correctional environments—incarceration, community corrections, and juvenile corrections—the collection of essays discusses working in prisons or prison systems, probation and parole, and juvenile residential and community corrections.

Each essay tells an interesting and important story. The essays go beyond simple storytelling, however, as discussions of experiences are grounded in scholarship. At the same time, they keep academic and professional jargon to a minimum and avoid excessive citation. The essays are necessarily subjective, containing a great deal of advocacy and critique, but arguments are based on concrete experience and scholarly analysis. It is not the intention of this book as a whole to advocate any particular views or opinions, nor to dictate practice, but to use practical experience to illustrate concepts and demonstrate how to connect academics and practice. Additionally, although the authors are very frank and straightforward in narrating, evaluating, and contextualizing their experiences, the book is intended to be optimistic. It is intended to help prepare future corrections workers by giving them a view into the many possible challenges in this type of work, not to make them pessimistic about working in corrections.

This book's readability and "real life" analyses will help instructors generate student interest and involvement in their courses, helping those that find it difficult to see the practical relevance of academic knowledge. The essays put a "human face" on the study of corrections, without sacrificing learning quality (without "dummying down" material). They bring core corrections books to life by offering real life professional experiences and concept applications. Students may enjoy the book's personal touch and appreciate its relevance to their career interests. This book simultaneously serves two important instructional purposes that may often seem contradictory to students: disseminate academic knowledge and prepare them for the professional workforce.

The book contains three special pedagogical features. First, each essay chapter begins with an Editor's Introduction written to prepare readers to learn from the essay. These introductions identify general points in each essay regarding the author's work, challenges faced, type of scholarship applied, and overall lesson. Second, each chapter, including the introduction and conclusion, ends with three discussion questions. These are designed to assist instructors in developing group discussions, assignments, and exams or quizzes and assist students with a study aid for digesting the material in the chapter. Third, each chapter, including the introduction and conclusion, also ends with author recommended related readings. These are intended to help students further explore the subjects of the essays, providing them with possible sources for papers and instructors with possible additional readings to assign.

❖ ACKNOWLEDGMENTS

Let me begin by saying thanks to all of the contributors for making this book happen. It was an honor and a pleasure to work with you. I am thankful for the opportunity to gather your work into this volume, and I learned much from your essays. Next, thanks go to Jeff Ross, John Fuller, Michael Braswell, and Jerry Westby for their encouragement and much needed assistance in helping me develop a clear vision and viable proposal for the book. Also, thanks go to reviewers for providing constructive criticism and suggestions that led to significant improvements throughout the book. Finally, thanks go to Ellen M. Coenen, Esq., for her thoughtful and helpful reviews of my chapters.

1

Introduction

*Connecting Academics and Practice
in Corrections*

Lee Michael Johnson

T he essays to follow are written by professors with practical experience in corrections. Each essay contains the author's valuable and insightful reflections on their efforts to achieve important objectives while employed in the field. Like academia, the workplace is an environment in which important knowledge is produced and disseminated. The advantage of drawing from academic scholars with practical experience in corrections is that they can combine "real world" and academic knowledge and show the relevance between the two. The authors use their real world experiences to illustrate theoretical and methodological concepts and to demonstrate approaches to practice. In retrospectively applying their theories and perspectives to corrections, the authors contribute to the development of a bridge between academic scholarship and practice.

This first chapter is designed to introduce the reader to the book's two main tasks. First, it seeks to establish the value of integrating course work and practice by discussing some of the key benefits, difficulties, and general strategies involved in making connections between academics and practice. Second, it provides a preview by describing the general nature and purposes of the collection of essays, including an identification of the types of issues covered by the authors.

❖ THE VALUE OF INTEGRATING ACADEMICS AND PRACTICE

Many if not most educators, professionals, and students would agree that it is important to be able to make connections between academic course work and everyday life, including professional practice. Instead of simply hoping that students will find a way to apply what they have learned in school after graduation, their abilities to use academic knowledge in practice must be cultivated while they are still in school. Relating concepts taught in courses to real world scenarios in assignments, tests, and other activities is good practice for applying them "for real" at work and in other environments. It cannot be assumed that the ability to make connections between academics and practice comes naturally. It can be difficult to make connections between what is learned in courses and what happens in practice even in studies oriented more toward professional practice. For example, social work students may find it difficult to see the relevance of theory to their experiences at internship or practicum sites (partly because of conflicting goals between the agencies and the academic discipline), even though making theory–practice connections seems to be one of the main purposes of such programs (Lewis & Bolzan, 2007). Also, students have their own backgrounds and theoretical orientations that may clash with some of the people they work with or under when entering the field, which could create interference or lack of support in attempts to connect academics and practice. Thus, to truly understand the usefulness of connecting academics to practice, studies must also be directed toward learning *how* to apply academics to practice and vice versa, not just *about* academic and practice subjects. The authors of this collection of essays assist here by exhibiting some connections between scholarship and practice.

Often, the relevance of social scientific concepts to practice is not immediately obvious. For example, one of the contributors to this volume, N. Prabha Unnithan, points out in an earlier article (1999) that it can be difficult to make connections between abstract criminology and criminal justice policy, although they can become clear upon a careful examination of the relationships between certain theories and policy types. ("Get tough" policies, for instance, are based in deterrence or rational choice and "just desserts" punishment theories.) Policies and programs created to deal with crime have their foundation in some kind of crime causation theory, and social research methods are used to test their effectiveness (Unnithan, 1999). It is important for students to understand the relevance of criminology to practice, but intensive steps must be taken to make connections between the two clearer. To achieve this goal, instructors use various methods to bring discussions of practice into course work. These methods include analyses of policy-relevant readings and assignments that require students to make the connections between criminological theory and criminal justice policy. For application assignments and reading materials intended to connect coursework with practice to work, however, they must be embraced (Unnithan, 1999). Often, instructors hear the complaint that information taught in their courses, such as theory, is not relevant or useful to real life or prospective careers. This view may be supported by organizational cultures wherein academic knowledge clashes with workplace norms, values, beliefs, and objectives. While educators, professionals, and students equally share the burden of making academics practical, students will hopefully be open to the possibility that it is the reluctance to learn academic material and how to apply it that ultimately renders it useless to some people.

Stohr (1999) argues that a partnership between academics and practice can improve ethical behavior in corrections. Professor Stohr reveals that while she was an undergraduate criminal justice student, she did not fully realize the relevance of her ethics studies to employment in corrections. Later, after working as a correctional officer and prison counselor, she experienced this relevance firsthand: "On virtually a daily basis at the prison, I was faced with both minor and/or major ethical considerations" (p. 91). These considerations included ensuring the consistent and fair treatment of inmates and reporting violations by "friendly" inmates as well and by reporting verbally abusive staff, racist comments by supervisors, harassment (sexual and otherwise), staff's failure to perform duties, and supervisory approaches that threaten security (Stohr, 1999, p. 91). While Professor Stohr admits that at times she struggled to make the right choices, she believes that her professors helped forearm her to confront ethical dilemmas. Her experiences thus have very important implications regarding the connection between theory and practice. When thinking abstractly about how we will conduct ourselves in our prospective careers or not thinking about it at all, we may assume that because we are good people, we will do the "right thing" and clearly know what the right thing is. However, without some kind of early practice struggling with ethical issues and other matters presented in criminal justice courses, students remain inadequately prepared for the challenges of the workplace. Indeed, the process of transforming formal book knowledge into practical knowledge begins while one is _ ··· ·- school, especially if the formal knowledge is being applied to authentic problem solving (Collin & Tynjälä, 2003). Thus, as Stohr (1999) demonstrates, academics have much to offer in promoting ethical conduct in work environments, which means very real benefits for both staff and management.

Some academic subjects have more direct relevance to the workplace, including ethics and social scientific studies of organizational environments and their broader institutional contexts. Workers who understand the social structures in place and social processes operating beyond their immediate positions and specific organizational units (departments or programs, for example) are better prepared for career success and making beneficial contributions to the organization and community. It is important to avoid approaching practical experience with tunnel vision, concentrating merely on the duties of one's job and the functioning of one's unit. This principle seems to be apparent in Gordon and McBride's (2008) *Criminal Justice Internships: Theory Into Practice*, a popular text used to prepare students to learn from their internships, including making connections between academics and practice. In this book, three chapters in particular cover subjects that place practical experiences within larger philosophical and social scientific contexts. Ethics are covered in Chapter 8, including discussions of corruption, misconduct, quality of job performance, confidentiality, appropriate interpersonal relationships, reporting unethical behavior, the role of personal values, and, generally, ensuring justice and fairness in the criminal justice system. Organizational structures (formal and informal), a topic of great interest to sociologists and social psychologists who study formal organizations, are covered in Chapter 9. Noting that organizational variables affect group and individual behavior, the authors spend much of the chapter applying pioneering sociologist

Max Weber's "ideal type" organizational framework to two hypothetical criminal justice agencies (one public, one private). In Chapter 10, the author draws from the disciplines of political science, economics, and law to discuss topics such as politics and power, globalization, budgeting, legislation, and social control. The subjects covered in these three chapters are those that criminal justice–social science students will likely come across several times before graduating.

Social scientific knowledge has important implications for practice and policy; it is relevant to the real world of work if persons actually employ it and do so wisely. But practice also informs scholarship, creating a reciprocal relationship between academics and practice. As McNeill (2000) argues, theory and practice should "interrogate" one another. This interrogation must be localized, meaning that the relevance of one to the other must be viewed within each unique context in which practice takes place. The people, places, variables, and relevant theories that are present across situations are very diverse, so while some patterns can be found across contexts, theoretical-practical understandings that emerge in some situations may not apply to others (at least not without modification). According to McNeill (2000), "criminology performs a service for practitioners by sharpening their grasp of the relationships between values, understandings of crime and criminalisation, policy and practice responses to them, and evidence of the effectiveness of these responses" (p. 113) while practice in turn offers criminology "the detail and depth of individual and local experience" (p. 113).

In corrections, several offending reduction strategies target the possible causes of crime; by eliminating or neutralizing the *criminogenic* factors acting on some individuals, it is hoped that they will discontinue offending. Many of these strategies are influenced, at least in part, by theories proposing causes of crime. If these strategies work, if they lead to beneficial outcomes, theories on which they are based can be validated to some extent, but if they do not work (or do not work very well), then the theoretical bases must be reevaluated. Hence, theory influences practice, and practice in turn influences theory. People working with offenders serve important social welfare and justice functions by working to reduce harm to victims, potential victims, and offenders (McNeill, 2000). In doing such work, however, one may slip into becoming concerned only with administrative routines that maintain criminal justice systems (not that these are unimportant) and not the causes of crime and what to do about them. Criminology enables practitioners working with offenders "to think differently about their work and to develop their practice" (McNeill, 2000, p. 108).

Practice and academics not only inform one another but also overlap. In fact, one does not have to work as a teacher or researcher in a collegiate setting *to be* a criminologist, political scientist, anthropologist, sociologist, psychologist, and so on. The work of some field professionals is defined by the practice of academic disciplines, making them *practicing* criminologists, political scientists, anthropologists, sociologists, psychologists, and so on. The common ground between academics and practice should not be surprising. The study of human behavior and society for the sake of solving real world problems has been a cornerstone of social scientific disciplines, such as sociology, since their early development. Social scientists working primarily in academic settings also tend to be quite concerned with the applicability of their work to solving problems, and many are making deliberate attempts to increase the applied value of their disciplines to meet the needs of current populations (Ruggiero & Weston, 1991).

Because they use social scientific knowledge extensively in the field, social science practitioners are in a strong position to recognize and discuss the practical value of academic disciplines. Practicing sociologists who participated in a survey conducted by Ruggiero and Weston (1991) identified academic topics, including deviance, social control, and criminal justice, as relevant to their work and stressed that it is important for students to learn about practicing sociology and be exposed to examples. It was clear that they perceived that their work fit into many of the subjects traditionally taught in introductory sociology courses. The practitioners identified "what sociological practice is really like," "the importance of research and theory for practice," and "the fundamentals of sociology" as the most important issues to be taught to introductory sociology students (Ruggiero & Weston, 1991, p. 216). Further, they considered three aspects of what sociological practice is really like to be especially important for students: "that practice can have a positive impact on society and often is oriented toward social change," "that there is a wide variety of potential applications," and "that sociological practice actually exists and one can be a sociologist outside academic settings" (Ruggiero & Weston, 1991, p. 216). In many cases, college students will not become formal practitioners of the disciplines they study. Still, social science coursework is based on the hope that all students taking social science courses, in some way, will become social science practitioners—that they will use their studies to improve their performance at work and make contributions to society.

Integrating school-based and work-based learning, theory, and practice, for example, is essential in developing expertise in one's employment field. More specifically, actively engaging in problem solving is the key to being able to use formal educational knowledge in the workplace (Collin & Tynjälä, 2003). While students may value the knowledge they are gaining in their courses and hold the belief that it has the potential to be applied in practice, how to use this knowledge to solve problems in the workplace may not be readily apparent (Collin & Tynjälä, 2003). Real life examples of persons applying academic knowledge to practical problem solving, both successful and unsuccessful, can be helpful to students developing their problem-solving abilities.

In addition to internship and practicum work experience, there are a variety of ways that real world knowledge of the field may be brought into course work—for example, field trips, guest speakers, service learning projects, and brief experiences in practical settings (such as police ride-alongs). These learning strategies are effective ways to demonstrate the concepts being taught in the course and therefore bridge theory and practice, and they help students make more informed career choices (Payne, Sumter, & Sun, 2003). By using practical experience to illustrate theoretical and methodological concepts and research trends, it is easier to see the connection between academics and practice. (Robert F. Meier and Teresa F. Smith cover internships and experiential learning in-depth in Chapter 16.)

Further, professors and instructors often bring practical knowledge into their courses using their own field experiences. College teachers have extensive formal educational backgrounds. Much of the knowledge that they impart in courses stems from their own formal learning experiences. However, like anyone else, they have also learned from workplace experiences. Many were at one time in the same position as their students participating in internships or practicum or working in jobs related to their studies. Their experiences often have a great deal of relevance to the material taught in courses, such as when an event or situation can or cannot be explained by a theory, illustrates a concept, or is consistent with or an exception to a research trend. A teacher's practical experience is therefore a very valuable teaching resource. Drawing from personal experience has at least three benefits: It helps capture students' attention by adding a "human touch" to lectures, provides concrete examples to help clarify concepts, and offers students insights into potential areas of work. Thus, students can benefit from the practical experiences of their teachers as well.

❖ A PREVIEW OF THE ESSAYS

This collection of essays offers another way to bring the field into course work. The authors use their personal experiences to help teach academic knowledge. The book is a blend of a more traditional way to present course material (readings from a book) with a more real world approach, as each author is a type of presenter with personal experience in the field. The reciprocal relationship between academics and practice is inherent throughout the essays, as they provide students with knowledge that can be related to the field but do so by applying practical experience to the academic study of corrections. As stated earlier, problem solving is essential to making connections between academics and practice. The authors of the essays often discuss their attempts to solve problems at the workplace and explicitly or implicitly offer possible solutions to current problems. While the authors identify several problems in corrections work, it should be noted that the book has optimistic intentions.

Often, when professors and instructors create activities intended to help students make connections between course work and practice, they require students to report on practical experiences and find common ground between academics and practice. This book does the opposite: Professors report on *their* experiences and place them within scholarly frameworks. The essays also exemplify how to learn from personal experience—how to use personal experiences as evidence of reality without making false generalizations. The authors apply general theories, principles, and empirical trends as frameworks for understanding their experiences (reason deductively, from the general to the specific), while avoiding the opposite—making broad generalizations based on their unique personal experiences. Their discussions of their experiences are grounded in scholarship; the essays go beyond simple storytelling, although each tells an interesting and important story. While the essays contain a great deal of advocacy and critique, arguments are based on concrete experience and scholarly analysis.

Throughout the essays, authors tackle questions such as the following:

- What challenges or problems arose in dealing with correctional clients or employees? What ethical concerns did you have? Were you properly prepared to deal with offenders? What might have you done differently?

- What was your initial experience like? Did the assumptions that you had about working in corrections turn out to be realistic? Did you have to modify your approach to your work?

- What specific strategies or general approaches to treatment, management, or administration did you use and were they effective? Were there any theories or perspectives supported or negated by personal experiences?

- Which harmful and/or helpful conditions and situations did you experience? Which conditions and/or situations inhibited or facilitated your efforts?

- What intrapersonal tools did you use to cope with your correctional experience? How did you relieve stress, deal with frustrations, and handle the many contradictions inherent in a corrections job?

- What kinds of empirical issues did you encounter? How did your experiences compare to broader research trends? If you were involved in policy or program evaluation, what kinds of challenges did you face—where did you and the agency succeed, and where did you and the agency fall short? Does your experience have any research and/or policy implications?

- Were there interesting relationships and interactions with system-involved persons and/or other employees worthy of discussion? Were there any interesting characters?

- What did you learn about yourself?

While the authors chose and developed their own topics, writing style, and structure, each essay includes pertinent personal background information, a workplace overview (descriptions of the agency, relevant programs, specific sites, and employment positions held), a narrative analysis of experiences (conditions, routines, and events serving as evidence supporting the author's arguments), and the lessons learned from the experiences. Further, each chapter, including this introduction and the conclusion, ends with sets of discussion questions and recommended readings. The questions are designed to facilitate discussions and assist in digesting the material in the chapter. The recommended readings identify related literature that offers further exploration into the subjects of the essays.

Several specific issues will be encountered throughout the essays. Some essays deal with operating correctional organizations—with administration, management, supervision, frontline staff, and even prisoner advocacy and protection issues. Some deal with services such as mental health care, therapy and counseling, treatment programs, and education. Some deal with interpersonal relationships at work, such as relationships with superiors and coworkers and rapport and proper social distance with sanctioned persons. Some essays deal with personal struggles—such as workplace stress and coping, personal journeys and self-discovery, tinkering with problem-solving strategies, and assessing if one is truly making a beneficial impact (making a difference)—while others deal with connecting corrections to larger social issues, such as social inequality, discrimination, social change, social justice, and working with women and minority populations. Finally, the essays occasionally offer a bit of corrections history. In terms of the types of corrections covered, the essays offer a sampling from the three general areas of incarceration, community corrections, and juvenile corrections, as authors worked in prisons or prison systems, probation or parole, and residential or community juvenile corrections.

Also, the types of scholarship that authors associate with their practical experiences are very diverse. Because of the nature of the book—reflective essays on personal experiences—its mission is not to impose theoretical, methodological, or philosophical standardization but to draw from the unique experiences of authors with different scholarly and professional backgrounds. The nature of the book also means that the authors will be more subjective. The essays are quite different from what crime and justice scholars typically write. The authors often take sides on contested issues, and their views may seem controversial at times. In fact, several other scholars and practitioners will disagree with them. The essays may draw several kinds of reactions from the reader, including agreement and disagreement as well as anger, sadness, and surprise. All of these feelings, however, can accompany learning. While each essay offers, in some way, a persuasive argument, it is not the intention of the book as a whole to advocate any particular views or opinions. Rather, the book intends to reveal what the authors went through while working in the field and what they now think of their experiences in an effort to bring scholarly concepts to life and demonstrate the relevance between academics and practice.

Two more important points need to be raised before ending this chapter. First, while it is hoped that the essays help prepare readers for corrections work by offering a sort of window into what it can be like to work in the field (through the eyes of professors), it is not the intention of this book to offer advice, expert or otherwise, on how to practice *specifically*. Rather, it intends to help prepare readers by helping them to see the connections between academic studies and practice. This book does not pretend to be a technical training manual for practicing corrections, and it is not intended to interfere with professional field training. It does not intend to *direct* readers to think, feel, or act in certain ways, although essays may compel them to approach corrections work with conviction, determination, and intelligence. It is hoped, then, that this book serves the corrections profession by playing a role in educating its workers.

The second point has to do with optimism. The following essays offer frank and honest accounts of the tough conditions experienced by persons working in corrections. As some authors state, the reality of working in prison is often very different from workers' preconceived ideas. In some way, the authors may often be revealing what they perceive to be the "ugly truths" of the corrections profession. Some of the stories have to do with persons who entered the field as idealists, fueled perhaps by their college education, only to have their idealism severely threatened by rude awakenings in the form of hostile interactions with persons in custody as well as fellow employees, the inability to have a positive impact, frustration with the administrative failings of the system, and/or social injustices. It will become clear that these conditions played a significant role in some authors' decisions to leave corrections. It is not the intention of this book, however, to make one pessimistic about working in corrections and striving to achieve its goals. While this book intends to give readers insights into the many challenges and obstacles in corrections work, it also intends to offer possible solutions and hope. The frank stories are better interpreted as warnings of some of the struggles that may be encountered—warnings that may help others prepare to meet the challenges that threaten to strip the professional of ambition and compassion.

Corrections workers are charged with controlling, punishing, and changing individuals, which makes adversarial relationships almost inevitable. Consequently, workers must take caution and protect themselves and others from manipulative, harmful behavior on the part of persons under correctional supervision. Additionally, it can seem that peers and superiors do not take a conscientious approach to their work and that they are there mostly for the paycheck. All too often, coworkers engage in misconduct themselves, creating moral and ethical dilemmas for colleagues who disapprove of such behavior. But while one should avoid being naive about these types of matters, it is also important to avoid the other extreme of becoming cynical because persons under correctional supervision often have honest intentions and engage in prosocial, or at least harmless, actions, and the field is full of many honest hardworking professionals who persistently believe in the goals of good corrections. It should be recognized that the following essays also offer accounts of successes, rewarding experiences, or even the bright side of problematic situations.

❖ REFERENCES

Collin, K., & Tynjälä, P. (2003). Integrating theory and practice? Employees' and students' experiences of learning at work. *Journal of Workplace Learning, 15*(7/8), 338–344.

Gordon, G. R., & McBride, R. B. (2008). *Criminal justice internships: Theory into practice* (6th ed.). Cincinnati, OH: Anderson.

Lewis, I., & Bolzan, N. (2007). Social work with a twist: Interweaving practice knowledge, student experience and academic theory. *Australian Social Work, 60*(2), 136–146.

McNeill, F. (2000). Making criminology work: Theory and practice in local context. *Probation Journal, 47*, 108–118.

Payne, B. K., Sumter, M., & Sun, I. (2003). Bringing the field into the criminal justice classroom: Field trips, ride-alongs, and guest speakers. *Journal of Criminal Justice Education, 14*(2), 327–344.

Ruggiero, J. A., & Weston, L. C. (1991). Teaching introductory sociology students about the practice of sociology: The practitioner's perspective. *Teaching Sociology, 19*(2), 211–222.

Stohr, M. K. (1999). Clearing and maintaining an ethical path in corrections: The contributions of practice and theory. *American Jails: The Magazine of the American Jail Association, 13*(4), 90–91.

Unnithan, N. P. (1999). Criminological theory and criminal justice policy: In search of pedagogical connections. *Journal of Criminal Justice Education, 10*(1), 101–110.

❖ RECOMMENDED READINGS

Gordon, G. R., & McBride, R. B. (2008). *Criminal justice internships: Theory into practice* (6th ed.). Cincinnati, OH: Anderson.

Hachen, D. S., Jr. (2001). *Sociology in action: Cases for critical and sociological thinking*. Thousand Oaks, CA: Pine Forge.

Langton, P. A., & Kammerer, D. A. (2005). *Practicing sociology in the community: A student's guide*. Upper Saddle River, NJ: Pearson.

Ross, J. I. (2008). *Special problems in corrections*. Upper Saddle River, NJ: Pearson.

Stohr, M. K. (1999). Clearing and maintaining an ethical path in corrections: The contributions of practice and theory. *American Jails: The Magazine of the American Jail Association, 13*(4), 90–91.

DISCUSSION QUESTIONS

1. What kind of work are you interested in? Do you have a specific job or career in mind? How important is a college education and degree to your career goals? Explain your answer.

2. Do you think that the material covered in social science and criminal justice courses (theories, concepts, principles, research methodology, empirical trends, etc.) will be useful to you at work? Why or why not? Does anything from your studies so far look like it might be relevant to practice—a certain theory, for example—and if so, how?

3. What are the difficulties in making connections between academics and practice? For example, what are potential problems in trying to apply material learned in class to work? What kinds of problems do you think you personally will have in connecting academics and practice?

2

Looking Back

Reflections of a Probation and Parole Officer

John Randolph Fuller

Editor's Introduction: Professor Fuller held the combined position of probation and parole officer. He offers a frank and honest account of the pressures of his job and the problems that occurred while trying to help his clients. Fuller describes how he drew from established theories of crime causation and counseling in his work and argues that corrections work should have a theoretical basis. However, he also shows that applying social science to achieve desirable results is difficult and warns that disappointment contributes to job stress, not to discourage people from working in corrections, but to prepare them to deal with its challenges and become more successful. The good news is that Fuller's experiences also show that probation and parole officers can have a beneficial impact on the lives of people in trouble with the law.

After almost 40 years working in or teaching about the criminal justice system, I have gained a certain perspective that allows me to recognize the value of both experience and mistakes. This essay is an attempt to evaluate the positive contributions and regrettable errors I made as I began my criminal justice career. I was naive about my ability to change someone's behavior and about the bureaucratic nature of criminal justice institutions. I should have been much more aware. At the age of 25, when I began my first job as a parole and probation officer, I had already flunked out of college; gotten drafted; spent 2 years and 7 months in the army, including 1 year in Vietnam; returned to college; and graduated. Yet I was still an idealistic young man who wanted to save the world and make a name for myself.

On graduating from the University of New Mexico in 1973, I went to work for the Florida Probation and Parole Commission. I moved to Florida mainly to terminate a personal relationship. At that time, my motto was "There is no problem so big and so complicated that it cannot be run away from." Although I have always regretted leaving New Mexico (but not the girlfriend), it was refreshing to move to a new place and make new friends.

I almost did not get the job. Before graduation, I had gone to Tallahassee, Florida, to interview with the commission's human resources department. Later, having heard nothing from Tallahassee, I went to visit my brother in south Florida and dropped by the West Palm Beach office to apply for a job. When the gentleman there found out I had already interviewed in Tallahassee, he made a phone call. After speaking with the human resources department in Tallahassee, he explained to me that although I had interviewed quite well, they had concerns about one question: Was I willing to enforce the marijuana laws of the state of Florida? This question took me aback because I thought I had already cleared that hurdle. The gentleman in the first interview had asked me, "If one of your parolees called you and said that they were having a party at their house and they had plenty of booze and dope, would you attend?" I had answered, "No. I think it would be inappropriate to socialize with individuals who are on my caseload." That seemed, at the time, a reasonable answer to me, but upon reflection, it is clear that I should have said I would have gone to the party and busted them for using illegal drugs.

Once I clarified this with the supervisor in the West Palm Beach office and assured him that I would indeed enforce the state's laws regarding marijuana, he offered me the job. I was given my choice of three counties: Dade (Miami), Broward (Fort Lauderdale), and Palm

Beach (West Palm Beach). I chose Fort Lauderdale for no reason other than I knew it had a famous beach.

❖ THE JOB

In the 1970s, probation and parole functions were lodged under the Florida Parole and Probation Commission. This included both the parole board, which decided when inmates were released, as well as the supervision services for parolees and probationers in the state courts. At this time, it was thought that separating the probation and parole functions from the corrections function provided a better division between the rehabilitation and punishment goals of the criminal justice system. Today, the probation and parole supervision services are under the Florida Department of Corrections. This organizational placement can still be debated, but given the punitive nature of contemporary criminal justice policy, it is likely that the present system will continue.

The Broward County office was one of the largest in the state. It consisted of over 50 officers across three offices: the central office in Fort Lauderdale, a northern office in Deerfield Beach, and a southern office in Hollywood, Florida. I was in the central office, which was located in the Broward County Courthouse. Not only was it located near the county jail, but it had also the advantage of being a few floors above the courtrooms. The workings of such a major office were very different than they are today. Our offices were situated around the circumference of a large central room called the bullpen where approximately 20 women typed the probation officers' reports. The few offices with windows belonged to the senior officers.

One unique feature about this job was that it entailed dealing with both probationers and parolees. The typical caseload was 100 to 120 cases with about 15% being parolees. Many of my colleagues believed that parolees were easier to work with because they had already been to prison and were anxious not to return, whereas probationers had been given a break by the court system and did not fully appreciate how drastically their lives would have changed had they gone to prison. On the other hand, parolees tended to have longer criminal histories and more serious offenses under their belts.

When I began my job in August 1973, I was one of three new officers. During our 3-week training period, we followed one of the senior officers who explained the decisions he made on his cases. We also learned the commission's policies and forms and watched court proceedings. A bigger group would have been more formally trained, but this on-the-job training seemed effective to me because we could ask questions about real cases and observe how parolees and probationers interacted with the officer.

At the end of the training session, a stack of 100 case files landed on my desk. These were my new clients. Because the turnover rate of probation and parole officers at the time was about 50% a year, our office had not contacted many of these clients for 3 or 4 months. I quickly devised a form letter advising my new clients that I was their new probation or parole officer and instructed them to make an appointment to come and see me. Within days, I heard from about 80% of the clients and began to meet with each to acquaint myself with their cases and their adjustment to supervision.

The other 20 cases took more effort. For the next 2 weeks, I combed through their files for phone numbers and addresses and tracked down all but 3. When I reported to my supervisor that I was not able to make contact with the last 3 cases, I was instructed to take out arrest warrants. I made one last phone call to these clients' families to advise them of the warrants, and 2 of the clients, who were probationers, immediately contacted me with profuse apologies.

The last client, a parolee, was picked up 3 months later on a traffic violation and sent back to prison for 3 months to wait for a parole board hearing. When he was reinstated on parole, he told me that he was not happy that I had taken out a warrant on him. I explained that this was the consequence of not keeping in touch with the parole officer and that if I had any more trouble with him I would be forced to take out another warrant and he would probably be in prison for a much longer time. This case gave me an appreciation for just how much a parole officer can affect the lives of those under supervision. This parolee had spent 5 years in prison and 4 years on parole, and had gone through five parole officers. He had become lax in maintaining contact with our office because of the high turnover. When he went back to prison, he lost the construction job that he held for 2 and a half years. At his request, I contacted his supervisor and got him reinstated in his job, but he still lost 3 months of wages. Eventually, I developed a good professional relationship with him, and he gave me no more problems.

❖ THE WORK ENVIRONMENT

In 1973, the nation's correctional philosophy was in the midst of a paradigm shift. For years, corrections, probation and parole in particular, operated on a rehabilitation model. By the time I began my job, this philosophy was beginning to become more punitive. This new way of dealing with offenders and ex-offenders was the result of two primary pressures. The first was the belief of many policymakers that the rehabilitation philosophy had failed. The second had to do with intermediate sanctions, such as intensive-supervision parole, house arrest, drug testing, and so on. There was a backlash to the perceived liberalization of society as exemplified by the excesses of the 1960s. Recreational drug use, sexual promiscuity, and the flaunting of traditional values were being counteracted by a conservative agenda aimed at reclaiming the country from the clutches of the hippies.

I was too young and naive to understand this conservative shift as I started my criminal justice career. Coming out of college, I just wanted to "help people" even though I had little idea about exactly what that meant and was ill equipped to do so anyway. I came to the job focused on rehabilitation and was quickly confronted with supervisors wanting me to concentrate on the public safety aspect of the probation and parole mission. This meant that I spent much time ensuring that my clients filled out their monthly reports, maintained stable employment and residency, and stayed out of trouble. Any rehabilitation was couched in the supervision agenda. For instance, putting a client in a drug rehabilitation program was considered a good way to transfer some supervision responsibility to another agency. If the client showed up regularly and participated well in the program, the probation officer could safely assume the client was making good progress. In actuality, although the client may have been adhering to the program's rules, the probation and parole officer could not know for sure whether he or she was actually off drugs and out of trouble. Drug testing was not a feature of probation and parole at this time, and officers depended more on their intuition and experience in deciding if someone was adjusting to mainstream society.

Then, there was the intermediate sanctions issue. Florida was starting a pilot program on intensive-supervision probation, the intent of which was to relieve prison overcrowding by dealing with at-risk offenders in a much more comprehensive and efficient manner. We were told at the time that this was one of the first such programs in the country, and Florida was committed to developing alternative strategies to enhance the effectiveness of probation. A few officers in several counties received reduced caseloads and were told to increase the level of supervision in an attempt to reduce the high rates of recidivism. In Broward County, some of our senior officers received caseloads of 35 clients. They were required to contact the probationers on a much more regular basis and ensure not only that they were meeting their conditions of probation but also that they were in rehabilitation programs. The clients chosen for intensive probation were serious offenders who were most likely to violate their probation and return to prison. The idea behind intensive-supervision probation was that if these clients got more help and more regular supervision, then they were increasingly likely to successfully complete their probation.

At this point, the law of unintended consequences kicked in. Because these clients were monitored more closely, the probation officers became aware of probation violations that had escaped detection under traditional probation. Rather than reducing the number of violations, this program helped uncover even more, and probation officers revoked these clients' probation at a much greater rate than normal. Once the central office in Tallahassee became aware that intensive-supervision probation was sending more people back before the judge than traditional probation, these officers were instructed not to follow through on these violations. The central office was under political pressure to demonstrate that the program was successful, and the intensive-supervision probation officers had to adjust their policies. For minor infractions, such as marijuana use, these officers were told not to formally charge the offenders but to pressure them to adhere to the law. There was quite a bit of consternation and confusion among the officers as to what was expected of them as they supervised their caseloads.

In the end, increased supervision meant greater awareness of not only the probationers' legitimate activities but also their illegitimate ones. The organization had a vested interest in ensuring the experiment's success so that it could be replicated in other counties, but it had to alter its policies to do so.

❖ APPLYING SOCIAL SCIENCE

One thing that surprised me most about my training was that it had no theoretical basis. I had taken a number of classes in college that were useful to my work, including juvenile delinquency, criminology, speech communication, philosophy, political science, and sociology. On the job, I found that most of my colleagues lacked social science degrees. The majority of them seemed to have business and education degrees. In my criminology class, we used Edwin Sutherland and Donald Cressey's (1960) *Principles of Criminology*, and I was well versed in differential association as an explanation for the delinquent behavior.

One day at lunch, we were discussing why people become involved in antisocial behavior, and I pointed out that one explanation was peer pressure, which we saw a lot of in our office. My fellow officers had never heard of differential association. Back at the office, they were amazed when I showed them the book. I asked what theoretical basis they used to supervise clients, and their answer was "whatever works." Basically, they were winging it.

In one of the counseling classes I took at the University of New Mexico, I was exposed to William Glaser's reality therapy. I found this to be a particularly good approach to dealing with parolees and probationers because the therapy did not show them as deficient or sick but rather as individuals who made poor choices. Reality therapy fit nicely with our supervision mission because it encourages individuals to make a plan and break it down into small stages. It seemed that this was what most my colleagues were doing without understanding the theoretical basis behind the instructions they gave their clients. My colleagues quickly rejected any excuses the probationers and parolees gave—which is part of the reality therapy philosophy—but the officers were also quick to punish those who did not follow their plans. Reality therapy encourages the therapist with a problematic client to help the client make new, more realistic plans rather than punish. This part was a hard sell to the officers who saw punishment as one of their main tools for eliciting acceptable behavior.

The lack of a theoretical basis for how the officers approached supervision meant their work was plagued with inconsistencies. We had 50 officers supervising their clients in widely disparate ways. Although some norms emerged, they were not theoretically based. Looking back, I now see that *why* the clients got in trouble was not the main concern of our office but rather that the clients were detected and punished when they did get in trouble.

My supervisors did not always appreciate my efforts to provide treatment for my clients. The range of treatment facilities was limited and in many ways discouraged. Over time, an adversarial relationship developed between our office and many of these treatment facilities. Once the client was referred to a drug-treatment program, that program took ownership of the client and viewed the probation and parole officer as problematic. Rather than working closely with each other to ensure effective treatment, a distrustful relationship developed in which the treatment programs would not alert the officers of further drug use or crime because they feared the officer would revoke the probation or parole and send the client to prison. This competition for control over the case resulted in many probationers and parolees not being referred to suitable treatment. In an attempt to get around this, I attempted to treat and counsel my clients myself. Now, I realize that I was ill equipped for treating clients, but my heart was in the right place, and I had plenty of energy. I would spend hours talking to my clients and attempting to use reality therapy to help them take control over their situations. My goal was to keep them busy in jobs or in educational pursuits. I determined that if they were gainfully employed or seriously pursuing a GED or college program, they would have less time to break the law.

❖ HARD LESSONS

Manipulative Clients

Often, I was not successful in helping clients. The one thing I was not prepared for was my clients' dishonesty and manipulation. I can see now that I was extremely naive to believe that these thieves, rapists, and armed robbers would not lie to me. Often, I thought I had established a good rapport with them only to find out later they were telling me what I wanted to hear. I had one case in which a 20-year-old male seemed to have a lot of discretionary money to buy boats, cars, and clothes. He was self-employed doing detail work on cars. He traveled around in a van to his clients' cars and put on pinstriping, waxed and buffed them, and cleaned the interiors. He was so successful at this that he hired his brother and cousin and equipped them with vans also. Later, I was surprised when his cousin was arrested for selling drugs. A sheriff's investigation revealed that the three guys were using the vans to deliver cocaine and marijuana. I had completely missed all the signs of drug dealing because I wanted to believe that I was successful in helping this client establish a viable business.

On another occasion, another young probation officer, Paul, and I decided we would try group therapy. We had 12 young offenders who all seemed to be at the stage in their lives in which with a little guidance, they might go on to lead successful and productive lives. They were all 18 to 23 years old and on probation for larceny, marijuana use, or fighting in bars, and all seemed like decent people who had made bad choices but were not committed to criminal careers. On Tuesday evenings, we would gather these young men in the probation department's conference room for a 2-hour meeting, and I would lead them in a discussion about careers, relationships, and staying out of trouble.

I looked forward to the meeting because it seemed we were making real progress with these young men who seemed so receptive to the group sessions. They showed up regularly, enjoyed each other's company, and seemed to speak freely not only about their past criminal activities but also about their hopes and goals. More than one time, one young man helped another get a job or introduced him to a girl. After the session, Paul and I would talk about the conversations and develop ideas for finding positive activities for each client.

I was particularly proud of this group-treatment activity, and it was not until I had quit my job to return to graduate school that Paul called me and told me how we had once again failed to detect criminal behavior. The young men did not know each other before the group sessions, but they quickly bonded, and each night after the session they would go out and break into homes and businesses. Paul and I had unwittingly created a gang of burglars who learned to work together to be more effective criminals. According to Paul, each Tuesday evening, one participant would come to the group with a place to burglarize that he had already investigated. Typically, it would be his place of employment, so he had inside knowledge of where valuables and money were. The man would establish his alibi by visiting his employer's home while his friends burglarized the business. When the police called the employer, the young man would accompany him to the business and typically destroy any evidence his friends had left.

I was heartbroken when Paul told me what had been going on. I was so sure we had established a connection with the young men and helped them become productive citizens. Looking back, I wonder how many other times I had been wrong about my clients.

Frustrating Bureaucracy

I spent 3 years in the military during the late 1960s. I thought I had seen all the idiocy that a bureaucratic organization could promote to stifle creative thought and efficient service, but the Florida Probation and Parole Commission frustrated me even more. I think that one of the main impediments to effective administration of the office was the practice of promoting good probation and parole officers to administrative positions without teaching them how to manage law-abiding employees rather than parolees and probationers. A good probation and parole officer must always be on guard against clients who lie. Everything must be verified and nothing taken at face value. However, administrators brought this distrust to dealing with the officers and treated them with skepticism even after they had proven that they were dependable and honest workers.

With over 50 officers, adequately overseeing the work of so many individuals was challenging, and a number of internal checks existed to ensure that everyone was doing their job. However, some policies demonstrated a level of distrust that offended many of the officers. One of the rules was that everyone had to be there by 8:00 a.m. The administrative assistant would then walk around the office, note who had not arrived, and report them. To be safe, everyone would arrive at 7:45. Unfortunately, this policy got in the way of adequately supervising cases because early morning was one of the best times to check on clients at home as they were getting ready to go to their jobs or at their places of employment to ensure that they were indeed working. Thus, a petty administrative rule destroyed a valuable and effective way to supervise clients.

Another grating rule was the requirement that a mileage log be maintained each day the officer was out of the office supervising clients. Although we all used our own cars, we had to log the miles between each visit to a probationer's home or place of employment. We were not reimbursed for these miles, but the supervisor simply wanted to oversee our activities. Many officers felt they were too busy to maintain mileage logs and simply estimated (fabricated) how many miles they traveled each day. Although I never saw a supervisor actually go out and verify the mileage logs, we all knew it was possible, so many of us religiously adhered to this policy. These types of policies made many of us feel that we were as distrusted as a probationers and parolees.

❖ CONCLUDING OBSERVATIONS

My experiences as a probation and parole officer have been an asset to my career as an academic criminologist. The perspective that I developed has helped me to teach my students that what they encounter in the field will not always live up to what they learn in the classroom. Any organization has an occupational culture that devalues what is learned in the classroom. When the army sent me to work in a hospital in Vietnam (I was an X-ray technician), one of the first things I was told was "Forget everything you ever learned in basic training; this is the real world, and we do things differently." I saw this same attitude at the probation and parole office. Rehabilitation, treating clients with respect and dignity, and using one's own judgment were discouraged in lieu of following policies designed to stay off the radar screens of

supervisors and judges. We were not encouraged to think for ourselves and were always advised to get our supervisors' approval for
any difficult decisions. Our supervisors were unwilling to take any
type of risk and consistently erred on the side of caution.

After a year as a probation and parole officer, I resigned to return
to graduate school at Florida State University. I did not see working in
probation and parole as a viable career. The pay was abysmal and the
chances of advancement limited. Furthermore, I did not appreciate
being treated by my supervisors with the distrust and suspicion they
had developed for their clients. Still, I had learned valuable lessons
about dealing with offenders, and, more important, I had learned valuable lessons about myself. I'm glad I had this experience because it has
informed my teaching and writing in criminology.

In my 30 years as a university professor, I have had many students
who have gone on to probation and parole careers. I am confident that
most have been effective in their jobs in part because I have been able
to alert them to some of the pitfalls of this occupation. My goal is to
impress on them the importance of this type of work and equip them
with the skills and attitudes necessary to survive. Occupational burnout is a major problem for probation and parole officers. It's very easy
to become cynical because one must deal with both offenders and a
government bureaucracy. It is my hope that my students are equipped
with better skills, a more realistic idea of the occupation, and a better
sense of themselves than I was when I became a probation and parole
officer so many years ago.

❖ REFERENCES

Sutherland, E., & Cressey, D. (1960). *Principles of criminology*. Chicago: Lippincott.

❖ RECOMMENDED READINGS

Braswell, M., Fletcher, T., & Miller, L. (1998). *Human relations and corrections*
(4th ed.). Prospect Heights, IL: Waveland Press.

Clear, T. R., & Dammer, H. (2003). *The offender in the community*. Belmont, CA:
Wadsworth.

Cromwell, P., Alarid, L. F., & del Carmen, R. V. (2005). *Community-based corrections* (6th ed.). Belmont, CA: Wadsworth.

Cullen, F. T., & Gilbert, K. E. (1982). *Reaffirming rehabilitation*. Cincinnati, OH:
Anderson.

Kratcoski, P. C. (2000). *Correctional counseling and treatment* (4th ed.). Prospect Heights, IL: Waveland Press.

Petersilia, J. (2003). *When prisoners come home: Parole and prisoner reentry*. New York: Oxford University Press.

DISCUSSION QUESTIONS

1. Which major paradigm shift did the author identify, and how did it affect his work environment and him personally? How will the current social and political climate affect you and your job?

2. Which theory and type of therapy did the author apply in his work, and how did he apply them? If you were working with offenders, which social scientific concepts would you apply, and how would you apply them?

3. Briefly, which "hard lessons" did the author learn? How can you use these lessons in your work while still striving to help your clients and the organization for which you work?

3

Presentence Officers as Beasts of Burden

Coping With Drug Mule Cases in an Age of Punitive Sentencing

Staci Strobl

Editor's Introduction: Professor Strobl worked as a federal presentence officer, a type of probation officer. She discusses the challenges of sanctioning drug couriers, often called "drug mules" because they are used to transport illegal drugs on their person, often across borders. Many couriers in Strobl's caseload were impoverished women from different countries who in many ways were victims, while the law tended to treat them simply as offenders. Placing corrections in a global context, she identifies the part that political-economic globalization and inequality plays in making low-income

(Continued)

(Continued)

women more vulnerable to criminal exploitation. Strobl thinks that recent legal developments giving the courts more discretion to use mitigating social circumstances to decide drug sentences may increase the importance of the work of presentence investigators and lead to more fairness in determining the criminal responsibility of drug couriers.

❖ INTRODUCTION: FEDERAL PROBATION AND DRUG COURIER CASES IN NYC

In the Eastern District of New York (EDNY), where I served as a federal probation officer, the presence of John F. Kennedy (JFK) International Airport in the jurisdiction led to a good percentage of our presentence investigation caseload to consist of drug couriers, also known as "drug mules." These couriers, often poor, female, and hailing from underdeveloped countries, undertook the trip to the United States with cocaine or heroin secreted into balloons that they swallowed. Should any one of the balloons break inside the courier's body system, it was almost certain death due to the toxic levels of these drugs in even one balloon. In other instances, the drugs were lined in their luggage, shoes, or elaborate drug-filled wigs. These couriers were most often freelance operators compelled by poverty and hardships to fall victim to a persuasive recruiter who bore a greater role in the drug operation as a whole. To be a presentence investigator in the EDNY was to become intimately familiar with the typical hardscrabble stories, which led otherwise ordinary women to travel to an unfamiliar country with toxic drugs in their systems, breaking the law.

What many could not have known, given their typically limited education and little experience in the drug trade, was that for a good 20 years in the 1980s, 1990s, and early 2000s, the penalties for drug couriers were almost entirely driven by the weight of the drugs they carried with only limited mitigation of a sentence for the fact that they were minimal participants in the drug trade. The weight of the drugs was a fact almost never known to the couriers themselves. Those who swallowed their drugs could hold up to 400 grams of heroin or cocaine in their digestive tracts.

In these "bad old days," the U.S. sentencing guidelines locked judges into draconian sentences under the auspices of creating like sentences for like offenders throughout the nation. In addition, law-makers hoped to achieve *truth in sentencing* by tying sentences directly to specific factors that characterize the offense. Data on federal sentencing indicate that between 1984 and 1990 the guideline's effect was to create longer prison sentences as well as widen the net of the offenses to which imprisonment would be the response (Meierhoefer, 1992). The average sentence length for convicted drug traffickers increased from 23 months before the guidelines to 78 months in 2001 (Nachmanoff, 2009). In 1997, approximately one in four federal inmates was a nonviolent, low-level drug offender, often couriers (Sevigny & Caulkins, 2004); this ratio was higher for cases coming out of the EDNY. Half of the cases in our jurisdiction involved drugs and a majority of these were drug mules.

For drug courier cases, the guidelines created almost no judicial wiggle room. Rather than simply sending these couriers back from where they came, the typical drug courier defendant spent a year in detention awaiting trial only to ultimately plead guilty and then face up to 2 more years in federal prison, all at taxpayer expense. In the early 1990s, the EDNY sentenced over 400 drug couriers per year (Weinstein, 1993), a number that continued to grow throughout the decade.

Drug courier cases were how new presentence officers cut their teeth. The application of the sentencing guidelines was relatively easy, the details of the cases were hardly substantially different from the others, and the investigation itself took minimal effort. Until officers graduated from drug courier cases, they would never see anything more interesting, and there were a handful of more exciting cases to be had—complicated Racketeer Influenced & Corrupt Organizations Statute (RICO) cases involving famous crime families, such as the Bonannos or Luccheses; bank fraud cases with multiple defendants; and drug-related murders.

❖ HANDLING DRUG COURIER CASES

I joined the presentence division of the EDNY in 1999 after the sentencing guidelines had been in effect for almost 15 years. I wanted not only to be in a law enforcement job but also to use my writing skills and journalism background. Being a presentence investigator seemed to have the right combination of street and office duties. As investigators, we visited defendants' homes and interviewed their family members while also spending a good amount of time in the office writing reports and applying the guideline formulas. I liked to tell my friends that the job afforded me the opportunity "to meet people I wouldn't otherwise have a chance to meet." Indeed, I interviewed and visited the homes of a wide array of defendants, from identity thieves living in the projects in Queens to sex offenders residing in their mothers' basements in Brooklyn. There were crack sellers and child pornography distributors, charity fraudsters, and arsonists. But mostly, there were drug couriers, one after another. Even when officers had earned the right to take on the more exciting complex cases, they would always have a few drug couriers on their caseloads at any given time—there were simply too many of them, and the entire presentence office of approximately 30 members had to pitch in and keep cranking out these boilerplate investigations to keep up.

One of my early drug courier cases involved Alice,[1] a mother of four from Kingston, Jamaica. Her story was not only difficult to hear but also not so different from many stories heard by presentence investigators. After the father of her last child walked out on her (the father of her first three children was already long gone), it had become nearly impossible to make ends meet. She could not find regular work in the poor neighborhood of Kingston where she lived, and she had to pull her children from school because she could not pay their school fees. Although her sister's family had been able to help out for awhile, it also hit hard times when the family's breadwinner lost his job. Unable to pay any rent or provide food, Alice moved her family in with her sister, creating a crowded, impoverished situation made all the worse by her account of being raped by her brother-in-law. When approached by a drug courier recruiter, she could not turn down the chance to make the $700 being offered, which could help her regain a place to live and food for her children. All she had to do was get a Jamaican passport, swallow some balloons filled with drugs, and get on a flight to New York.

Meanwhile, customs agents at JFK airport closely monitored passengers hailing from certain "known drug midpoint and source locations" of which Kingston was one. Part of the drug courier profile was disembarkation from a flight from Accra, Lagos, Bogotá, Manila, Panama City, or Port au Prince, among other cities. For probable cause to seize a passenger for further questioning, agents had to also observe another red flag—the nervous passenger, ascertained by profuse sweating, nervous eye-darting, or fidgeting. In other cases, the passenger with a brand-new passport, having never traveled to the United

---

[1]Name has been changed.

States and claiming no familial ties, would become the object of suspicion. Once seized, a passenger was questioned, searched, and asked to submit to an abdominal X-ray. If balloons were visible on the X-ray, agents had the task of monitoring the detainee through the process of excreting the balloons, which were then retrieved for laboratory analysis. In many cases, by this point, the courier would be in tears, explaining that she was so sorry. She just needed the money. She rarely had any information about her recruiter or the organization to which the recruiter belonged that she could use in exchange for leniency. All she had was a cell phone number to call once in New York or the name of a low budget airport motel where she was to rendezvous with the drug receivers. In a few cases, this information would lead to a successful operation to apprehend the receivers, but often, these accomplices would be tipped off by the amount of time that had transpired between the flight's landing and the passenger's making contact. Suspecting that the courier had been apprehended, accomplices would abandon their plans, leaving the courier alone and enmeshed in the drama of prosecution, guilty pleas, and sentencing.

Alice was caught up in the same drama. As she awaited sentencing in New York, no amount of apologies or reiteration of her story to agents, lawyers, or probation officers could stop the course of events. Meanwhile, her children were left in the care of her sister in less than desirable circumstances and now absent both parents. As a presentence officer, I was required to ask a number of detailed questions about the couriers' family situations, which inevitably triggered emotional outpourings about children left behind, sick parents, or family members who had died since the couriers' arrests. I had nothing to offer. I wrote these details down and maybe said an empty "I am so sorry to hear that." The presentence report included this type of information in a profile of the offender, but it hardly mattered to sentencing at that time. Sentencing used a strict grid, which cross-referenced the offense calculation, a numeric assignment of the seriousness of the offense and its related conduct, with the defendant's criminal history, pursuant to a range of sentencing options in months from which the judge could only depart in unusual circumstances. Poverty, abuse, exploitation, and family emergencies never qualified.

Part of the job of a presentence officer is also to verify with any institutions as to the defendant's personal history, whether that be schools, employers, or hospitals, but only if the verification involved an entity located in the United States. What made drug courier cases so easy was the usual lack of any verification inquiries because they had not lived in the United States. The careful retelling of the defendant's social background, education, health, and employment painted a comprehensive, though unverified, picture for little purpose. In the end, these couriers were just couriers, flatly defined by the weight of the heroin or cocaine they trafficked.

Given the lack of verification of many of these stories, a cynic could argue that they were convenient sob stories told by people caught red-handed. But over the years, these stories came to the EDNY in the thousands, and even if a few accounts here or there were patently false, the overall story was in bold relief. Professor Steven Wasserman (1995) started out his essay calling for sentencing reform for drug couriers with the generally accepted facts:

> A typical [EDNY] drug courier prosecution involves a foreign defendant, often a woman, working for an unapprehended supplier who is operating from abroad. The defendant is arrested at Kennedy airport, pleads guilty and is sentenced in proportion to the quantity of drugs secreted into her digestive tract, shoes or luggage. (p. 643)

The overall narrative, heard by presentence officers again and again, underscored how exploited many of these couriers were lured into a trap by recruiters offering relief from desperate socioeconomic circumstances. In Alice's case, the $700 payoff represented several months of living expenses for her family, more if budgeted wisely. In countries where jobs are scarce, and for women who can qualify only for low-skilled labor unlikely to pay much above the poverty level, recruiters can count on a ready supply of couriers to do their bidding. According to Olga Heaven who runs a not-for-profit Hibiscus Foundation that has interviewed hundreds of drugs couriers in prisons and in West Africa where they are recruited,

> What we found was that these women were not motivated by greed, but by desperation. Usually the drug barons identify women who are single parents struggling to raise their children. Their husbands may have died; they might have deserted their wives—various scenarios. But the one constant is that these vulnerable women, who simply want to feed their families, put a roof over their heads, clothes on their backs, shoes on their feet and get them an education—are offered an "easy way" to earn some money. Little do they realise the risks they run nor the kinds of long sentences they will serve if they get caught, leaving their children without a mother and without support while they serve their time in a foreign prison. (Williams, 2008, p. 24)

Hearing these women's stories consistently pointed to the dark side of the globalized context in which we live. On one hand, globalization has brought the world in closer contact through international mass communication, trade, investment, and travel. On the other hand, it widens the gulf between the rich and the poor as those without access to the means of participating in a global economy become increasingly isolated and ripe for exploitation. Further, socioeconomic inequalities are crosscut with issues of sexism and patriarchy. Alice, for example, faced the compounded difficulties of being a single mother in a society that expects her to care for her children by herself while simultaneously lacking avenues for female employment or affordable child care. Women in many underdeveloped societies are dependent on men even as their societies see increasingly high rates of single-mother households.

❖ THE LARGER ECONOMIC AND POLITICAL CONTEXT

Globalization also creates circumstances that ratchet up the speed and intensity of smuggling. The flow of people across borders provides a means for major drug players to move their product while simultaneously distancing themselves from criminal responsibility. The relative ease with which drug couriers were caught is in stark contrast to the complicated investigation required to net so-called drug kingpins. Yet couriers are the least culpable. Wasserman (1995) argues that drug weight should not be the main concern at sentencing for drug couriers because they have little knowledge of the specifics such as weight or type of drug of what they are carrying. Other scholars have empirically shown that using weight-centric sentences creates uniformity across sentences despite variations in roles and therefore culpability (Osler, 2007; Sevigny, 2009). Therefore, many have suggested that their minimal participation should be the paramount factor to consider.

Famously, Judge Jack B. Weinstein in the EDNY registered his dismay at the overly punitive state of drug sentencing by refusing to hear any drug cases for a period in the 1990s. His rationale for this particularly bold rebellion from the bench was explained in a 1993 op-ed piece he wrote for the *New York Times* in which he stated that the guidelines were particularly harsh on drug couriers whose sentences on average in the EDNY nearly doubled after the guidelines were implemented. He noted that over 60% of those in federal prisons have been convicted of drug offenses. He wrote, "Largely because of mandated and unnecessarily harsh sentences for minor drug offenders, which fail to deter, I have exercised my option as a senior Federal judge not to try minor drug cases" (p. A19).

Interestingly, for many years, the sentencing guidelines manual, the presentence officer's Bible, did not even mention rehabilitation in its list of the goals of sentencing policy. Deterrence, incapacitation, and retribution ruled the day, and as Judge Weinstein noted, programs that were rehabilitative in nature, such as education and counseling, were drastically cut in the post-Martinson world of "nothing works" in corrections.

Within probation, however, the debate over the appropriate model for probation, whether as a means of crime control or a type of social work, continued despite the nothing works attitudes (MacKenzie, 2011). Probation officers tended to fall into one orientation or the other in the EDNY presentence division despite the pendulum swing of politics. Some officers hooked into their presentence investigations as a means of holding offenders accountable through a verified litany of the characteristics of their offenses and the details of their criminal histories. Others hoped to put a human face on these offenders and provide verified information for the sake of addressing a number of problems offenders might have from health concerns to drug addiction. Regardless, it was nearly unanimous that drug courier cases represented a failure of the criminal justice system for a wide variety of probation officers—another drug courier case on one's caseload, another day in the salt mine. And to what effect? For the crime control–oriented officers, these nonviolent offenders represented a wasteful use of resources on low-level offenders who directly posed no threat to public safety (though the overall drug trade itself is dangerous) and potentially diverted the system from focusing more intently on bigger fish. For the social work–oriented officer, the detailed write-up of these couriers' sad stories was a depressing exercise in futility as almost none of the social or economic problems detailed made one iota of difference in sentencing. With the Bureau of Prisons offering limited rehabilitation and educational programs—and certainly not in the wide range of languages these offenders spoke—the presentence report acted as the classic bureaucratic rubber stamp rather than an opportunity to identify and address problems. But if the root cause of the problem was global inequality, then what could the federal criminal justice system really do anyway?

❖ PERSONAL REFLECTION

Any officer who thought too deeply about drug couriers was bound to be dissatisfied in his or her chosen employment. My career was looking like hard time—a 20-year sentence of drug courier report writing. If I moved up the chain of command within the presentence division, I would graduate from writing drug courier reports ad nauseam to reading them ad nauseam in a supervisory role. Although there are worse fates, I could not help but question whether I could truly be satisfied interviewing drug courier defendants and then delivering their words to a cold system caught in the throes of a tough-on-crime obsession. Like judges, probation officers had very little discretion in interpreting the guidelines. Every so often a case would come along that offered an opportunity to explore a gray area—such as whether a particular batch of child pornography constituted sadomasochism (S-M), or whether a defendant who built a wall to hide the drugs stashed in his Brooklyn factory should receive a sentencing enhancement. However, these opportunities were too rare and often not exciting enough to lull oneself out of a monotonous drug courier coma.

In essence, the job, like many government jobs, was attractive in its stability. With a fairly good paycheck and steady advancement, one could make a solid, middle-class life. But it was a middle-class life acting on behalf of a system warehousing defendants so that they would be out of the way of other middle-class people, a type of postmodern social sanitation in which the poor are criminalized and then isolated from everyone else. I began to suffer from a keen awareness of the social vertigo and existential emptiness that characterizes the theorizing of Jock Young and Zygmunt Bauman. The line between me and global inequality was thinner by virtue of this job; it became harder for me to see poor women from underdeveloped countries as not-my-problem. Human rights reports from the likes of Christiane Amanpour were no longer so abstract. The "ascriptive inequalities," or the inequalities that people are born into, which Willem Bonger eloquently wrote about in the early 20th century and were a passing landmark in my graduate school education, suddenly cropped up in full relief. With drug couriers, I became intimately familiar with the structural web of doom some were caught in by virtue of class, gender, and nationality.

Like many contemporary law enforcement war stories, 9/11 figures into my narrative. When the attacks occurred on the World Trade Center I was sitting in the basement of Federal District Court in Brooklyn waiting for the U.S. Marshals to produce a drug courier I needed to interview. I waited longer than usual for a 9:00 a.m. interview. The marshals seemed strangely understaffed for a Tuesday morning in the "pens," the detention and interview area. By 9:20, everyone had cleared out of the marshals' office, and an attorney who passed by was in a strange frenzy. "The World Trade Center is on fire! An airplane hit one of the towers!" he told me. In the chaos that ensued, our workday was soon cancelled, and the probation officers were sent home in government cars since public transportation was frozen. Many officers wanted to help at Ground Zero. As we were federal officers, shouldn't there be a role for us? We couldn't just sit there idly, could we? Our leadership instead instructed us to stay away, advice that later made sense in light of how little first responders were able to do to help people and how many secondary-style responders, such as counselors and clergy members, had shown up.

When we returned to work 3 days later, a meeting was called. Still reeling from the emotional trauma of the attacks and many of us knowing or related to people who worked in the Twin Towers, we assumed the meeting was a check-in as to how everyone was holding up. Instead, the meeting introduced us to a slight modification in the format for drug courier presentence reports. Although this was what I would consider only some misguided leadership on the part of our division, I couldn't help but be stuck for some time on the fact that in the wake of the biggest foreign terrorist attack on American soil, which had ignited a mere 2 miles away from our offices, it was business as usual, drug couriers as usual. Many people have stories of 9/11 as a wake-up call, and this was mine. In the aftermath of 9/11, many other things in the world of criminal justice seemed infinitely more important than sentencing drug couriers, and yet not even the 9/11 attacks could cause much of a pause in it. Shortly thereafter, I resigned from my position as a presentence officer and returned to graduate school full-time.

❖ CONCLUSION

Today, drug couriers continue to come through Kennedy airport and into the arms of the federal criminal justice system. Developments in the guidelines since my time as a presentence officer, however, have slightly improved the fate of couriers. In particular, *U.S. v. Booker* (2005), *Gall v. U.S.* (2007), and *Kimbrough v. U.S.* (2007) were the products of more widespread judicial rebellion against the constraints of the guidelines than Judge Weinstein's admirable one-judge crusade. The Supreme Court effectively established through these cases that the sentencing guidelines are advisory and not mandatory. In *Kimbrough,* an offender's sympathy inducing personal history spurred a judge into the rebellious position of sentencing below the guidelines a First Gulf War veteran who sold crack. Kimbrough had grown up very poor and had few advantages in life. After serving in the war, he developed a drug habit and then went on to support his habit through drug selling. These potential mitigating factors could not be considered under the guidelines as originally conceived, but the time had finally come to give judges back the discretion to rule on not only the weight of the drugs but also the totality of circumstances, including an offender's characteristics and role in the offense. In the post-*Booker* era, as this new age in federal sentencing is known, the length of sentences for drug offenders has decreased, particularly for drug couriers. Statistics from EDNY indicate that in 2009, below-guideline sentences have been handed out by judges in a quarter of the cases (U.S. Sentencing Commission, 2009a; see also U.S. Sentencing Commission, 2009b).

The *Booker* case created an opening for the presentence investigation to once again put a human face on offenders and to allow a variety of circumstances to influence criminal sentencing. I imagine that if I were a presentence officer post-*Booker* that my level of satisfaction as to the relevance of my job to the people I interviewed and to their ultimate sentences would be greater. In the debate over social work versus crime control in the probation world, it seems that the mandatory guidelines experiment showed that striking a balance is fundamentally important. As peace officers, probation officers assist the court in creating public safety through verified information about offenses and offenders, but they also potentially provide assistance to offenders by verifying circumstances that tailor sentences and programs to them. Although sometimes wearing two hats makes the job more complicated, overall, the more options we can give the court in responding to offenders, the better our system of justice will be. The *Booker* case cannot solve the problem of global poverty nor stem the supply or demand for drugs in the United States, but it can make our response to that global reality more humane and, in the process, more cost effective.

❖ REFERENCES

MacKenzie, D. L. (2011). Probation: An untapped resource in U.S. corrections. In L. Gideon & H. Sung (Eds.), *Rethinking corrections: Rehabilitation, reentry, reintegration* (pp. 97–128). Thousand Oaks, CA: Sage.

Meierhoefer, B. S. (1992). The role of offense and offender characteristics in federal sentencing. *Southern California Law Review, 66*, 367–399.

Nachmanoff, M. S. (2009). *Booker* five years out: Mandatory minimum sentences and Department of Justice charging policies continue to distort the federal sentencing process. *Federal Sentencing Reporter, 22*, 96.

Osler, M. (2007). More than numbers: A proposal for rational drug sentences. *Federal Sentencing Reporter, 19*, 326–328.

Sevigny, E. L. (2009). Excessive uniformity in federal drug sentencing. *Journal of Quantitative Criminology, 25*(2), 155–180.

Sevigny, E. L., & Caulkins, J. P. (2004). Kingpins or mules: An analysis of drug offenders incarcerated in federal and state prisons. *Criminology & Public Policy, 3*(3), 401–403.

U.S. Sentencing Commission. (2009a). *2009 Federal sentencing guidelines manual.* Washington, DC: Author. Available at http://www.ussc.gov/2009guid/TABCON09.htm

U.S. Sentencing Commission. (2009b). *Statistical information packet: Eastern District of New York, 2009 datafile.* Washington, DC: Author. Available at http://www.ussc.gov/JUDPACK/2009/nye09.pdf

Wasserman, S. (1995). Toward sentencing reform for drug couriers. *Brooklyn Law Review, 61*(2), 643–656.

Weinstein, J. (1993, July 8). The war on drugs is self-defeating. *New York Times*, p. A19.

Williams, S. (2008, October 1). Black women drug mules in foreign prisons. *New African Woman*, 24–25.

❖ RECOMMENDED READING

Bauman, Z. (2006). *Liquid times: Living in an age of uncertainty.* Cambridge, UK: Polity.

Gideon, L., & Sung, H. (2011). *Rethinking corrections: Rehabilitation, reentry, reintegration.* Thousand Oaks, CA: Sage.

Young, J. (2007). *The vertigo of late modernity.* London: Sage.

DISCUSSION QUESTIONS

1. What are the larger political and economic forces identified in this essay, and how do they seem to impact both federal probations work and the lives of drug couriers?

2. Can the drug couriers discussed in this essay also be considered victims? If so, in what ways are they victims, and what should we do for them? If not, why are they not victims, and how should they be dealt with?

3. Based on this essay, what would you propose as a solution to the problem of drug smuggling? For example, would changes to the criminal justice system significantly reduce the problem, or do we have to do something outside of the system?

4

Experiencing the ISP Movement

The Good, the Bad, and the Ugly

Eric J. Wodahl

Editor's Introduction: Professor Wodahl worked in community corrections as an intensive supervision program (ISP) agent. Intensive supervision is a more restrictive type of control placed mostly on probationers and parolees considered to be at higher risk of reoffending. Using a creative offender typology that he devised—"the Good, the Bad, and the Ugly"—Wodahl assesses the effectiveness of his ISP in achieving the goals of reducing prison overcrowding, saving money, providing more appropriate punishment, improving public safety, and promoting rehabilitation. He found the ISP to be successful in achieving many of its goals but that this success varied according to type of offender. Wodahl's analysis shows the importance of accounting for several contingencies when judging programs and gives reasons to be optimistic about ISP and community corrections.

❖ INTRODUCTION

The final decades of the 20th century witnessed the development and mass implementation of intensive supervision programs (ISPs) across the country. These programs were marketed as the panacea for a correctional system experiencing massive overcrowding and budget shortfalls. Two decades later, however, it has become evident that ISP has largely failed to deliver on the promises of its advocates. This essay offers one perspective on this phenomenon by intertwining important ISP research with my personal experiences in the field.

My experiences in the corrections field began in the 1990s following the completion of my undergraduate degree in criminal justice. My first "real job" was as a youth worker in a juvenile correctional facility. It was in this position that I first realized that academic study, while important, cannot take the place of practical experience. I learned more about the criminal justice system and interacting with offenders in the 15 months on this job than in my previous 4 years of college.

I later applied for and was hired as a probation and parole officer responsible for the supervision of adult felony offenders. I would remain in this position for the next 7 years. During this time, I had the opportunity to gain a variety of experiences, including supervising traditional caseloads, writing presentence investigation reports, and overseeing offenders in a halfway house facility. My most memorable experiences, however, came during the 4 years I spent as an ISP agent. It is these experiences that I draw upon for this essay.

❖ OVERVIEW OF THE AGENCY AND PROGRAM

My experiences in community corrections, including my time as an intensive supervision program agent, came during my employment with the Wyoming Department of Corrections. The Wyoming Department of Corrections (WDOC) is a state-level agency responsible for carrying out the sentences of adult offenders convicted in the state of Wyoming. The agency comprises two main divisions, the Division of Prisons and the Division of Field Services. The Division of Prisons, as the name suggests, is charged with managing offenders incarcerated in the state's various correctional institutions, while the Division of Field Services is responsible for the supervision and management of offenders in the community.

Consistent with national trends, the vast majority (over 75%) of offenders under correctional custody in Wyoming are managed in the community under probation or parole supervision. This supervision is carried out by probation and parole agents, who are assigned to various field offices located throughout the state. Most offenders under community supervision through the WDOC are under traditional probation or parole supervision, which generally consists of monthly or bimonthly meetings with their supervising agent and sporadic home visits. Agents who supervise traditional caseloads are responsible for managing caseloads of 60 to 100 offenders. In addition, many agents also have the responsibility of writing presentence investigation reports for newly convicted felony defendants.

Up until the mid-1990s, aside from a few privately operated halfway house facilities, traditional supervision was the only method of supervision used to manage offenders in the community. In 1996, however, the Wyoming Department of Corrections' Intensive Supervision Program (WDOC ISP) was created. As in many other states, one of the primary motivations behind the creation of the WDOC ISP was to slow prison growth by targeting prison-bound offenders. This was not the only reason for its development. The department also recognized a need to broaden its continuum of sanctions and provide cost-effective alternatives to prison for certain high-risk offenders.

The WDOC ISP is a program primarily for adult felony-level offenders. The program accepts both probationers and parolees, and there are no restrictions based on gender. To be considered for placement, the offender must be classified as high risk and/or high need as determined by the department's risk and need assessment instrument. Three types of offenders have been identified as priority offenders due to their historically poor performance under traditional supervision and their overall threat to public safety. These include youthful offenders who have graduated from the WDOC's boot camp program, sexual offenders, and methamphetamine users.

Offenders can be placed into the WDOC ISP by one of three methods: court diversion, parole, and enhancement. *Court diversion* is considered a front-door placement. This occurs when the sentencing judge directly orders the offender to complete the ISP. *Parole placement* occurs when an offender is placed on ISP as a condition of their release from incarceration. In this instance, the parole board rather than the sentencing judge is considered the release-granting authority and maintains jurisdiction over the offender until completion of his sentence. *Enhancement* involves the movement of a probationer or parolee from traditional supervision into the ISP. Wyoming probation and parole agents, with the approval of their supervisor, can enhance noncompliant offenders into ISP as an alternative to revocation.

The WDOC ISP is designed to last approximately 1 year, during which time offenders progress their way through a series of three levels that vary in supervision intensity. While on the program, they are subjected to intense supervision, including frequent home visits, random drug testing, and electronic monitoring. Participants are expected to abide by a broad array of supervision conditions. In addition to the standard conditions of community supervision, such as abstaining from drugs and alcohol and maintaining employment, they are required to abide by additional rules and regulations, which include curfews, restrictions on visitors, and adherence to a weekly schedule. The ISP also places a heavy emphasis on treatment and programming. Offenders are required to attend a broad array of treatment programs such as substance abuse and sex offender treatment to address their criminogenic needs.

My particular experience as an ISP agent occurred in the Cheyenne field office. Cheyenne is the largest city in the state and also serves as the state's capital. While Cheyenne is the most populated city in the state, its population is just over 50,000, which can hardly be considered an urban environment. My caseload as an ISP agent typically ranged between 12 and 15 offenders. This low caseload afforded me the opportunity to give each offender a substantial amount of attention. It was not uncommon to have daily visits with offenders, especially when they first entered the program. Most contacts with my caseload occurred in the field through home visits and schedule checks rather than office visits. These visits were intended in part to ensure that ISP participants were following the rules of the program as well as to gain a better perspective into how the individual was coping under supervision.

There was no typical workday or workweek during my time as an ISP agent. I was given broad freedom in determining my schedule, which often included night and weekend hours. It was common to be out until 1 or 2 in the morning doing home visits, as well as to come in early in the day to call offenders in for random urinalysis drug testing. In addition to the surveillance aspects of being an ISP agent, there were therapeutic aspects as well. I maintained close communication with counselors and other treatment providers to ensure that offenders were attending required therapy sessions. In addition, I was responsible for administering criminal-thinking and cognitive-behavioral groups to ISP offenders. These groups are designed to assist offenders in identifying and disrupting distorted thinking patterns and assist them in learning new ways of interacting in their environments.

❖ THE GOALS OF ISP

The main purpose of this essay is to critically reflect on my experiences as an ISP agent in order to explore the ways in which my supervision of offenders either contributed to or detracted from program success. Accomplishing this task, however, requires that a framework be developed by which both success and failure can be judged. During my time as an ISP agent, I had a very narrow and incomplete view of this issue. Successes and failures were judged exclusively by individual outcomes. The program was successful when offenders completed the WDOC ISP without committing a new crime or being revoked, while the program was deemed unsuccessful when offenders were revoked or arrested for a new offense. The limitation of this perspective is that it fails to take into account the varied goals ISPs are meant to accomplish that may or may not be directly related to whether or not an offender completes the program. Thus, to develop a framework for determining the success of ISP, it is important to first ask, What goals are ISPs intended to achieve?

A primary goal of ISPs is to reduce prison crowding and correctional spending (Clear & Hardyman, 1990; Petersilia, 1998). ISPs swept across the country during the 1980s and 1990s due largely to the belief that these programs could ease the financial costs and burdens associated with massive prison growth and crowding experienced by many correctional systems in the final decades of the 20th century. It was believed that strict conditions of supervision coupled with intense monitoring practices would allow ISPs to supervise even high-risk offenders in the community who would otherwise be in prison. Since the cost of supervising offenders in the community under ISP supervision is substantially lower than the cost of incarceration, ISPs have the potential to both reduce prison growth and save taxpayer money.

A second goal of ISP is to expand the continuum of sanctions available for law violators (Tonry, 1996). Prior to the development of intermediate sanction programs, such as ISP, the two primary options available to the court for punishing offenders was probation and prison, which are viewed at opposite ends of the punishment continuum. Probation is regarded as suitable response for low-risk offenders involved with minimal crimes, while prison is often considered an appropriate sentence for serious offenders who deserve severe punishment for their transgressions. The problem, however, is the lack of options available for offenders whose actions do not readily justify a prison sentence but who deserve more than a probation sentence. ISPs were developed in part to fill this gap in the sentencing continuum by providing a sentencing option that is more punitive than traditional community supervision but less severe than incarceration.

The ISP movement was also fueled by a desire to enhance public safety by ratcheting up the supervision of offenders in the community. Influential research conducted in the 1980s revealed that serious offenders were sentenced to probation supervision and that many of these offenders were responsible for a substantial amount of new offending, which included many serious offences (Petersilia, Turner, Kahan, & Peterson, 1985). This research led many to question the capacity of traditional probation services to handle high-risk offenders without jeopardizing public safety. ISP proponents claimed that unlike traditional supervision, ISP supervision could manage these offenders in the community and limit risks to the community (Erwin, 1986). ISP supervision is intended to promote public safety in two ways. First, the restrictive structure of ISP was meant to incapacitate offenders by limiting their access to the community. Second, the intense supervision practices were meant to act as a specific deterrent by sending the message that offenders who violated would be caught and punished (Petersilia & Turner, 1993).

A final goal of at least certain ISPs is to promote the rehabilitation of offenders. The vast majority of the early ISPs implemented in the 1980s lacked a rehabilitative focus and concentrated exclusively on surveillance and incapacitation aspects of supervision. Other programs, however, combined intensive supervision practices within a framework that also recognized the need for offenders to address underlying problems that contributed to their criminality. The merger of ISP with the goal of rehabilitation gained legitimacy with research revealing that programs that incorporated a therapeutic component were more effective in reducing recidivism than those that relied solely on close monitoring of offenders (Paparozzi & Gendreau, 2005).

❖ A TYPOLOGY OF ISP OFFENDERS: *THE GOOD, THE BAD,* AND *THE UGLY*

As I reflect on my experiences as an ISP agent to explore the ways in which my supervision of offenders contributed to or detracted from the program goals, I find there is an inherent complexity associated with this task. This complexity emanates from two sources. First, as we saw in the previous section, the goals of ISP are diverse, ranging from punishment to rehabilitation. Not only are the goals of ISP diverse, but in certain cases, they are also conflicting. In other words, sometimes achieving one goal such as enhancing public safety detracts from other goals such as diverting offenders from incarceration or promoting rehabilitation.

A second and perhaps more formidable obstacle associated with the task of assessing program success stems from the realization that the ISP offenders themselves are very diverse. During my time as an ISP agent, I supervised a varied group of offenders with offenses ranging from murder to shoplifting. I supervised offenders as young as 17 to as old as 75. I supervised some individuals who couldn't read and others who were college educated. Some persons on my caseload had deep-seated issues with mental illness and addiction, while others appeared rational and calculated. This lack of uniformity makes any general discussions of program success very difficult. The program, for example, may have been very effective in promoting rehabilitation for certain offenders but very ineffective with others.

Thus, before beginning any general discussion about my successes and shortcomings as a WDOC ISP agent, I will first reflect on my experiences to develop categories, or a typology, of ISP offenders. The majority of offenders I supervised as an ISP agent can be grouped into one of three categories, which I refer to as *the Good, the Bad,* and *the Ugly.*

The Good refers to the group of ISP offenders who presented the lowest threat to public safety. They were most commonly involved in lower level, nonviolent criminal offenses, such as property crimes or drug-related offenses. While this group of offenders did not represent a substantial threat to the public, they did present a substantial risk to themselves as well as to those close to them, such as their close friends and families. Their self-destructive behavior, which included their criminal behavior, stemmed from some type of underlying issue such as an addiction to drugs or alcohol or severe mental health problems. I refer to this group as the Good largely because of their potential to become contributing members of society. The Good were typically compliant and likable individuals who had the greatest capacity to lead productive, law-abiding lives if they could get a handle on their addictions and other underlying problems. Despite their potential, the Good were often persistent offenders who cycled in and out of the system. They often found their way into the WDOC ISP after having been unsuccessful under traditional supervision and were placed on ISP because it was believed that they would benefit from the added structure of the program.

While I supervised many individuals who fit the Good type, one individual stands out who personifies this type. I will refer to her as Lucy. Lucy was in her early to mid-40s and had been in the criminal justice system much of her adult life. Her involvement with the legal system stemmed almost exclusively from her heroin addiction. Lucy's most recent conviction, which led to her placement in the WDOC ISP, involved forging checks. The profits from her crime were used to support her drug habit. In addition to her problems with heroin, Lucy had long-standing problems with depression and anxiety that stemmed from the sexual abuse she suffered as a child. Lucy had made several suicide attempts in the past and, as a result, had spent time in several mental health facilities. Lucy was a pleasant and likable individual who sincerely wanted to change and get her life on track. Her motivation for change was driven largely by a desire to regain custody of her two children, who were placed in foster care after her most recent arrest. She was very compliant with the rules of the ISP and seemed to thrive under the structure of the program. Much of her supervision focused on addressing her addiction and mental health issues, which included frequent contact with her counselors and monitoring her medications.

The group of offenders most commonly supervised under the WDOC ISP was *the Bad*. These individuals, unlike the previous group of offenders, presented at a more substantial risk to public safety due both to the seriousness and frequency of their offending. Their criminal activities varied but often included offenses such as burglary, assault, and drug dealing. While drug and alcohol use was common among the Bad, most were not considered addicts. We often referred to them as criminals who liked to use, as opposed to addicts who committed crimes. These individuals were typically younger offenders who often had little impulse control. Many of their problems involved their peers, who also tended to be young and impulsive. Not surprisingly, the Bad were often a challenge to supervise. They were not strongly committed to changing their lifestyles and often pushed the boundaries of the program to see how much they could get away with, which often resulted in an antagonistic relationship between the agent and offender. The Bad were typically placed into ISP for one of two reasons, the first being that they failed under traditional supervision and were placed in ISP as a response to that failure. Second, it was felt that the nature of their offense coupled with their prior criminal history warranted a punishment that was more severe than traditional probation, but they were spared a prison sentence through their placement in ISP.

"Bill" is a prime example of an offender who could be classified as Bad. Bill was 19 years of age when he was placed on the WDOC ISP. Bill was sentenced to ISP following his conviction for his involvement in a string of home burglaries. While this was his first adult-level felony offense, Bill was well-known to local law enforcement and court personnel due to his extensive juvenile court history. He had spent a large portion of his teenage years locked up in various juvenile facilities. Bill liked to drink and smoke a little pot, but his main problems stemmed from his impulsiveness and temper, which hampered his ability to function in the community. He struggled maintaining a job and had very poor relationships with his family. Bill's impulsive nature also affected his capacity to function on ISP. He accumulated a number of technical violations on the program for things such as staying out past curfew, drinking, and not following his weekly schedule. Bill was required to attend counseling to address his problems with impulsiveness and anger but had a hard time making it to his appointments on a consistent basis.

The third group of offenders under ISP supervision was *the Ugly.* *The Ugly* refer to the ISP offenders who presented the greatest risk to public safety. These individuals are most often violent and sexual offenders who were placed on ISP after spending considerable time in prison. Their placement in ISP typically came as they neared the end of their prison sentences, and it was believed that ISP would offer the best environment to assist them in their reintegration into the community, while also limiting the threat to public safety. Individuals in this group often had a difficult time readjusting to life outside of prison. These offenders often found it difficult to find a job due to their limited job skills and the stigma of their conviction. The Ugly were often subject to more intense levels of supervision than other ISP offenders because of the risk they presented to the public. Treatment requirements were also common among this group of offenders. Many had substance abuse issues that prompted referrals for drug and/or alcohol treatment. Sexual offenders were required to attend sex offender counseling, which is a very intense and confrontational form of treatment. The offenders' attendance and progress in treatment was closely monitored by their ISP agents.

"Richard" was an offender who fit the profile of the Ugly. Richard came to the WDOC ISP after spending over a decade in prison following his conviction for rape. Aside from his most recent prison sentence, Richard had spent time in prison for various other violent and sex-related crimes. All in all, he had spent most of his adult life in correctional institutions. Richard's ISP supervision consisted of a combination of intense monitoring and life skills training. Owing to years of incarceration, Richard was institutionalized and thus struggled with even the most basic tasks. I remember picking him up from the bus stop on the day he was released from prison. His bus came in around lunch time, and I took him to a local fast-food restaurant. I offered to buy him lunch and told him to order what he wanted. Richard had not had a choice about what meal he would eat for over a decade and was completely overwhelmed by the prospect of ordering his own lunch. As I glanced over at him, I saw his hands trembling, and he had a look of panic on his face; I ultimately had to order for him. Despite being over 40 years old, Richard had never held a legitimate job and had few job skills to offer a potential employer, making it very difficult for him to find work. He was required to attend sex offender counseling as part of his release, as well as substance abuse treatment due to his history of drug and alcohol abuse. However, his counseling was hampered by his strong distrust of treatment providers and authority figures in general.

❖ ASSESSING THE EFFECTIVENESS OF ISP SUPERVISION

Now that a typology of offenders has been established, I can begin to examine the ways in which my supervision of offenders either contributed to or detracted from goals of ISP. I begin with the goal of punishment. As discussed earlier, ISPs were developed in part to expand the continuum of sanctions by creating a punishment option that was more severe than traditional probation but less onerous than prison. I can confidently say that the WDOC ISP was effective in achieving at least part of this goal. ISP was unquestionably more punitive than traditional supervision. The strict conditions of ISP coupled with intense supervision practices created an environment that offenders found unpleasant to say the least. This was most apparent in the supervision of offenders classified as the Bad. As mentioned above, many of the Bad came to ISP after they were unsuccessful under traditional supervision and thus had a reliable reference point for assessing the punitive nature of the program. These offenders often began the program skeptical of the true nature of the program and would often test the boundaries. However, they quickly realized that conditions of supervision would be monitored and strictly enforced.

I am less confident that the WDOC ISP was successful in creating an environment that was less punitive than incarceration for all offenders. On the surface it seems absurd to assert that ISP even with its strict conditions and aggressive supervision practices could be considered more punitive than incarceration. However, for a considerable number of offenders, this seemed to be the case.[1] The burdens of ISP supervision were substantial. In addition to the strict monitoring, participants were expected to work full-time, maintain sobriety, attend treatment, and provide for their own food, housing, and other living expenses. Incarceration, by contrast, creates no such obligations. The difficulty of ISP was often compounded by a lack of resources in the community to assist offenders in meeting their obligations. Programs to assist individuals with needs such as housing or employment were in limited supply and in some cases excluded ISP participants due to their legal status. Thus, at least for certain offenders such as those who are unemployed and lack economic resources, the advantages of incarceration are understandable.

Understanding why offenders might not view ISP as being less punitive than imprisonment can be better understood by considering the supervision of the Ugly. The Ugly most commonly came to ISP after having spent considerable time in prison. For these individuals, prison was familiar and, while not pleasant, was at least comfortable. Additionally, prison did not require a substantial amount of effort; everything was done for them. ISP, by contrast, was unfamiliar and required them to be more than passive participants. In addition to normal responsibilities of life, such as maintaining a job and paying bills, ISP offenders were often required to attend treatment, perform community service, and attend groups and meetings at the probation office. The difficulty of ISP for these offenders was amplified by the fact that it took place in the community where temptations and distractions were abundant. An offender once told me that it was fairly easy to stay clean in prison where drugs and alcohol were not always readily available, but staying clean in the community was much more difficult because of the constant temptations. Thus, for many offenders, especially the Ugly, ISP was perceived as being more onerous than spending time in prison.

Next, I turn my attention to the goal of enhancing public safety. The strict and intense nature of ISP is meant to enhance public safety by both limiting participants' abilities to commit further crimes (incapacitation) and sending a message that all transgressions would be caught and punished (deterrence). On the surface, my experiences suggest that there is strong reason to believe that ISP was extremely effective in this regard. During my time as an ISP agent, I can recall only two cases in which offenders under my supervision were arrested for serious crimes. One involved an offender who stole a car and absconded from supervision, while the other involved an attempted sexual assault. In both cases, the individuals were revoked and quickly returned to incarceration, which is not surprising given the emphasis placed on deterrence. Aside from these instances, most other arrests involved relatively minor offenses, most of which were traffic related. This observation is consistent with findings from studies of other ISPs, which show a relatively small proportion of offenders commit new crime violations while under ISP supervision (Petersilia & Turner, 1993).

While the lack of serious criminal offending by offenders under WDOC ISP supervision is encouraging, I have to be cautious before unequivocally asserting that the program enhanced public safety for all types of offenders. It is important to recognize that the public safety goal of ISP is premised on the belief that ISPs are composed of high-risk offenders who present a substantial risk to public safety. In reality, however, many offenders I supervised were not high risk at all. Most notable are the Good offenders, whose destructive behavior tended to be directed inward rather than outward. These individuals, regardless of the type of supervision they received, were unlikely to engage themselves in behavior that represented a substantial threat to the well-being of the community. Thus, for this group of offenders, it is unlikely that ISP contributed to public safety in any meaningful way.

The WDOC ISP, like other ISPs, was intended to promote the rehabilitation of offenders by combining intensive supervision practices with therapeutic interventions aimed at addressing offenders' underlying problems. Because rehabilitation involves long-term behavioral change, it is admittedly difficult to assess the degree to which my efforts as an ISP agent were successful in achieving this result. What I can say with confidence, however, is that the program was successful in promoting the goal of rehabilitation in more than a superficial manner. Legitimate emphasis was placed on ensuring that offenders had access to and were engaging themselves in the appropriate treatment programs, such as substance abuse counseling, sex offender treatment, or job training programs. I was expected to maintain regular contact with counselors and other treatment providers to monitor offenders' progress in therapy. Offenders who failed to meet their treatment obligations were held accountable through sanctions or other methods. In short, treatment was a priority in the supervision of offenders in the WDOC ISP.

Did this emphasis on treatment and rehabilitation result in long-term behavior changes in offenders? While this is a difficult question to answer, the answer seems to be yes, at least for some. As a group, the Bad seemed to be the least amenable to treatment and thus benefitted the least. While these offenders would attend counseling when mandated, they rarely engaged in any meaningful way. Most of my rehabilitative successes were from the Good. The combination of strict supervision with intensive therapy created an environment that was often beneficial to this group of offenders. One case that stands out involved a woman who had developed an addiction to prescription pain medication. She had been dealing with this addiction for several years, and by the time she began ISP, she was taking between 40 and 60 pills a day. She struggled severely when she first started the program as a result of her addiction, which resulted in a number of sanctions, such as time in jail and placement in a 30-day in-patient substance abuse program. Over time, she began to improve. She continued with her treatment, stayed clean, and was able to complete her ISPs. Several years after she had finished ISP, she came to my office to thank me for all I had done for her. She was still clean, had a good job, and had regained custody of her children. She credited ISP with "saving [her] life."

ISPs were developed largely with the aim of reducing prison crowding and soaring correctional costs through the diversion of prison-bound offenders. Prior research suggests that ISPs in general have not been successful in achieving this goal (Petersilia, 1998; Tonry, 1996). A primary reason for this finding is that ISPs have largely been occupied by probation-bound rather than prison-bound offenders (Petersilia, 1998; Tonry, 1996). In other words, ISPs most commonly are composed of offenders who would have been on traditional probation supervision had the program not existed, which does little to reduce prison growth and correctional costs.

Of all of the ISP goals, this is the most difficult to assess from my experiences. It is simply difficult to know what proportion of offenders I supervised would have gone to or remained in prison had the program not existed. I can say with at least some assurance that a good proportion of the Ugly would have remained in prison had they not been given the opportunity to be supervised on ISP because of the serious nature of their offending. Consequently, for this group of offenders, ISP was successful in reducing the prison population by facilitating the early release of these high-risk offenders. It is more difficult to assert with any confidence what effect the supervision of the Good and the Bad had on this goal. As discussed previously, many of these offenders were not high-risk individuals, and it is likely that they would have remained in the community under traditional supervision had WDOC ISP not existed.

A further reason for the failure of ISPs to suppress prison growth and correctional spending is due to the high revocation rates experienced by ISP offenders. The strict conditions of supervision combined with the aggressive supervision practices used in ISP have created an environment in which large numbers of technical violations are perpetrated and detected. And these technical violations are the most common basis for revocation of ISP offenders (Petersilia, 1998; Tonry, 1996). This finding is consistent with my experiences with the WDOC ISP. Vast numbers of technical violations were detected, especially for certain offenders. As one might expect, the Bad was the group most likely to violate program rules. These young and impulsive offenders found it very difficult to confine their behavior to the structure of the program. Common transgressions among this group included staying out past curfew, associating with unapproved visitors, and drinking alcohol. While it was rare to revoke offenders following their first violation, it was typically the accumulation of these technical transgressions over time that led to their removal from the program.

❖ CONCLUSION

Nearly 30 years has passed since the ISP movement first began, and these programs remain a dominate feature of the community-corrections landscape. It would be easy to end this essay on a critical note by espousing the ways in which ISP has failed to live up to the promises of its advocates. However, as I reflect on my experiences as an ISP agent, I find that there are reasons to be optimistic. ISP, while not a panacea for the failings of the correctional system, does have the capacity to achieve promising results for at least certain types of offenders. The ISP movement, for example, has shown that incarceration is not the only method available to punish offenders; rather, punishment can be effectively meted out in the community. ISP has also shown that even high-risk offenders can be managed in the community without sacrificing public safety. Finally, and maybe most importantly, ISPs that incorporate intensive supervision strategies with a commitment to rehabilitation can produce long-term behavioral changes.

❖ ENDNOTES

1. It is important to recognize that this finding is not unique to the WDOC ISP. Research focusing on perceptions of punishment severity has revealed that many offenders do not view certain community-based sanctions, such as ISP, to be less punitive than prison confinement; see for example, Petersilia and Deschenes (1994) and Wood and Grasmick (1999).

❖ REFERENCES

Clear, T. R., & Hardyman, P. L. (1990). The new intensive supervision movement. *Crime and Delinquency, 36*, 42–61.

Erwin, B. (1986). Turning up the heat on probationers in Georgia. *Federal Probation, 50*(2), 17–24.

Paparozzi, M. A., & Gendreau, P. (2005). An intensive supervision program that worked: Service delivery, professional orientation, and organizational supportiveness. *Prison Journal, 85*, 455–466.

Petersilia, J. (1998). A decade of experimenting with intermediate sanctions: What have we learned? *Federal Probation, 62*(2), 3–10.

Petersilia, J., & Deschenes, E. P. (1994). Perceptions of punishment: Inmates and staff rank the severity of prison versus intermediate sanctions. *Prison Journal, 74*(3), 306–328.

Petersilia, J., & Turner, S. (1993). *Evaluating intensive supervision probation/parole: Results of a nationwide experiment.* Washington, DC: National Institute of Justice.

Petersilia, J., Turner, S., Kahan, J., & Peterson, J. (1985). *Granting felons probation: Public risks and alternatives.* Santa Monica, CA: RAND.

Tonry, M. (1996). Stated and latent functions of ISP. In T. Ellsworth (Ed.), *Contemporary community corrections* (pp. 185–202). Prospect Heights, IL: Waveland Press.

Wood, P. B., & Grasmick, H. G. (1999). Toward the development of punishment equivalencies: Male and female inmates rate the severity of alternative sanctions compared to prison. *Justice Quarterly, 16*(1), 19–50.

❖ RECOMMENDED READINGS

Clear, T. R., & Hardyman, P. L. (1990). The new intensive supervision movement. *Crime and Delinquency, 36*, 42–61.

Paparozzi, M. A., & Gendreau, P. (2005). An intensive supervision program that worked: Service delivery, professional orientation, and organizational supportiveness. *Prison Journal, 85*, 455–466.

Petersilia, J. (1998). A decade of experimenting with intermediate sanctions: What have we learned? *Federal Probation, 62*(2), 3–10.

Petersilia, J., & Deschenes, E. P. (1994). Perceptions of punishment: Inmates and staff rank the severity of prison versus intermediate sanctions. *Prison Journal, 74*(3), 306–328.

Tonry, M. (1996). Stated and latent functions of ISP. In T. Ellsworth (Ed.), *Contemporary community corrections* (pp. 185–202). Prospect Heights, IL: Waveland Press.

Wood, P. B., & Grasmick, H. G. (1999). Toward the development of punishment equivalencies: Male and female inmates rate the severity of alternative sanctions compared to prison. *Justice Quarterly, 16*(1), 19–50.

DISCUSSION QUESTIONS

1. How is intensive supervision different from other types of community interventions? What is or are the main purpose(s) of ISPs? How are they connected to probation and parole?

2. What does the author mean by "*the Good, the Bad,* and *the Ugly*"? (Be able to describe the categories and identify the types of people to whom the author is referring.) What do persons in each category need as a counter to offending, and to function well in the community?

3. What appear to be the strengths and weaknesses of ISPs? Should there be more ISPs? Why or why not?

5

Patient Evaluations R Us

*The Dynamics of Power Relations in a Forensic
Psychiatric Facility From the Bottom Up*[1]

Jeffrey Ian Ross

> *Editor's Introduction*: Professor Ross was a psychiatric assistant in a
> correctional facility hospital that provided mental health evaluation
> and care for individuals charged with crimes, sentenced to jail or
> prison, or about to be released from correctional facilities. He
> identifies and discusses the power dynamics within the forensic unit
> from a frontline staff perspective and provides a frank retrospective
> narrative and analysis of contradictions between the mission of the
>
> *(Continued)*

[1]Special thanks to Bruce Arrigo, Natasha J. Cabrera, Steven Hughes, Therese
Jones, Catherine Leidemer, Bridget Muller, and Dawn Rothe for comments.
Charquis Meadows was helpful with research assistance.

(Continued)

organization and its actual operation, including a failure to truly implement a Total Quality Management (TQM) style. Ross identifies specific problems in the course of providing lessons for staff–management relations, and he points out some sources of employee stress and responses to them (good and bad). Although his coworkers and he found it difficult to achieve the ideal goals of their unit, Ross's experience as a shop steward demonstrated how dissatisfied employees can work toward improving the workplace.

Over the past 4 decades, a hybrid organization incorporating elements from both hospitals and correctional facilities has been created in most advanced industrialized countries. These are generally called *forensic units* and are typically located in selected jails, prisons, or hospitals. There is considerable variability with respect to their missions, policies, procedures, workers, and clientele. Some are primarily detention centers, while others are pass-through institutions that psychologically assess individuals with criminal charges or convictions and then remand them (i.e., send them to another organization in the criminal justice system).

In 1980, I enrolled at the University of Toronto as a "mature student." I had successfully completed a special program that allowed individuals like myself who had never finished high school to be conditionally admitted to the university after having completed a bridging course. I was slightly older than the average student and had more work-related experience. I began with a course of study that would result in a psychology degree, with the hope of becoming a clinical psychologist.

To gain a bit of firsthand experience in my desired career, I did some volunteer work in the psychogeriatric unit at Queen Street Mental Hospital—which was, at the time, one of the oldest and largest mental health facilities in the province of Ontario. I quickly discovered that I did not care for this type of clinical setting, which primarily consisted of feeding and listening to psychotic patients, and moved on to the volunteer program at the Clarke Institute of Psychiatry. Here, I worked on the forensic ward, which served me better than my previous volunteer experience but not by much, as opportunities for interaction with patients were limited. Over time, I grew dissatisfied with the Clarke volunteer program, so I tried yet another opportunity offered by the

Crisis Intervention Unit at the East General Hospital in Toronto. This was a much better fit than the other two experiences—it was fast paced, and the patient's concerns were more pressing (i.e., violence toward oneself and others). In June 1982, I began working as a psychiatric assistant (pejoratively referred to as a head banger) at Midway Forensic Evaluation Center,[2] the pseudo name I will use for a forensic mental health evaluation facility located in a major city in Canada and run by the provincial government. I held this job until August 1986. During the school year, I worked part-time; during the summer, I worked full-time. Between January and August 1986, I also worked full-time.

Throughout my 4 years at Midway, I had the opportunity to work on both the ward and the division's Brief Assessment Unit (BAU). These locations allowed me to experience the inner dynamics of a unique organization that was one part hospital, another part correctional institution, and still another part teaching facility. My access and expertise enables me to provide an in-depth analysis of the function and inner dynamics of Midway and the role of a psychiatric assistant (or P.A. for short). I worked all three shifts—days, evenings, and nights (also referred to as the graveyard shift)—so my narrative is not simply confined to a single time of day. Although my experiences may be akin to a snapshot in time and there may be jurisdictional and cultural peculiarities, considerable lessons can be learned from my experience.

The P.A. position is generally akin to that of a psychiatric orderly. However, the latter term does not adequately address the so-called professionalism of the position. In general, my job was, along with the correctional officers, to assist the nurses with unit or ward management (in other words, to maintain order). In many respects, the P.A.s were the most important day-to-day workers on the ward because (1) they had the most interaction or contact with the patients; (2) they mediated among the patients, nurses, correctional officers, and psychiatrists; and (3) they helped to keep the unit functioning smoothly (i.e., with a minimum of conflicts among patients and staff).

It is possible that the reader may see this reflective essay as simply self-serving—a manifestation of my overly cynical personality; some version of sour grapes on my part; an opportunity to blame, poke fun

---

[2] I struggled with identifying the institution by its proper name or keeping the institution anonymous (as I have so done). Although using a pseudonym is a bit disingenuous because anyone scratching below the surface into my bio would immediately recognize the institution, in the interests of editorial preferences I have gone with the pseudonym.

at, or belittle others; or an unconscious need to elicit sympathy from readers. To safeguard against some of these possible perceptions and to sharpen my analysis, I sent drafts of this chapter to former Midway colleagues for comment and review. Although some of the institution's policies, procedures, and problems have changed since the time I worked there, my sources tended to indicate that my interpretation remains relevant and valid.

❖ OVERVIEW OF THE INSTITUTION

Midway was established in 1977 by the province to assist the provincial criminal courts by providing "fitness/competency to stand trial" evaluations of individuals who had been charged with criminal offenses. Midway also evaluated felons to determine their proclivity for violence during the presentence, postsentence, prerelease, and postrelease stages of their criminal cases. The institution, physically located within another provincial hospital in the economically depressed part of the city, was jointly supervised by the Ministry of the Attorney General, the Ministry of Health, and the Division of Corrections. It was also part of a larger psychiatric institute, which I will call Parent Psychiatric Institute, that maintained research and teaching functions associated with a large prestigious university.

In most Anglo-American democracies, many people who are charged with a crime and who appear to be suffering from a mental illness are remanded to a state-appointed psychiatrist to be examined. More typically, these individuals are sent to a forensic facility for a 1-, 30-, 60-, or 90-day assessment. The length of the evaluation depends on the particular jurisdiction's law and the difficulty involved in determining the mental health diagnosis. In addition to the psychiatric evaluation, doctors may identify other health-related issues (e.g., diet, medical, or dental problems). If the accused individual cannot understand the nature of the charges or the proceedings and/or if one is unable to adequately work with one's legal counsel, then the person can be declared incompetent, or unfit, to stand trial. When this happens, the legal proceedings are typically suspended, and the individual is confined to a mental hospital for an indefinite period until a review board decides that he or she is fit to stand trial.

The decision-making process that determines if a person is fit to stand trial is often flawed. Unfortunately, situations occur in which a person may spend a considerable period of his or her life in confinement for a relatively minor crime because she or he has been identified as being unfit to stand trial. A sentence that involves confinement within a mental hospital can potentially mean a longer stay than the person would have received had she or he been found fit to stand trial, found guilty, and sentenced to time in jail or prison.

Although the majority of patients who came through our institution were diagnosed with antisocial personality disorders or labeled psychotic or delusional, a considerable number of them were charged with or had committed what many of us considered to be heinous or bizarre crimes (e.g., bestiality, sexually assaulting senior citizens in a retirement home, and dropping babies from apartment balconies). Because those who were admitted were not quite patients and not really inmates—and since they were not in a traditional correctional facility—we often fell back on referring to them using the nondescript term *clients*. Perhaps motivated by trying to stay out of jail or prison, some patients faked mental disorders, and it was our ward's duty to determine if these individuals were in fact suffering from underlying mental illnesses.

❖ REFLECTION FRAMEWORK

This reflective essay contributes important contextual information concerning management in corrections. Started in 1966 by the Federal Bureau of Prisons (FBOP), unit management is designed to break the correctional facility into small parts, push decision making downward, and try to increase contact between correctional workers and prisoners (Seiter, 2005, pp. 317–318). During the 1980s, building on this initiative and recognizing that the old style of managing correctional officers would not work so well, state Departments of Corrections (DOCs) started experimenting with and in some cases implementing both corporate and participatory methods for running their correctional facilities. The corporate management model "emphasizes modern management techniques and participant management. Lines of authority and accountability are clear; feedback and quantitative evaluations are widely used" (Bartollas, 2002, p. 261). The most dominant change was called Total Quality Management (TQM). It emphasized "work force empowerment, process improvement, customer obsession, and strategic planning" (Anschutz, 1995, p. 1). In general, TQM is intended to improve staff–staff and staff–inmate communication and improve employee morale. This is fostered by having the staff offices located right on the tiers (i.e., the floors where the prison cells are located). This innovation was supported by the FBOPs National Institute of Corrections, and in 1993, it started offering TQM training (Stinchcomb, 1998). Nevertheless,

> it did not take long for correctional administrators to discover that the new management theory did not solve the problems they faced in American prisons. By the late 1980s, most of these correctional administrators saw that in spite of private-sector management theory, most prisons had more violence, worse conditions, and fewer programming opportunities than they had had under the autocrats of old. (Bartollas, 2002, pp. 261–262)

During the 1980s, many DOCs abandoned the shared-powers model. They started moving toward a system where inmates yielded considerable power. The problem with this state of affairs was that prison gangs made up the power vacuum (Bartollas, 2002, p. 262). TQM was not without its problems, including "employee resistance," "negative attitudes," "fear," "lack of leadership support," "finding sufficient time to" introduce TQM, and lack of money for implementation (Stinchcomb, 1998, pp. 133–134). But almost completely ignoring staff input and treating it symbolically is sometimes worse.

People going into corrections and similar environments must be prepared for these kinds of problems, whether or not they go into management. This chapter identifies several difficulties that occur when management disregards the actual and potential contributions and well-being of frontline staff, especially when it does not involve staff in important decision-making processes. The general lesson here is that when management treats staff members poorly and does not take their input seriously, it ignores valuable "frontline knowledge" that management may not have and ends up fostering poor morale among a large number of employees who are essential to achieving the goals of the institution. This all comes back to hurt managers, who then have the daunting task of dealing with the ensuing headaches. Moreover, my coverage of my role as shop steward illustrates how effective a frontline worker can be in improving the quality of the workplace. In the end, management cannot just give lip service to egalitarianism; otherwise, it will have negative repercussions to the organization. A managerial ideology or set of principles that calls for an increased role of staff in decision making—something that contrasts with authoritarian styles—is needed.

❖ MY EXPERIENCES

The Front Line: P.A.s, Nurses, and Correctional Officers

Most of the psychiatric assistants were young white males ranging in age from their mid-20s to their mid-30s. Nearly all were full- or part-time university students in their last few years of undergraduate studies or recent bachelor's degree recipients. There were also a few master's students and doctoral students who did not finish their dissertations. Although Midway had a human resources department located as a geographically separate entity, most P.A.s were recruited through word of mouth. Whenever there was a vacancy, one of us usually told the head nurse that we had a friend who might be appropriate for the job. In these matters, she usually heeded our recommendations. Training was minimal and basically consisted of learning on the job through a trial-and-error process. Granted, we were eventually taught basic first aid and cardiopulmonary resuscitation (CPR), but the daily duties—how to chart on patients' behavior and how to deal with patients (interchangeably referred to as clients or inmates)—were usually learned only from experience.

Some of the more entrepreneurial P.A.s started their own part-time businesses on the side, specializing in consulting or importing and exporting. If they could do most of their hustling during the day, then at night they could kick back and read the newspaper or catch up on paperwork or accounting. Many of my fellow P.A.s, feeling that it was time to move on, were constantly applying for other jobs. But the flexibility of the work—especially if you had a child, were going to school, or were starting a part-time business—was an undeniable draw. On an evening shift, it was entirely possible to squeeze in at least an hour of studying or balance your small company's books. On a night shift rotation, for example, if you did not sleep much, you might be able to do at least 3 hours of personal work.

The majority of a P.A.'s time was spent facilitating the patients' progression through the daily schedule. We charted their behavior (typically at the end of the shift), restrained them when needed, and escorted them in and out of the ward. We also accompanied nurses on their rounds (to ensure the safety of the unit); essentially, we, along with the correctional officers, were "the muscle." A considerable amount of this work involved opening and closing locked doors and continuously counting patients/clients, to make sure everyone was accounted for. To our credit, the patients often saw us as being more reasonable than the nurses and correctional officers. In fact, for P.A.s, it seemed that the biggest obstacles on the job were not the patients but rather the head nurse and middle management.

On any given day, patients would be allowed to exercise, watch television, or participate in *group time* (a process that borrowed some features from group therapy). Although the rationale for the regimen was rarely questioned, these activities offered only mundane opportunities to observe the clients in different settings or situations and chart on their behavior. Similar to the practice of *diesel therapy* or "tuning up" identified in corrections literature, it seemed that many interactions were designed to agitate and observe, or as we pejoratively called it, to "provoke and chart." For example, a patient might be confronted by frontline staff who presented a low-level stressful situation (like a bedroom search). The patient's response was then observed and recorded. If the client became upset, it would give us something to include on his or her chart. It then became part of the official record. In short, the job entailed a lot of observation, recording, and the occasional restraint of patients.

Each P.A., correctional officer, and nurse was assigned a group of patients (2–8) for each shift. At the end of an 8-hour rotation, we were responsible for charting on all patients under our supervision. The chart typically identified several categories of behavior that served as a guide for staff to observe, record, and comment on the patient's behavior. Each patient was assigned a psychiatrist, and it was assumed that over the course of the patient's stay, the assigned psychiatrist would not only periodically interview the patient but also regularly read the individual's chart. Each patient would normally require a social worker's report, a physical education report, and a psychometric evaluation. Although the charting seemed like a logical, straightforward task, it was difficult (for many P.A.s and correctional officers) to see any noticeable relevant behavior with the selected items because the patients' behaviors were not easily categorized into discrete events. A considerable amount of time was spent by staff in the nursing station, located in the central portion of the unit. Most of the time, staffers were either responding to patient's mundane requests, charting, or chatting amongst themselves.

Many P.A.s (and nurses) were under the impression that most of the nurses had chosen the field of psychiatric nursing because they either did not like the classic *bed pan nursing* (i.e., being at the beck and call of needy patients) or because they had a fascination with patients' bizarre behavior. Although management liked to tell us that we were the nurses' equals and that we engaged in milieu therapy, most of the

P.A.s recognized that they lacked the training and experience the nurses possessed. Many of the nurses were unnecessarily quite rigid and provoking in their approach to patients and coworkers. Their demeanor often led to unnecessary conflicts with patients and fellow employees. Alternatively, female nurses who were single and seen as attractive were often "hit on" (i.e., asked out on dates) by patients, P.A.s, and correctional officers. It was not uncommon for single nurses to date their fellow workers.

Most of the correctional workers were men with rough demeanors. They typically were *seconded* to us (i.e., temporarily lent) because the Ministry of Corrections was grooming them for more senior-management positions. Thus, they wanted to broaden their experience, and a stint at Midway could provide cross-training that might be useful in their future work endeavors. Alternatively, the position provided a place where they could be "parked" if they had an administrative problem with the Ministry of Corrections. Many seconded workers had difficulties adjusting to the new work environment where the inmates—whom they were now instructed to refer to as patients—were afforded more liberties than that traditionally given to convicts.

Management

Although Midway's chain of command was rather simple on paper, there was considerable ambiguity in reporting relationships. This gave management ample room to manipulate (i.e., confuse) the P.A.s and other frontline staff. For example, no one was quite sure who was in charge. In general, P.A.s and correctional officers answered to nurses. Charge nurses on each shift were supervised by the head nurse. The head nurse (who worked only days), in turn, answered to the unit administrator and to other senior administrators. The senior administrators were accountable to Parent Psychiatric Institute, and the three provincial ministries (Solicitor General, Corrections, and Health).

During my employment at Midway, there were two successive head nurses. The first was, by the time I joined, a seasoned nursing administrator in her 40s. She appeared to have mastered all the ambiguous catch phrases as to why we could or could not do something on the job. One of my most salient memories of her involved her display of dissatisfaction with the way a desk counter had been recently installed around the interior walls of the nursing station—she chose to slam her clipboard into it several times. When she retired and her successor was announced, we knew we were in for trouble. Her replacement was a fellow nurse with minimal supervisory experience, someone with whom some of us had socialized. It was apparent that, at least initially, she lacked the necessary training and experience to successfully carry out the required duties her position entailed. For instance, she had a temperamental disposition and appeared to be unable to write an articulate memo.

The unit administrator spent the majority of the day inside his office with his door closed. Like a groundhog in spring, he periodically came out of his office to see what was happening on the ward. This was not your textbook senior management walk around. Invariably, he would find something that we had done wrong, which he would interpret as "goofing off." He would make a public spectacle and then retire to his office. The unit administrator, along with other members of management, would periodically reprimand us in front of the patients, which we interpreted as a sad effort to undercut our perceived minimal authority and reassert their power.

Middle- and upper-management jobs were designed so these individuals are rarely present on the ward. Most of the senior psychiatrists were rarely visible. They were absent because they either needed to attend meetings at the Parent Psychiatric Institute or were distracted by the pressures of running a private practice, testifying in court, or conducting research and presenting papers at conferences. Midway was physically separated by two floors; the inmates/clients, were housed on the second floor, and the administrators, psychiatrists, and psychologists were located on the first floor. This arrangement symbolically represented and reinforced middle and upper management's lack of visibility and care. This perception was reinforced by their periodic inane or irrelevant comments and diagnoses that appeared to be made on the fly during their infrequent visits to the unit. This increased our perception, and maybe the reality, that management did not care enough about what happened on the ward. In general, the nursing staff considered them to be rather incompetent and out of touch with the day-to-day issues involved in running a psychiatric ward. To keep up pretenses, the professional staff (i.e., psychiatrists and psychologists) would periodically lead a group. Under the label of group therapy, this "drama" was really another opportunity to provoke and evaluate patients, as otherwise quiet patients might speak up, which would be a chance to develop content for the patients' files. And for this reason, it became clear to many of us that this process was a coercive display of sleight of hand. In sum, we got the impression that senior management really did not care about the patients.

Contradictions

Because Midway is a government institution, many of the factors that go into cost-benefit decisions appear to be much different than those traditionally expected in the private sector. For example, decisions to admit individuals for psychiatric evaluations over a longer period of time were not necessarily made based on the demand presented by the patient (i.e., how complicated the symptoms appeared and the necessity of providing an accurate diagnosis) or at his or her lawyer's request, but rather on the availability of bed space. It appeared as though if upper management determined that we needed more beds filled to keep our enrollment numbers high, then there would be a greater pressure to admit rather than reject candidates. Also, while management complained about the fact that P.A.s were putting in a lot of overtime, nothing realistic was done to resolve the root problems such as the inflexibility of management in granting leave time.

My fellow P.A. employees and I had difficulty understanding the underlying logic of administrative decisions and thus accepting the numerous and contradictory policies, procedures, and job expectations of the institution, as well as the behavior of most of the nurses, supervisors, and administrators. Inevitably, this contributed to an us-versus-them mindset and unnecessary stress. Specific problems included the following:

1. Ward policies and practices were constantly in a state of flux. Many were not written down in a policies and procedures handbook, posted on an announcement board, or generally available for patients and workers to read. This caused an incredible amount of confusion for patients and nursing staff alike. As a result, administrators were able to manipulate the patients and some workers who didn't know any better because they weren't aware of the appropriate ward policies and practices and past practices.

2. Midway, through its job descriptions and periodic subtle communications, emphasized the professional nature of the P.A. position. However, administrators were willing to hire people who lacked a counseling or psychology background. Indeed, the duties of the job did not truly require a bachelor's degree, but candidates needed to be reasonably rational adults.

3. The institution was established to provide high quality mental health assessments. Ironically, some of the staff appeared to suffer from character flaws, and at least one of the administrators seemed to have

a serious anger management problem. Additionally, some employees engaged in poor work-related decision making. For instance, on several occasions, female nurses would, without hesitation, go into an interview room alone to speak with an alleged or convicted sex offender, which was considered to be institutional taboo.

4. Although we were responsible for patients' health and safety, it took management a considerably long time to put us through any sort of appropriate training (including the previously mentioned first aid and CPR courses). Moreover, the safety-related equipment that we were issued for out-of-unit escorts and visitor searches was typically broken. When we went on external transport duty, the walkie-talkies we used to keep in contact with the nursing station were rarely functional. The same could be said about the handheld metal detectors used when patients had visitors. Despite the number of times we complained to supervisors about these problems, the equipment was not fixed or replaced. On the other hand, we were told (in a reassuring fashion) that although the devices did not work properly or were broken, they nevertheless served as symbolic deterrents.

5. Midway assessed and cared for the mental health of patients, but was unwilling to grant days off for staff, even if they were requested reasonably well ahead of time. Consequently, the burnout rate seemed high and naturally contributed to distress and lower staff morale.

6. Although the institution claimed that it used milieu therapy, this was more symbolic than an actual practice. Milieu therapy emphasizes the idea of an egalitarian workplace in which decisions concerning patient care and unit management are made collectively. It was clear, however, that there was a professional hierarchy and that, in reality, psychiatrists actually called all of the shots. P.A.s and correctional officers clearly remained on the bottom of the job ladder. Lip service was given to employee participation in ward management and to workplace decision making. Once a week, we were required to attend the nurses' meeting. Most employees found convenient excuses to miss the meeting (e.g., emphasizing the need to maintain a certain level of coverage on the unit), which was typically treated as a joke by most attendees because none of the problems raised (particularly safety issues) would be addressed by the head nurse or senior management. For newcomers, these meetings were usually a means of blowing off steam and often involved middle management making

excuses. Since we were technically not nurses, it was difficult to hold management accountable. Although minutes were judiciously taken at these meetings at the beginning of my P.A. career, in the final half of my tenure at Midway, this practice was abandoned. Mysteriously, old minutes of the meetings began to disappear from the binder located in the nursing station. Although they may have been misplaced, most of the nursing staff interpreted this as another way that management was controlling dissent or minimizing accountability.

7. Periodically, academic researchers would visit the unit to conduct a study, and we would later obtain the resulting report or publication (e.g., journal article). The findings were often replete with what we believed were outlandish interpretations that reflected a rudimentary understanding of ward procedures and practices. This underlined the practitioner–researcher dichotomy found in many fields.

The contradictions of the work environment encouraged the loss of commitment to the ideals of the organization and, ultimately, disengagement. The differences between what was said (policy) and what was done (action or practice), led to absenteeism, apathy, cynicism, and antagonism. After witnessing or experiencing numerous conflicts or contradictions within the organization, frontline staff—P.A.s, correctional officers, and nurses—either increased their participation in union activity or began to mentally and emotionally disconnect or disengage. Part of the response may have been demonstrated through recreational drug use, alcohol use, and sexual promiscuity among staff members. Staffers would also *work to rule*, or do no more than what was required.

Loss of commitment was also manifested in passive-aggressive behavior. For example, each year management asked employees to fill out the self-evaluation section of their annual performance evaluation—initially a typical source of anxiety among many of my coworkers. With the union's blessing, I as shop steward at the time instructed our staff that this was no time for modesty and to give themselves As for each of the categories listed. When confronted by the head nurse regarding this alleged act of "self-deception," as she put it, we coyly asked for an explanation of why we didn't in fact deserve such high marks for our performance. Also, in an attempt to deal with the head nurse's failure to grant a shift change, P.A.s would often phone in sick with short notice or at the last minute. Although most of this sickness was legitimate, some was also the result of a passive-aggressive response toward the head nurse and institution as a whole and was actually a somewhat effective method used to adequately manage a healthy social life. The thought, though rarely verbalized, was that if management wouldn't grant a request for a day off, then the worker would simply phone in sick—though upon returning to work, the P.A. would most likely have to endure inane questioning by the head nurse.

P.A.s also took advantage, as much as possible, of their unused sick days; they would often combine sick days with vacation time. Although this employee strategy became a headache or nuisance for the charge nurse (and, in turn, the head nurse), coworkers believed that if middle management had been more flexible, then staff would not resort to these more devious methods. Alternatively, those who had lost faith in the organization would try, as much as possible, to work the evening or night shift, which would reduce the hours of contact we would have with not only the head nurse and middle management but also the patients.

When shift changes took place, the charge nurse would brief the incoming team. During this time, the nurse would orally review each patient's progress with the incoming staff. Periodically, the charge nurse would go into elaborate detail about a patient. In an attempt to inject some levity into the situation and perhaps to make an under-handed comment on the futility of the process, some of us would say, in unison, "no significant change." In all seriousness, it was difficult to find something new to say about many of the patients from one shift to the next. Similarly, in the context of reviewing what happened with a patient who had a history of *acting out* (a euphemism for being aggres-sive), the nurse related a story about how the person had been a pain that day. Alternatively, we would roll our eyes when the nurse would use catch phrases like the person is "coming to grips with the situa-tion," or is "showing insight" into his or her difficulties. It seemed as if all we were doing was processing people all day, and the ability to make meaningful contact or promote individual change was next to impossible.

Getting Involved

During the time that I started work at Midway, I also became more interested in politics. Specifically, I was interested in how a majority of mental health problems seemed to be a result of poor funding, an unequal distribution of wealth, and other socioeconomic, political, and social problems. I also came to question if people in positions of power in mental health agencies (e.g., psychiatrists, many of whom became administrators) had a vested interest in maintaining but not necessarily changing the system. In September 1982, I entered my 3rd year at the University of Toronto and went on a part-time, on-call status at Midway. I continued at this level for another 2½ years, working full-time in the summer and over the Christmas and winter breaks and part-time during the school year. In January 1986, after I finished my undergraduate studies, I attempted to switch to full-time status. Following my previous boss's footsteps, the new head nurse—in violation of the collective bargaining agreement—blocked my candidacy. Consequently, in an effort to redress the perceived wrong, I told a number of coworkers that I planned to launch a grievance. Within 24 hours, I received a call from the new boss with the job offer. I accepted and almost immediately asked the unit's shop steward if I could take over his position. He happily agreed, as he found the responsibilities of the position to be an unnecessary burden.

The P.A.s, along with the cleaning crew and kitchen workers, belonged to the Service Employees International Union (SEIU). Despite the SEIU's current strength in the American labor movement, it was probably mismatched for the type of work we did. Nevertheless, most P.A.s were averse to involving the union in their labor disputes. The situation later reminded me of Lukes's (1974) and Gaventa's (1980) theoretical and empirical work concerning the "Third Face of Power," in which people, after having been beaten down numerous times, became resigned to not participating in political matters. Also, it appeared as if everyone perceived themselves to be white-collar workers who would soon leave the institution, and thus, they did not want to speak up, or *make waves*, out of fear that it would lead to a negative job recommendation.

I assumed the role of shop steward in an effort to retain a modicum of sanity and to protect workers from threats, violations of the collective agreement, and unfair labor practices by supervisors. I was responsible for representing 22 workers, including P.A.s, cleaners, and kitchen help. I memorized the union's collective agreement, took a steward training course, and shortly thereafter launched the first grievance in the 9-year history of the institution. As frontline personnel, we were required to attend the weekly nurses' meeting. The head nurse would schedule staff meetings in the mid-morning hours. This meant that if someone on the evening or night shift had a complaint, he or she would have to come in on off hours. For some, the meeting occurred during the time that they would normally be sleeping, going to school, or taking care of their children. More importantly, those who came in to attend the meetings were never reimbursed for their time. Since this had been a recurring bone of contention, I used the issue as a test case for not having to work certain days of the week and for being properly reimbursed. While management was trying to figure out its response, I helped one of my coworkers—a 40-something Jamaican man who was suspended without pay for leaving work early because of a demonstrable sickness—get his job back without loss of pay and a permanent negative memo being added to his personnel file.

My fellow workers subsequently felt more empowered and came to respect my analysis, actions, and intent regarding our collective workplace justice issues. Shortly after these incidents, a business agent position (similar to that of a regional manager) opened up in the main office of the union. When I told my business agent about my desire to apply, he appeared to be very uncomfortable. Although it appeared as if it was an open competition for the job, the senior management at the union seemed to have already selected someone to fill the position. Eventually, I learned that both management and the labor union were, in effect, playing games with workers in their local (i.e., part of the union). To make matters worse, the chief shop steward worked out of Parent Psychiatric Institute and thus was not physically present in the same building as us. He was notoriously unreliable. When a grievance arose, both he and the union business agent were typically out of town. (This perception of disengagement was reinforced when the chief shop steward told us that his most favorite pastime was golf.) This incident and its outcome allowed me to better understand the political and organizational culture of my union.

❖ CONCLUSION

In many respects, this chapter depicts a workplace where most of the managers are either ill-informed, poorly skilled, disingenuous, and/or corrupted by power. Indeed, an alternative explanation might be that the management- and work-related systems that were in place were well designed but had unintentional negative consequences, that some of the managers were well-meaning and tried their best with the constraints. Yet in my recollection, I cannot find any evidence to support this point. Most decisions were made a priori by the management and either announced to the frontline staff or introduced to my fellow workers as it was something management was considering, and if there was some opposition, the language but not the essence was passed through a wordsmith, or carefully massaged. Management, to the best of its ability, also waited out the individuals whom it thought would be opposed to specific policy changes. Management hoped that employee fatigue and eventual quitting or retirement would help it prevail in the long haul. In general, however, managers used what one might consider to be a neglectful, authoritarian, routinized managerial approach in which staff members were treated disrespectfully and excluded from decision making, which led to low morale, poor working conditions, and tougher management tasks. Perhaps if a genuine TQM kind of approach had been taken, many of the problems could have been avoided and institutional management would have improved. In situations like this and all too often, typically staff respond to "the screwed up institution" with deviant adaptations (destructive to the agency and self)—calling in sick, manipulating sick and vacation days, exhibiting cynical and/or passive-aggressive behavior, excessively using alcohol and drugs, and so on. My work as shop steward, in which I helped my fellow employees, shows the beneficial impact that staff can have on the workplace. Also, it is a good example of a legitimate adaptation to unjust circumstances; instead of just griping about problems, I attempted to do something constructive about them.

In the end, most of us P.A.s got lucky. Some transferred to the forensic ward at Parent Psychiatric Institute. This provided a change of scenery and a temporary respite from the characters, policies, and practices that we had to deal with at Midway. Others finally graduated from their courses of studies and found different and hopefully better (i.e., more rewarding) jobs. As for me, I went to graduate school in the United States. In retrospect, the experience at Midway was not all dim. It provided me with the opportunity to rule out my desire to be a clinical psychologist. My stint as a P.A. also gave me an introduction to an often neglected branch of the criminal justice system that I had previously not encountered. Moreover, having practical experience in the criminal justice system has also allowed me a measure of legitimacy in my profession. As an added plus, my time spent working at Midway provides me with a source of countless anecdotes on which I occasionally rely during social functions and/or in my criminology–criminal justice classes. Midway allowed me to further understand the contradictions of the workplace and served as a good source of training for work as a college professor.

❖ REFERENCES

Anschutz, E. E. (1995). *TQM America: How America's most successful companies profit from Total Quality Management*. Bradenton, FL: McGuinn & McGuire.

Bartollas, C. (2002). *Invitation to corrections*. Boston: Allyn & Bacon.

Gaventa, J. (1980). *Power and powerlessness*. Urbana: University of Illinois Press.

Lukes, S. (1974). *Power: A radical view*. London: Macmillan.

Seiter, R. (2005). *Corrections: An introduction*. Upper Saddle, NJ: Prentice Hall.

Stinchcomb, J. B. (1998). Quality management in corrections: Implementation issues and potential policy implications. *Criminal Justice Policy Review, 9*(1), 123–139.

❖ RECOMMENDED READINGS

Dias, C. F., & Vaughn, M. S. (2005). Bureaucracy, managerial disorganization and administrative breakdown in criminal justice agencies. *Journal of Criminal Justice, 34*, 543–555.

Goffman, E. (1961). *Asylums: Essays on the social situation of mental patients and other inmates*. Garden City, NY: Doubleday.

Kesey, K. (1962). *One flew over the cuckoo's nest*. New York: Viking.

Menzies, R. (1989). *Survival of the sanest*. Toronto: University of Toronto Press.

DISCUSSION QUESTIONS

1. If you worked with prisoners in a psychiatric unit or hospital, how would you view them—mostly as prisoners, mostly as patients, prisoner–patients, or something else? Explain your answer. Also, describe how your view of them might affect the way you act toward them.

2. If you had an entry-level job (with limited power) in a correctional facility and you thought that there were problems with supervision, administration, or organizational policies and procedures, what would you do in response to them? Explain why you would choose this response.

3. Imagine that you are a supervisor in a correctional facility and will be holding a staff meeting intended to teach staff members how to better get along and work together in reaching the organization's goals. Based on Ross's experiences, what advice would you give to the staff?

6

Re-discovering Possibility

Humanistic Psychology and
Offender Treatment

David Polizzi

Editor's Introduction: Professor Polizzi worked as a psychotherapist in two maximum security prisons, practicing humanistic psychology, a client-centered approach, with prisoners. As one may imagine, he faced several challenges working on behalf of his clients in an environment geared toward punishing and controlling them. A person primarily concerned with helping prisoners will likely be viewed with suspicion and may face lack of support and even interference from staff and authorities who perceive caring for prisoners to be a threat to security. It is widely believed that offenders manipulate psychologists and fake treatment. Despite these obstacles, Polizzi finds that he was able to help prisoner clients undergo genuine change and identifies some who became actively involved in therapy despite having no chance of early release.

❖ INTRODUCTION

I began my predoctoral clinical internship having already accumulated approximately 8 years of clinical experience working with a variety of offender populations in the community. During that time, I listened to literally hundreds of client stories related to living under the difficult conditions imposed by penitentiary life. However, none of that accumulated perspective could accurately prepare me for what one actually experiences once behind the walls of a maximum security prison. I presumed that my past clinical experience would suit me well as I entered this new psychotherapeutic environment. After all, my clinical encounters with formerly incarcerated individuals allowed me the opportunity to witness sketches of the penitentiary experience through their eyes. Though penitentiary life was rarely the focal point of these individual sessions, the image of prison and the long shadow that it sometimes would cast was a helpful presence in my attempt to try to understand the effects of incarceration. As I would later realize, this observation was only partially correct.

Almost from the very beginning of the internship placement, my intellectualized knowledge of the prison environment was soon overwhelmed by the visceral reality of everyday penitentiary life. I was immediately reminded that there was a very obvious difference between listening to a client's account of his experience behind bars and actually witnessing some of those experiences firsthand. What my prior understanding of penitentiary life failed to appropriately recognize was the way in which the physical reality of the penitentiary dramatically influenced the way in which this experience would be perceived. Included in this failure was the way in which cultural and subcultural dynamics would often influence the psychotherapeutic process. Entering the penitentiary as an intern implied that I was not considered a permanent member of either of these communities and was held with some suspicion by both. What do I mean by this?

Trust is the essential foundation upon which any legitimate therapeutic relationship must be built. Given that I was a visitor and not a permanent member of either of these communities, I could not be trusted. Though I could be asked to leave the penitentiary at any time, I really could not be influenced in quite the same way as those whose lives were clearly part of the penitentiary system (Polizzi, 2010b). As a psychological intern, I was not trusted by some of the penitentiary staff because of my presumable liberal leanings, and I certainly could not be immediately trusted by the inmate population because I was staff and staff can never be trusted. The way I negotiated this difficult territory was to be faithful to both perspectives. As a psychotherapist, my imme-diate ethical concern was for the clinical care of my clients, and as an employee of the Department of Corrections (DOC), I was focused on the security concerns of the institution. Even though this stance still evoked suspicion from a variety of corners within the penitentiary, for the most part, I was able to keep them separate without incident.

During my first few days of employee orientation, I had the oppor-tunity to discuss my clinical placement with one of the sergeants involved with facility security. As he was describing the various logis-tics of the security protocols for the penitentiary, he acknowledged the decided difference in our professional duties and focus. He wanted to impress on me the importance of security while at the same time acknowledging that such issues were probably not that important to someone interested in doing rehabilitative work with offenders in a maximum security prison. I took away from this conversation the obvi-ous fact that psychotherapists were not necessarily held with the high-est regard within the correctional culture of the prison. Neither was I, however, all that surprised that many of the correctional officers in that institution held that opinion of psychotherapists as well. What was surprising was the realization that this attitude was also held by some of the very individuals whose job it was to provide psychotherapeutic care to the inmate population.

During one of my conversations with one of the full-time psycho-therapists on staff, he made the following observation. "Dave, the dif-ference between you and me is that I am an employee of the DOC who happens to be a psychotherapist and you are a psychotherapist who happens to be an employee of the DOC." My former colleague's state-ment made it very clear that to be a psychotherapist first implied a lack of fidelity to the DOC. It is important to note that this attitude was not shared by everyone who provided psychological care to inmates, and to be fair, neither was it shared by all correctional officers either. It would, however, certainly be fair to maintain that this perspective was one of the more predominant cultural attitudes of the penitentiary. I described this dynamic elsewhere as the struggle between the "us" and "them":

> The main psychological divide within this dynamic of the "us" and "them" is the obvious assumption that all of those identified as "them" represent some degree of threat to the attitudes, beliefs and normative values shared by the "us." If we generally believe that all inmates are incapable of genuine or honest interaction, we will likely view with suspicion anyone who does not share these rather obvious

views. Any attempt to establish a genuinely caring therapeutic relationship will be seen as naïve or perhaps will even be viewed as proof of the desire to collude with the inmate for some illegal or nefarious end. The logic of this type of meaning generating process is as simple as it is clear. The very practice of legitimate rehabilitative work fails to recognize the obvious dispositional character of all offenders: they are simply unwilling to change. (Polizzi, 2010a, p. 17)

The challenge, then, for anyone attempting to provide legitimate psychotherapeutic care within a penitentiary environment is to be able to negotiate this divide. Such a result is certainly legitimately reachable, but it is one that always demands the initial recognition of the problem. I found myself particularly challenged by this reality given my desire to work within a humanistic frame of reference, which demands that the therapist respect and support his or her client. Such a stance is either immediately respected or attacked with both contempt and suspicion. I have experienced both from treatment professionals and correctional staff alike. The purpose of this chapter will be to describe the way in which successful psychotherapy can be provided within the challenging environment of a maximum security penitentiary.

I will first provide a brief description of the two maximum security facilities in which I worked and then provide a more thorough discussion of the application of humanistic and phenomenological theoretical approaches to the practice of forensic psychotherapy. I will then explore these applications within the context of my specific treatment experience working with this clinical population. I will complete this discussion with some closing thoughts.

❖ OVERVIEW OF THE FACILITIES

A Brave New World: Psychotherapy in the Age of High Tech Incarceration

The State Correctional Institution at Greene County, or SCI Greene, as it is commonly known by staffers and inmates alike, was a relatively new facility in 1999 when I began my predoctoral clinical psychology internship with the DOC. The facility was opened in 1993 and was intended to serve as the state's first and only super-max institution. However, the facility's super-max classification was short-lived due to the drastic increase in inmate populations that began in the DOC during the mid- to late 1980s, a trend that has continued to the present day. The immediate need for more beds required that SCI Greene be redesignated as a maximum security penitentiary. As such, SCI Greene could be populated with inmates taken from all four classification levels: minimum, medium, maximum, and security confinement. Though no longer a super-max facility, it did retain its 400-bed segregation unit, which was often filled to capacity, making it by far the largest segregation unit at that time in the state system. The facility also housed a small number of death row inmates. Currently, the facility houses the vast majority of individuals who are awaiting their sentence on death row.

The layout and technical aspects of the facility were state-of-the-art, allowing for almost constant computer-generated surveillance of the entire prison population and penitentiary grounds. Every inch of the facility was secured by motion detection cameras and a seemingly infinite number of gates and computer operated doors that helped to increase security and control inmate movement. What was most disarming about this facility was that one rarely witnessed inmates in and around the penitentiary grounds. Inmate movement was tightly controlled, providing inmates no more than a 5- to 10-minute window to get from Point A to Point B. Once the "stop movement" call was announced over the prison's public address system, all movement was required to immediately cease. Any inmate caught disregarding this non-negotiable rule would be immediately sent to the disciplinary housing unit for a 30-day stay in the "hole." Each inmate was also required to have in his possession a movement pass that verified the next destination. The failure to provide a legitimate movement pass was also grounds for disciplinary sanction.

For example, every inmate would need to be issued a pass to attend the weekly psychotherapy session but would have to do so within the confines of the movement schedule. No passes were issued during mealtimes, and no pass would be honored until every block cleared inmate count. Failure to strictly adhere to the movement schedule would result in the cancellation of the inmate's pass. Each individual psychotherapist was required to submit a list of those individuals that were scheduled to be seen the following day. However, the request for an inmate pass did not necessarily imply that your inmate, or client, would actually attend the scheduled session. Given the relatively low priority given to inmate psychotherapy, a legitimate pass could be canceled for any number of reasons; one such example was when the officer on duty simply forgot or refused to give the inmate his pass at the appropriate time. The refusal to hand out passes was a pretty common strategy for certain officers who wished to disrupt an inmate's scheduled therapy session.

If SCI Greene represented the most technologically advanced facility in the DOC system at the time of my employ, SCI Pittsburgh represented its oldest and most historically significant. Pittsburgh Penitentiary was initially opened in 1882 and remained a working maximum security facility until its closing in 2005. Due to increases in prison population, the facility was reopened in 2007 and is currently used to house minimum to low-medium security prisoners in need of substance abuse treatment. Though given a minor face-lift in the mid-1980s, the facility retained most of its "historical character," resembling the type of facility we have all seen depicted on television and in the movies.

Stepping Into Shadows: SCI Pittsburgh

SCI Pittsburgh (also known as SCI Western) at the time of my internship and subsequent employment as a psychotherapist at that facility had a psychology staff of 10 masters or doctoral level clinicians who were responsible for approximately 1,800 inmates, which included following clients housed in the disciplinary units of the penitentiary. The facility also had a Special Needs Unit (SNU) for those stable individuals diagnosed with a chronic mental illness. The purpose of this cell block and program was to attempt to provide a level of protection to those inmates who could easily fall victim to the more predatory individuals found in the general population. The facility also housed one of the four mental health units (MHU) used by the DOC to treat inmates within the system who had more immediate mental health issues. If an inmate became psychologically unstable due to difficulties with medication or the symptoms of an undiagnosed or untreated mental illness, he would be legally committed and sent to either the MHU or transferred to a facility within the system that housed and treated the chronically mentally ill. Once stable, and no longer a threat to self or others, the inmate would be placed back into general population and returned to his previous cell block.

Unlike SCI Greene County's modern cell blocks, Pittsburgh's housing facilities reminded one more of an old Hollywood movie, complete with five stacked tiers of individual cells and catwalks approximately 75 feet in length. The cell block was also dimly lit and was often dank and poorly ventilated. Each psychotherapist was assigned to a specific cell block generally consisting of approximately

150 men, and each was required to visit the cell block a couple of times during the week to be sure that all individuals who required psychological services were being followed by the staff of the psychology department of the penitentiary.

Though the physical makeup of these two facilities was very different, the scope of my job responsibilities was very much the same. I was required to see any inmate who requested a referral to be seen by a psychotherapist, submit regular parole evaluations to the parole board to determine the psychological readiness of the individual for release, provide group psychotherapy when needed, provide crisis services when necessary, make regular rounds to my assigned cell block, and follow up with any individual from my cell block who was currently being held in administrative or disciplinary custody. I expanded my initial job description to include a regular individual psychotherapy caseload, which allowed me to hold approximately twenty-five 30-minute sessions per week; this schedule allowed me to see individual clients twice a month while at the same time working within the time frames provided by the facility. It is also important to note that I rarely had a cancellation, even though the individuals received no official benefit from the institution for their involvement in ongoing psychotherapy.

Most significant to my clinical experience at both of these facilities was the fact that neither of my two supervisors required me to use a specific theoretical model, or treatment philosophy. As a result, I continued to apply those theoretical approaches learned from my academic clinical training that exclusively focused on humanist and existential-phenomenological theory and practice. I found these theoretical approaches to be well suited to the clientele found in the penitentiary and believed that they afforded me the opportunity to construct strong therapeutic relationships with a number of my clients.

❖ FRAMEWORK: HUMANISTIC PSYCHOLOGY

Humanistic psychology, or client-centered psychotherapy, was initially created by the American psychologist and theorist Carl Rogers. Rogers sought to introduce an alternative clinical perspective to the one provided by Skinner's model of operant conditioning, which focused on the way in which we are controlled and influenced by outside social forces that determine our behavior. Rogers also took exception with Freud's classical psychoanalysis, which sought to reduce all of human experience to a set of complex drives and wishes that were also outside of our rational control. Rogers believed in the need to reorientate the practice of psychotherapy toward a more holistic understanding of human nature and experience. Such a stance attempted to situate personal meaning within the control of the individual who could then explore the psychological meaning of her or his current situation, absent the influence of learned expectations and unconscious desires and thus change his or her life (Goble, 1970; Maslow, 1968; Rogers, 1942, 1967). "By placing a greater emphasis on actual lived experience, humanistic psychology was able to liberate the possibility of human knowledge from preexisting concepts or categories which sought to limit the scope of that meaning" (Polizzi & Braswell, 2009, p. 5).

Rogers's central hypothesis reflected a belief that the individual has within the self the ability to transform existing self-concepts and attitudes when confronted and explored within the context of a facilitative psychological environment (Kirshenbaum & Henderson, 1989; Rogers, 1967). Rogers believed that the possibility for human growth was predicated upon the presence of three conditions, which he identified as essential to the process of psychotherapeutic development and maturity. These are genuineness, unconditional positive regard, and empathic understanding by the therapist of the client's experience (Rogers, 1942, 1951, 1967; Tudor & Worrall, 2006).

Genuineness implies the attitude that the therapist holds toward his or her client. Rather than hide behind a professional facade, the therapist strives to be open with the client so that an honest interaction can occur. Unconditional positive regard reflects the therapist's nonjudgmental stance toward the client. This condition, perhaps the most well-known of all of Rogers's concepts, requires that the therapist be able to accept the client without judgment and meet the individual where he or she is psychologically. The third condition identified by Rogers is empathy. "This means that the therapist senses accurately the feelings and personal meanings that the client is experiencing and communicates this acceptant understanding to the client" (Kirshenbaum & Henderson, 1989, p. 136).

The humanistic approach outlined by Rogers can be particularly effective when working with offender populations, insofar as it provides the theoretical frame of reference by which to explore issues of resistance and the lived meaning of their criminal life style (Cordess, 2002; Polizzi, 2009). By focusing upon the client's experience from his or her perspective, the treating clinician gains essential insight into the way in which the client understands this behavior, which in turn can become the foundation from which lasting change can emerge

(Spinelli, 2005). It also provides for the possibility for constructive confrontation, which invites the client to explore certain choices and beliefs that have been influential in perpetuating any number of self-defeating and self-destructive behaviors (Cordess, 2002; McMurran, 2002; Polizzi, 2009; Viets, Walker, & Miller, 2002).

Some have argued that attempting to apply a humanistic frame of reference to this clinical population is naive at best and certainly not effective (Martinson, 1974; Viets et al., 2002). The likelihood of client manipulation is believed to be high, and the lack of appropriate empathy renders any type of insight oriented psychotherapy useless with such clients. Though I would certainly agree that this observation has been true for a small number of individuals I have treated, it is hardly indicative of the total population (Maruna, 2001; Polizzi, 2009; Trotter, 1999; Ward & Maruna, 2007). Much of this "nothing works" ideology is predicated upon socially constructed profiles of the offender and offender psychotherapy that lead to what Reid Meloy has described as therapeutic nihilism (Meloy, 1988; Polizzi, 2007).

Meloy (1988) defines *therapeutic nihilism* as a countertransference response to inmate or offender treatment in its entirety: "It is the stereotypical judgment that all psychopathically disturbed individuals, or antisocial personality disorders, *as a class,* are untreatable by virtue of their diagnosis" (p. 325). The fact of criminality is seen as the overriding factor, which invalidates the legitimate possibility for lasting change among individuals in this population. Such a clinical stance almost guarantees the self-fulfilling prophecy of treatment failure. Aggressive and judgmental "treatment interventions" are deemed "necessary" given the presumed dispositional character of the offender, which is then conveniently used to identify the client as unmotivated, when "treatment goals" are not reached (Cordess, 2002; Trotter, 1999; Viets et al., 2002).

At issue here, for both research and ongoing clinical practice within forensic psychotherapy, is the way these disciplinary projects construct the image of the offender client. Is the client to be reduced to the sum total of his or her behaviors, which are to be assessed and constrained, or is the client to be seen as a human being capable of rehabilitative transformation? I have chosen and continue to work from the latter perspective. By engaging the client in a respectful and authentic manner, you greatly increase the likelihood that some degree of change will occur (Cordess, 2002; Polizzi, 1994, 2009). By inviting the client to describe his or her experience from his or her perspective, you may reduce the degree of resistance experienced in the therapeutic frame and gain a much clearer understanding of how the individual constructs the meaning of his or her lived world. For example, to deny the toxic effects of racism, sexism, or sexual abuse is to deny the lived reality from which these experiences emerge. Personal experience is not an excuse that seeks to deny responsibility but comes to represent the very foundation from which the possibility for responsibility is given its voice.

Once I have allowed myself to understand the perspective of the client, then and only then can I empathically enter that world. Most importantly, it provides me the necessary insight by which to facilitate lasting change in the client. If the client is able to experience the therapeutic relationship as respectful and caring, then he or she will also be much more inclined to respond to my clinical "confrontations" in a positive way (Polizzi, 2009). If lasting change is the legitimate goal of forensic psychotherapy, then the therapeutic process must be constructed in such a way that that does not get in the way of this process.

❖ CLINICAL EXPERIENCES

One of my most powerful clinical experiences occurred in the process of conducting a psychological evaluation to determine an inmate's eligibility for parole. The individual had served 8 years of a 12-year maximum sentence and was now scheduled to see the parole board. The indeterminate sentencing process used by the state required that an individual serve at least his minimum sentence before becoming eligible for parole; however, this did not guarantee that one would actually be granted a release. In fact, certain crimes such as rape had no realistic possibility for release given the violent nature of these types of offences. Though an inmate would become eligible for parole upon serving the minimum sentence, such an eventuality did not guarantee release at that time. Most inmates with violent offences were expected to serve approximately 85% of their total sentence before they would be given a realistic opportunity for release. Perhaps an extreme example of this process can be witnessed with Charlie Manson. Though Manson regularly appears before the parole board, it is highly unlikely that he will ever actually be granted parole.

I began our interview by stating up front that his chance for parole was zero, regardless of what I subsequently wrote in his report. The client, being well versed in the parole process, also understood that he was not going to be granted parole. In spite of the realities of the situation, he decided that he would still like to complete the evaluation process. I began the interview by asking him to tell me what happened.

He reported that he and a couple of associates were looking for an individual who'd failed to pay them for illegal drugs. Their search took them to a couple of known addresses where the individual was believed to live. At one of the homes, they confronted the individual's girlfriend who was unable to give them any information concerning her friend's whereabouts. Frustrated and angry over their inability to locate their target, they kidnapped the girlfriend and over the course of several hours raped and sodomized her in retribution for her boyfriend's failure to pay his bill. When he began describing the rape, he was momentarily silent and then began to cry uncontrollably. He was unable to speak, and tears and snot ran down his face. After a few seconds, he was able to compose himself and say, "I didn't think I was an animal." He continued briefly and once again burst into tears stating, "What if someone had done this to my sister?"

I feel that this event would have been completely different if my stance toward the client was judgmental and aggressively confrontational. Though this observation appears rather obvious, humanistic psychology and the other therapeutic approaches that emerge from this tradition, are the only clinical perspectives that clearly situate the importance of empathy and unconditional positive regard for the client as a central tenet of their theory. By relating to the client in an open and nonjudgmental manner, we were able to focus on the meaning of his actions and the power of his own self-imposed verdict. It would be very difficult for him to disagree with the conclusion, given it was his story as told by him, and its meaning was unmistakable. In the absence of direct confrontation between therapist and client, the most significant aspects of this clinical material were allowed to emerge. Though he was in fact denied parole and given an additional 20 months of incarceration before he would once again be able to go before the board, he did admit that our session allowed him to confront the difficult reality of his own actions and his determination and need to change.

Another example of the efficacy of the humanistic approach was witnessed in my work with a client who was suffering from a rather severe version of borderline personality disorder; this individual was infamous within the DOC system and was prone to regular bouts of very troubling behavior. He was well-known to the psychology staff with a history of self-mutilating behavior and an inability to tolerate the isolated environment of disciplinary custody. Though his infractions were minor when housed in general population, he would experience spectacular emotional "meltdowns" when housed in the Restricted Housing Unit, often accumulating months of additional disciplinary time.

I was assigned this individual at the beginning of my clinical internship and was informed that he would be a very difficult client to work with given the severity of his pathology. Though my actual experience of him was that of a shy and pleasant individual, there was no doubting the severity of his psychological condition. I worked initially to construct a sufficiently strong psychotherapeutic frame given the degree of personality pathology centering on issues of trust. It was essential that he experience the therapeutic frame as safe and feel free to share whatever feelings or emotions he felt were necessary. Not surprisingly, the environment of the Restricted Housing Unit became part of our weekly sessions: mirroring to some degree the same type of abusive interactions that he experienced as a child and adolescent.

As with any borderline client, I was particularly careful to construct clear boundaries with him that included a clear understanding that I would not come to the unit on a daily basis or answer his calls whenever he would deem to request my presence. However, I was also equally clear that I would attend our sessions at the agreed on times and would be ready to discuss any issue that he would bring to the session. This strategy was actually very effective and actually seemed to lengthen the period of time between "borderline events." He was able to trust the schedule we created and would work very diligently during our sessions on very difficult material. His ongoing trust in the therapeutic process allowed him to use our relationship as a container for his painful affect that was becoming more manageable over time.

I would like to conclude this section by simply stating that I saw a great deal of therapeutic change with a number of my clients that seemed to respond well to the experience of psychotherapy. The therapeutic presence afforded by the humanistic approach helped to disarm some of the natural defensiveness and suspicion that one would expect to experience with this population. I am not trying to argue here that this approach was always successful or always successful in the same way with different clients; what I am defending is the way in which this approach helps to create a therapeutic environment that can facilitate in the process of change (Cordess, 2002; McMurran, 2002; Polizzi, 2009; Viets et al., 2002). By removing the normal types of conflict and power struggles that are normally witnessed in this type of psychotherapy, therapist and client are better able to confront the more legitimate clinical concerns.

❖ CONCLUSION

The purpose of this chapter was to provide a brief exploration of my own person clinical experiences working within the environment of a maximum security penitentiary. Though oftentimes clinically challenging and personally demanding, this time was perhaps the most significant of my professional career. I found that it actually strengthened my belief in the power of the humanistic approach by witnessing its effectiveness when applied to offender populations. Too often, the process of forensic psychotherapy has been hijacked by erroneous assumptions and poor therapeutic practice, all of which resulted in negative therapeutic outcomes. Positive results are achievable, but they are also predicated upon the attitudes and beliefs researchers and psychotherapists bring to this very complex clinical setting.

By reintroducing the human back into the practice of forensic psychotherapy, we are forced into recognizing, if ever so humbly, that this suffering is real and tragically all too human. Psychotherapy, whether taking place in the comfortable setting of a private practice office or in the stark confines of a maximum security penitentiary environment, is still about coming to terms with the depth of human suffering and despair and the possibility for hope that forever lurks in those shadows.

❖ REFERENCES

Cordess, C. (2002). Building and nurturing a therapeutic alliance with offenders. In M. McMurran (Ed.), *Motivating offenders to change: A guide to enhancing engagement in therapy* (pp. 75–86). West Sussex, UK: John Wiley.

Goble, F. (1970). *The third force: The psychology of Abraham Maslow.* New York: Washington Square Park.

Kirschenbaum, H., & Henderson, V. L. (1989). *The Carl Rogers reader.* Boston: Houghton Mifflin.

Martinson, R. (1974). What works? Questions and answers about prison reform. *Public Interest, 35,* 22–54.

Maruna, S. (2001). *Making good: How ex-convicts reform and rebuild their lives.* Washington, DC: American Psychological Association.

Maslow, A. (1968). *Toward a psychology of being.* New York: Van Nostrand Reinhold.

McMurran, M. (2002). Motivation to change: Selection criterion or treatment need? In M. McMurran (Ed.), *Motivating offenders to change: A guide to enhancing engagement in therapy* (pp. 3–14). West Sussex, UK: John Wiley.

Meloy, R. (1988). *The psychopathic mind: Origins, dynamics, and treatment.* Lanham, MD: Jason Aronson.

Polizzi, D. (1994). Facing the Criminal. *Humanistic Psychologist, 22*(1), 28–38.

Polizzi, D. (2007). The social construction of race and crime: The image of the black offender. *International Journal of Restorative Justice, 3*(1), 6–20.

Polizzi, D. (2009). Developing therapeutic trust with offender clients. In D. Polizzi & M. Braswell (Eds.), *Transforming corrections: Humanistic approaches to corrections and offender treatment* (pp. 213–229). Durham, NC: Carolina Academic Press.

Polizzi, D. (2010a). Doing therapeutic work in incarcerated settings. In D. Polizzi & M. Draper (Eds.), *Surviving your clinical placement: Reflections, suggestions and unsolicited advice* (pp. 13–28). Durham, NC: Carolina Academic Press.

Polizzi, D. (2010b). Introduction. In D. Polizzi & M. Draper (Eds.), *Surviving your clinical placement: Reflections, suggestions and unsolicited advice* (pp. 3–10). Durham, NC: Carolina Academic Press.

Polizzi, D., & Braswell, M., (2009). Introduction. In D. Polizzi & M. Braswell (Eds.), *Transforming corrections: Humanistic approaches to corrections and offender treatment* (pp. 3–11). Durham, NC: Carolina Academic Press.

Rogers, C. (1942). *Counseling and psychotherapy.* Boston: Houghton Mifflin.

Rogers, C. (1951). *Client-centered therapy.* London: Constable.

Rogers, C. (1967). *On becoming a person.* London: Constable.

Spinelli, E. (2005). *The interpreted world: An introduction to phenomenological psychology.* Thousand Oaks, CA: Sage.

Trotter, C. (1999). *Working with involuntary clients: A guide to practice.* Thousand Oaks, CA: Sage.

Tudor, K., & Worrall, M. (2006). *Person-centred therapy: A clinical philosophy.* London: Routledge.

Viets, V. L., Walker, D. D., & Miller, W. R. (2002). What is motivation to change? A scientific analysis. In M. McMurran (Ed.). *Motivating offenders to change: A guide to enhancing engagement in therapy* (pp. 15–30). West Sussex, UK: John Wiley.

Ward, T., & Maruna, S. (2007). *Rehabilitation (Key issues in criminology).* London: Routledge.

❖ RECOMMENDED READINGS

Gadd, D., & Jefferson, T. (2007). *Psychosocial criminology: An introduction.* Thousand Oaks, CA: Sage.

Kirschenbaum, H., & Henderson, V. L. (1989). *The Carl Rogers reader.* Boston: Houghton Mifflin.

Leder, D. (2000). *The soul knows no bars: Inmates reflect on life, death & hope.* Lanham, MD: Rowman & Littlefield.

Maruna, S. (2001). *Making good: How ex-convicts reform and rebuild their lives.* Washington, DC: American Psychological Association.

McMurran, M. (2002). *Motivating offenders to change: A guide to enhancing engagement in therapy.* West Sussex, UK: John Wiley.

Polizzi, D., & Draper, M. (Eds.). (2010). *Surviving your clinical placement: Reflections, suggestions and unsolicited advice* (pp. 3–10). Durham, NC: Carolina Academic Press.

Spinelli, E. (2005). *The interpreted world: An introduction to phenomenological psychology.* Thousand Oaks, CA: Sage.

DISCUSSION QUESTIONS

1. What is humanistic psychology? How does treatment based on humanistic psychology differ from other approaches to offender rehabilitation? Does client-centered therapy contradict the other functions of prisons—punishment and incapacitation? Explain your answer.

2. Can the goals of offender treatment and punishment both be reached, or does one interfere with the other? For example, does offering therapy and counseling somehow make sanctions less punishing? Or does punishment like imprisonment somehow seem less "treatable"? Explain your answers.

3. Should rehabilitation remain a goal of prisons? (Can offenders be rehabilitated?) What evidence do you have that supports your answer? What are the reasons behind your beliefs regarding rehabilitation? Could they have anything to do with your values and social identities?

7

Administrative Work in Institutional Corrections

Kelly Cheeseman Dial

Editor's Introduction: Professor Cheeseman Dial held an administrative position that put her in charge of a state prison system research program examining staff morale, professionalism, communication, and offender climate. The purpose of the program was to gather information to be used to improve the prison environment for employees and prisoners. To gain the trust, faith, and participation of employees and prisoners, Cheeseman Dial employed human resource management, Total Quality Management (TQM), and leadership strategies grounded in the literature. While she encountered several difficulties in implementing the program, her experiences led her to believe that using these strategies helped her improve correctional work environments and to conclude that employee-centered management styles lead to a happier, healthier, more productive workforce.

Correctional institutions offer a unique work environment, and supervisors and administrators play a large role in the correctional experience for both offenders and line correctional employees. Prisons could be viewed as small cities in which large numbers of inmates eat, sleep, and recreate as well as learn. While most of the staff is composed of line personnel, such as correctional officers, supervisors and administrators also ensure the efficient and proper running of a prison or jail. Correctional administrators and supervisors include such individuals as ranking uniform personnel (i.e., sergeant, lieutenant, captain), nonuniform prison personnel (i.e., warden, assistant warden), and administrative support staff who operate in a prison system headquarters (i.e., division director, chief financial officer). Each correctional system relies on administrators to provide guidance, leadership, and discipline to line employees as well as offenders.

In this essay, I reflect on my experience working as an administrator with a southern prison system from January 2005 through July 2006. I discuss my role in the correctional system, the employees I interacted with, and the challenges and triumphs that I experienced in my administrative role. While this experience is in no way meant to represent the experience of all prison administrators, mine provides insights into what it is like to play a leadership role in introducing a new prison initiative to both prison employees and inmates. The purpose of this essay is to show how treating staff well and truly involving them in administrative decision making makes one a more effective leader.

❖ BACKGROUND

After graduating with my undergraduate degree, I went on to pursue a graduate education at Sam Houston State University located in Huntsville, Texas (also known as the prison capital of the world). While pursing my master's degree, I met a lieutenant for the prison system who encouraged me to apply as a correctional officer so that I could "learn about prison the right way." Consequently, my career in adult corrections began in the spring of 1998 when I was hired to become a correctional officer trainee. I began at the correctional academy in June 1998 and was assigned to work at a prison. I was assigned as a correctional officer to third shift and stayed in the position until July of 2000 when I took a job as a correctional officer in Pennsylvania. There, I was a senior officer until July 2002 when I decided to return to Sam Houston State to work on my doctorate degree. I was rehired as a state prison correctional officer in August 2002 and remained there until I was promoted in January of 2005.

In December 2004, I applied for an administrative position that would be implementing a new program in conjunction with the Prison Rape Elimination Act of 2003 (PREA). The job was a Program Specialist II position wherein the individual hired would be responsible for creating and carrying out an assessment of prison culture. The only correctional officer who had applied for the job, I interviewed for the position with at least 30 other applicants working at various levels within the agency, all at higher rank than I. Because of my degrees and ability to conduct research, I was hired for the position and promoted. The promotion was based on a scale that placed me between major and assistant warden. My position was one in which it was my job to oversee (administrate) a research program for the prison system.

The prison system was a large state correctional system situated in the southern part of the United States. The agency is divided into six regions throughout the state. I spent my career primarily working in Region I, which also housed the prison system headquarters. Region I has 13 prison facilities. My office, as an administrator, was located at the main headquarters complex, which meant that I was not a supervisor working at a prison facility daily. My job was one that required large amounts of travel across the state to visit prison facilities and train individuals across all the regions. My work environment was one of multiple locations. I spent an equal amount of time outside of headquarters at various prison units and training facilities.

❖ **PROGRAM DESCRIPTION**

My official administrative title was Program Specialist II, and my job was to carry out and implement the Unit Culture Profile Program (UCP). The goal of the program was to ensure compliance with PREA, examine the current conditions for both staff and inmates, and design realistic strategies to improve the overall prison environment for both the prison personnel and inmates. The UCP was designed to look at the prison environment through a four-pronged examination of staff morale, professionalism, communication, and offender climate.

Staff Morale

The overall morale or mood of the institution's staff is determined by an assessment (through observations, interviews, and records review) of staff perceptions in regard to the following:

- The performance appraisal process
- Training satisfaction
- Job resources
- The employee assistance program
- Staffing and workload
- Safety and security
- Staff turnover
- Job satisfaction
- Career opportunities and commitment
- Department morale
- Management's effect on morale
- The staff mentoring program

Professionalism

Professionalism is evaluated by examining the performance and competence of staff and management in such areas as the following:

- Staff professionalism
- Interaction with offenders
- Staff competence

Communication

The quality and methods of communication throughout the institution are assessed by examining areas such as the following:

- Management accessibility and responsiveness
- Labor–management relations

- Staff–supervisor relations
- Information accessibility and sources

Offender Climate

The character or mood of offenders is determined by an assessment (through observations, interviews, and records review) of offender perceptions in regard to the following:

- Staff and offender interactions
- Communication of institution issues
- Safety
- Sanitation
- Recreation
- Food service
- Health services
- Psychology services
- Mail service
- Commissary services
- Discipline process
- Work opportunities
- Educational opportunities
- Religious programs
- Visitation

The UCP itself consisted of a 1-week process that occurred at an actual prison unit. Prior to the site visit, supervisors and administrators were given an opportunity to talk to me and express concerns as well as set up logistics for interviews and observation. The UCP was divided into two distinct but equally important parts: interviewing and observation. Regional directors would choose prison units in their region for cultural assessment. During each year, two facilities from each region were selected to participate for a total of 12 facility assessments.

The interview process involved both prison staff and offenders. Fifty employees and 50 offenders were selected randomly from the rosters and were then given an opportunity to be interviewed about a variety of issues and topics relating to their prison unit. Potential participants were given an informed consent form as well as a brief description of the interview process prior to beginning the interview. Both staff and offenders were allowed to decline. If one chose not to participate, then another was chosen from a list of alternates. The interviewers were staff members selected from a pool of midlevel managers working in the central office or by regional directors. To ensure neutrality and provide confidentiality, UCP interviewers were not allowed to interview in their own region. The interviews of staff were to last approximately 1 hour, and interviews with inmates averaged between 30 and 45 minutes.

The second phase, or part, of the UCP was observation. Majors, captains, kitchen and laundry supervisors, and other prison unit administrators were all selected to be a part of the observation team. The team of 30 was trained on observation techniques and their specific roles in the UCP. Generally, from 7 to 10 supervisors would travel to a prison unit to conduct observations of prison operations as they occurred. Most teams were divided into two-person groups who would examine and observe every area of prison operations (food preparation and service, cellblock and housing units, laundry, administrative segregation, health services, education, shift turnout, officer and inmate interaction, pat searches, as well as many other areas). These two-person groups worked a variety of shifts that started at 3:00 a.m. and ended at midnight. If observation team members had serious concerns, they would approach me, and I would then report the issue to the warden or his or her designee. Observation would occur from Monday at 8:00 a.m. and continue until Friday at noon. Prior to lunch on Friday, all observation team members would meet together to present their observations to myself and the entire team. After lunch on Friday, I would then present the initial results to the warden. An official report would then be presented to the warden and regional director 2 weeks after the UCP was completed. I will now present the challenges I foresaw in implementing the program and the theoretically based practical ways in which I intended to overcome them.

❖ IMPLEMENTATION STRATEGIES

One of the greatest challenges in my career as an administrator was implementing the new program and getting correctional employees to "buy into" it and new ways of thinking. In this section, I discuss management and leadership approaches that I attempted to implement to get employees and inmates to buy into the Safe Prisons Program and the UCP. I had to take an approach that would instill trust in me and the program by the prison system employees.

Human Resource Strategies

Human resource approaches to management suggest that if you take care of your people, they in turn will take care of you. Table 7.1 presents an overview of human resource strategies.

Table 7.1 Overview of Human Resource Strategies

Strategy	Implementation
Develop a long-term human resource pilosophy	• Build the philosophy into the corporate structure and incentives • Develop measures of human resource management
Invest in people	• Hire the right people and reward them well • Provide job security • Train and educate • Share the wealth
Empower employees and redesign their work	• Provide autonomy and participation • Focus on job enrichment • Emphasize teamwork • Ensure egalitarianism and upward influence

In getting employees and supervisors to believe in a new program, getting their participation was important. Teamwork was a key component, and individuals were encouraged to share ideas. I recognized that starting a program would take the passion and support of the midlevel supervisors. Consequently, the program had to be one in which supervisors were able to express their concerns, ideas, and input and also feel that not only was their feedback heard but also that it would influence the shaping and execution of the UCP. I am not implying that human resource strategies would be effective in every situation, but they were a way to increase employee autonomy and participation. The goal was to allow employees at each level of the organization to have input into the UCP and explore ways that I could strengthen their prison units and agency.

TQM

One of the greatest challenges in being an administrator is that many correctional employees seem to believe that the agency or prison unit level administrators (wardens) do not have a vested interest in them. Another popular form of administrative management is Total Quality Management (TQM). While TQM is normally practiced and used in manufacturing and private corporations, administrators in public agencies have used it, and I used approaches tied with TQM. TQM intends to increase customer satisfaction, aim for modernization, and ensure that workers have the highest level of training. It is often associated with the development, deployment, and maintenance of organizational systems that are required for various business processes. Deming (2000) felt that there were 14 essential points that needed to be implemented for an organization to achieve TQM. In addition to human resource strategies, some of these 14 points seem most relevant to achieving TQM in the correctional environment: adopt a new philosophy, improve constantly and forever the system of production and service, institute training on the job, institute leadership, drive out fear, and break down barriers between departments. Below is a list of the ways in which I attempted to incorporate these TQM strategies into the UCP program:

1. Adopt a new philosophy

   Implement an assessment of our unit culture and examine ways we can improve prison environment for employees and offenders.

2. Improve constantly and forever the system of production and service

   Review and encourage constant feedback in the UCP process. Individuals on both the observation and interview teams were constantly asked to reflect on how the program could be strengthened and improved, and better meet the needs of prison employees and offenders at each prison unit. The UCP program and all individuals involved within it (especially myself) had to assess the effectiveness and efficiency of the UCP and if our process was both manageable and meaningful to those around us.

3. Institute training on the job

   Train employees on various elements of the Safe Prisons Program: sexual assault prevention and eradication, why sexual assault in prison is a wider societal issue, prison culture, prison cultural assessment, how to conduct an interview of prison staff or an offender. Train all levels of employee—from executive director to line correctional officer.

4. Institute leadership

I chose the philosophy of leading by example. During most UCPs, I would meet the team at 3:00 a.m. at least once and stay until midnight to ensure that the team knew that I was going to lead by example. In the same way, I expected them to be leaders in setting a tone of professionalism and belief in the UCP. If they felt they could not or did not want to be a part of the UCP, they were not forced to be on the team. Establishing a new program is best done when people believe in the vision of what you are doing and are willing to follow the leader (myself). I also felt strongly that team members needed to feel empowered to share ideas, suggestions, and changes, giving them a concrete role in being leaders.

5. Drive out fear

A new program means uncharted territory and many midlevel managers were skeptical about "another program that won't do anything or provide any real results." Driving out fear was not an easy task, and much of my time was spent in a marketing campaign of why this program was important and how we could use it to make our institutions better environments for everyone. Through training and actually working together to create the UCP, the team members really "bought" the UCP and what it could do for employees and inmates. Many supervisors saw the power it had in informal and formal ways of dealing with issues and commending employees who were doing great things. The UCP team members then served as ambassadors who would essentially sell the UCP to their coworkers and wardens, and instead of a dreaded process, in some cases, wardens requested that a team come and provide suggestions.

6. Break down barriers between departments

Another challenge in the UCP process was to break patterns of thinking into an "us versus them" mentality. Some prison employees felt that by asking inmates their opinions about the unit, all we would get would be complaints and false information. Surprisingly, inmate statements of concerns or complaints were often found to be confirmed by members of the observation team. Additionally, corrections employees who were in security might not see the prison environment the same as medical, educational, or psychological personnel. Essentially, personnel had to embrace an idea that we were all part of the same team, regardless of our job descriptions. Although this can never be achieved completely, one of the goals of the program was to get people working together who under normal circumstances might not interact or share information.

Some correctional agencies have been able to effectively break down barriers between security and treatment staff (Webb & Morris, 2002). Most correctional agencies seek to avoid change, and the implementation of even minor changes might upset a fragile balance that is present in the correctional environment. Change often occurs slowly in corrections, and to say that every prison unit or staff member was impacted or believed in the UCP would be a gross overstatement. The UCP did, however, begin the process of examining where we were as an agency and if change was needed, how we could or should implement it.

Leadership Strategies

In their research on correctional leadership, Stojkovic and Farkas (2003) define *leadership* as "a process by which an organizational culture is engendered such that tasks, objectives, and goals are achieved through the coordinated effort of supervisors and subordinates" (p. 7). Early on, after many years of working in the prison environment and seeing both good and bad supervisors in my career, I knew that to have a program with meaning and substance I would have to ensure that I empowered my team members through strong leadership. Public agencies are unique in that they have more than just one set of managers. I was in charge of my team members for only 1 week; then, they would return to their prison units and resume their regular duties. Being a part-time leader or sharing a supervisory role presents special challenges. Because the program was unique, many wardens and high ranking supervisors were skeptical of the program and vocalized this to team members. While working for me, they might have had to follow different rules on how to interact with inmates, talk to staff members, and so on. This can cause tension for employees who have multiple sets of supervisors. While a prison may have a warden and administrators, the warden is subject to the policies of the agency itself and people in control of correctional budgets (i.e., legislators). Leaders must be able to transform individuals, elevate the interests of their employees to generate acceptance and awareness of organizational goals, and motivate them to look past their own interests and work for the good of the agency or organization (Bass, 1990). Bass also discussed four elements to transform employees as well as their environments, which apply to correctional institutions:

1. Individualized attention

2. Intellectual stimulation

3. Inspiring motivation

4. Idealized influence

I recognized early on that if I could give employees individual attention, stimulate them intellectually, and help motivate them, the UCP would have a chance at being successful. I spent a great deal of time and energy marketing the program to regional directors, wardens, and other administrators. Once a team member was assigned to me, I offered them time to ask questions and would spend time with each person individually, going over their roles and ensuring them that I would do my best to help them with what they needed. I was enthusiastic and tried to show team members that I believed in the program and that I believed in them. I did my best to lead them and empower them rather than just manage them. In their book on correctional leadership, Stojkovic and Farkas (2003) discuss the differences between correctional leaders and correctional managers. These are presented in Table 7.2.

One of the things that I was acutely aware of was the importance of getting my team members to trust me and get involved in the UCP. I always told them that this was "our" program and not just mine or the correctional agency's. Their feedback and honest input was necessary for the UCP to be a success.

Interestingly, one warden talked openly about how staff and inmates could and should interact within a prison environment. It has been noted by many that Dennis Luther, former warden of Federal Correctional Institution McKean, a federal medium security prison, was a correctional leader. Warden Luther believed that prison culture could change if officers and inmates saw each other as human beings.

Table 7.2   Differences Between Correctional Managers and
Correctional Leaders

Correctional Managers	Correctional Leaders
Operate within a structure	Deal with people in a structure
Are concerned with control	Inspire trust and involvement among employees
Live in the short term	Adopt a long-term perspective
Ask how and when	Ask what and why
Keep their eyes on the bottom line	Keep their eyes on the horizon
Imitate	Originate
Accept the status quo	Challenge the status quo
Are good soldiers	Are their own persons

To create this culture, Warden Luther, translated his mission into "28 Beliefs," which could be found posted around his prison (Peters, 1992). Some of these beliefs are as follows:

- Inmates are entitled to a safe and human environment while in prison.

- Inmates are sent to prison *as* punishment, not *for* punishment.

- Correctional workers have a *responsibility* to ensure that inmates are returned to the community no more angry or hostile than when they were committed.

- It is important for staff to model the kind of behavior they expect to see duplicated by inmates.

His vision for an institution where staff and inmates could respect one another was realized in results. In his 6 years as warden, there were no escapes, no murders, no suicides, and no reported sexual assaults (Peters, 1992). His prison was noted as one of the best run in the county, and his reputation as an effective correctional leader lives on. I took his example and realized that for a prison and an agency to have vision, we had to assess our prison culture and take an honest approach by putting our employees, at all levels of the agency, in a position to have input.

Warden Luther was not the only person who influenced how I examined my role as an administrator and leader in corrections. In his book *The Big House: Life Inside a Supermax Security Prison* (2004), former Warden James Bruton expressed his philosophy of corrections management. He believed, much like Warden Luther, that intimidation was not an effective strategy:

> Prisons do not run safely through intimidation. They don't run safely through fear of automatic rifles or corporal punishment. Prisons don't run safely by accident; they run safely by design. And it all starts with how you treat people. This is the most critical of all management principles in prison operations. It forms the foundation upon which everything else is built. Security and control—given necessities in a prison environment—only become a reality when dignity and respect are inherent in the process. (p. 75)

Bruton recognized the value of people in corrections, both staff and inmate. In approaching the UCP and my leadership position, I tried to remember to focus on people first and the actual program second. If people felt like they were valuable and truly seen as a human resource, then the program and prison cultural assessment would fall into place.

❖ IMPLEMENTING THE PROGRAM

Planning

Because the UCP was a new program, I spent from 6 to 8 months just getting a program plan of action and teams of people in place. The UCP was designed loosely on the Federal Bureau of Prisons Character Profile, although we attempted to carve this into our own unique process by making it qualitative in nature and the data very rich in depth. I spent an entire week with a consultant examining how we could create a program that was manageable yet provided information that wardens and regional directors could use for their facilities. Another part of the planning phase was to talk to wardens, supervisors, and correctional officers to get their input on the types of information that they wanted from a UCP (i.e., what types of information we could gather that would help the agency and employees understand the prison culture). Planning also involved discussions about logistics: what we could realistically and feasibly accomplish in a week and the types of resources we would need (e.g., access to computers, offices, personnel, etc.).

The UCP program was also run off grant funds, not from the same monies used for other public prison initiatives. Resources were not scarce, so I could pay my team members to stay in hotels and was able to buy new laptops for the team for data collection (this was met with resentment from many people who were unable to get anything for their prisons or employees). Our grant money had to be spent on the program and could not be diverted to other programs or initiatives. Planning for this project also meant that I spent a great deal of time with regional directors, the deputy director, and the executive director. As an individual who had spent her entire career as a correctional officer, I found it rather intimidating and nerve racking to spend time with people at the highest level of the agency. Additionally, because of my great jump from correctional officer to administrator, I felt a great deal of pressure to succeed and provide a great program.

Training

I spent much of my first 8 months traveling across the state explaining what a UCP was, how it was conducted, what we envisioned it would do, and how the program fit into the overall mission of the agency. The initial training was done with regional directors, and their feedback was then incorporated into the program itself and into further training. The regional directors chose two employees from each prison unit who were then sent to training with me to learn about their role in the process. This was the most intensive part of the training. Members were taught interviewing skills, such as how to remain neutral when interviewing, especially when interviewing inmates. After training, individuals were selected for teams based on interviewing skills, availability, and willingness to participate. Training time was also spent marketing the program. I learned a great deal in training about how people saw the agency (mostly negatively), new programs (very skeptically), educated people (very skeptically), and themselves. I also learned that change in any correctional agency is slow and that it takes time, effort, determination, and strength to keep pushing for change.

Running the Program

Actually, running the Unit Culture Profile Program was a major task. As such, I had to keep track of all team members, maintain awareness of my budget, schedule UCPs and UCP training, and coordinate my efforts with regional directors and wardens. One of the lessons I learned was that the world of administration is often tough to navigate.

One high level administrator wants things done one way, while another might prefer something different. I called it the upper administration obstacle course. Sometimes, I weaved my way through it, and other days, I would trip and fall. One of the hardest things I had to learn is that some people just did not like me or the program itself. In particular, when I had to share a report with the warden and the results were not positive, I was often accused of skewing the results or having a hidden agenda. It was often circulated, and totally untrue, that the UCP was a project that I was doing for my doctoral dissertation. My dissertation was on a corrections topic (correctional officer stress) but no UCP data were ever included in any of my research.

This is not to say that running a program and managing a team of people was a bad thing or did not have positive aspects. I loved having the opportunity to create a process that I really believed would help both staff members and offenders in a real and significant way. I was also afforded a great deal of autonomy in my schedule and appreciated the flexibility that the position afforded me. This autonomy was also presented to me in how I actually ran the UCPs, whom I was allowed to place on my teams, and how I wrote the final report that went to the regional director, deputy director, and facility warden. My supervisor, now a warden, understood that in order for me to become a leader, I had to make mistakes and plan without his micromanagement. If something in a UCP needed to be changed, I was given the power to change it without having to jump through bureaucratic hoops. One of the most enjoyable parts of my job was actually getting to know people.

Working With People

Of all that I learned in my experiences as an administrator of an assessment project, I learned the most about people in general and how to motivate and treat employees. My job, in reflection, was mostly about people—how they felt, what they liked and disliked, and how to get them to share their feelings and perceptions of the prison environment. One of the greatest things that came out of the UCP was something that I never really expected to be a benefit of the program. Many of my team members got to meet and exchange information with other people in the correctional agency that they would not have met but for the UCP. Many of them (mostly those on the observation team) expressed that when they saw immediate problems in the prison, they were able to work together to solve the issue or brainstorm ways to fix it. They were also able to see how other administrators ran their areas (i.e., laundry and food service) and take ideas back to their prisons and use them for greater efficiency, cost savings, and a better environment for staff and offenders. Observation team members really were impacted by the UCP process then. Not only were they able to help change prison unit cultures where they did assessments, but they were also able to take information back to their prisons to implement change.

One of my most striking realizations was that employees (and offenders) would talk honestly and openly about their prison units once they understood the confidentiality and anonymity of the survey and that their responses would not go directly to their supervisors or warden. It was originally expected that a great deal of employees would not be willing to talk about the unit, and we might not have a high completion rate. The employees longed to have a voice and talked at length with interviewers about the prison and issues that could or should be addressed by their prison and the agency as a whole. On many occasions, they thanked me or team members for talking with them and listening to their thoughts and ideas. The simplest and most concrete thing I learned was that correctional employees wanted to have a voice and be heard. Many said that they did not think anything would change but were glad that they got to talk to someone about their views and perceptions of their prison. I realized that no matter what job position I held, I would need to remember to give my employees a voice.

❖ REFLECTIONS AND CONCLUSION

I greatly appreciate my time as an administrator. The UCP was a modern approach to examining prison environments and one of which I was excited to be a part. Many southern prison systems are known for their tough approach to crime and corrections. Being part of a project that took an honest qualitative look at its prisons and how to best approach prison culture from the perceptions of both inmates and prison employees was a learning experience that taught me many new things about institutional corrections. The project was a highlight in my correctional career, and I consider myself very blessed to have been able to play a role in it. As an administrator, I was tasked with the program's creation, implementation, and long-term sustainability. It was an amazing experience, which helped me to see the power in listening to people and giving them a say in how the agency and prison could help them best do their jobs. Since much of the research in corrections focuses on stress, job burnout, and job dissatisfaction, I was thoroughly convinced that correctional supervisors and administrators who had an employee-centered approach would have a happier, healthier, and more productive work force. This is not to say that the job was challenge free. Administrators are tasked with many demands and have to make tough decisions that are not always embraced by employees. Many people disliked the UCP program, feeling that it was too "touchy feely" and believing that it would never produce any long-term results or benefits. I made enemies with wardens who felt that I was too hard on them or their prison. Essentially, sometimes doing a good job means that you cannot be everyone's friend and that you will not always make everyone happy. If my team reported issues and I reported them to the warden, I took the heat when the warden disagreed. When my team had issues, I had issues and felt that as their leader, part of my responsibility was to listen to them, process their comments, and be willing to do anything and everything that I expected of them.

After 1 and a half years, I left my position as UCP Coordinator with the agency to pursue a career in higher education. The program was put on hold and another person was hired, and the agency felt that a quantitative survey of employees would be more valuable so that it could generate statistics about how employees felt about their jobs. However, the value of the UCP could not be measured by charts and graphs. The true impact that the UCP program had on people will never be measured. I was sad to see the qualitative UCP program die because it reminded me of the comments made by so many employees such as, "is this just another passing feel good program the agency is doing and will you be around in another year?"

Regardless, my time as an administrator and program coordinator taught me much about people and correctional administration. Employees really are the backbone of any agency, and asking them what they need and giving them the power to implement change cannot be overlooked. Running a prison is also a major undertaking, and I respect the hard work of all prison supervisors and employees. Prisons are unique in that the clients are generally hostile toward agency employees, which adds another set of challenges for correctional administrators.

❖ REFERENCES

Bass, B. M., (1990). *Bass and Stogdill's handbook of leadership*. New York: Free Press.

Bruton, J. (2004). *The big house: Life inside a supermax security prison*. Osceola, WI: Voyageur Press.

Deming, W. E. (2000). *Out of the crisis*. Boston: MIT Press.

Peters, T. (1992). *Liberation management.* New York: Knopf.

Stojkovic, S., & Farkas, M. (2003). *Correctional leadership: A cultural perspective.* Belmont, CA: Wadsworth.

Webb, G. L., & Morris, D. G. (2002). Working as a prison guard. In T. Gray (Ed.), *Exploring corrections* (pp. 69–83). Boston: Allyn & Bacon.

❖ RECOMMENDED READINGS

Gregory, G. H. (2002). *Alcatraz screw: My years as a guard in America's most notorious prison.* Columbia: University of Missouri Press.

Horton, D. M., & Nielsen, G. R. (2005). *Walking George: The life of George John Beto and the rise of the modern Texas prison system.* Denton: University of North Texas Press.

Josi, D. A., & Sechrest, D. K. (1998). *The changing career of the correctional officer: Policy implications for the 21st century.* Boston: Butterworth-Heinemann.

Lombardo, L. X. (1989). *Guards imprisoned: Correctional officers at work.* Cincinnati, OH: Anderson.

Miller, T. D. (1996). *The warden wore pink.* Southeastern, PA: Biddle.

Ross, R. R. (1981). *Prison guard, correctional officer: The use and abuse of the human resources of prisons.* London: Butterworths.

Wilkinson, W. R. (2005). *Prison work: A tale of thirty years in the California department of corrections.* Columbus: Ohio State University Press.

DISCUSSION QUESTIONS

1. Do you plan on being a supervisor, manager, or upper-level administrator in a criminal justice agency? If so, what kind of positions are you considering? If not, why not? Imagine that you are in such a position of authority. What approaches will you take to get the most out of employees in your charge?

2. What are the literature-based theoretical strategies that influenced the author? Describe each of them.

3. Does this essay make working in corrections as a staff person, supervisor, or administrator seem attractive in any way? For example, could it make someone optimistic about working in corrections? Thoroughly explain your answer.

8

The Experiences of an Outsider Spending Time Inside

Gennifer Furst

Editor's Introduction: Professor Furst worked for an external agency that oversees and monitors a state prison system, a position that made her an advocate for prisoners' rights. She visited many prisons and found several problems with prison environments and practices and responded by recommending changes to authorities. Furst also observed problems associated with special populations: racial and ethnic disparity, different challenges for female prisoners, and the increasing needs of an aging prison population. Unfortunately, she cannot report that her work led to the desired changes, noting that prisons are bureaucratic systems and as such are resistant to change. However, Furst is thankful for the opportunity to work in corrections and learned much from her experiences, which is an inspiration behind her teaching.

❖ INTRODUCTION: A BRIEF HISTORY OF PRISON OVERSIGHT

Most prisons are publicly funded, yet they remain closed to the public. Still, outsiders have been visiting the inside of prisons since their inception. The earliest jails held those awaiting trial and sentencing, debtors, and even witnesses to crimes. People young and old, male and female, healthy and ill (physically and mentally) were housed together in underground tomblike structures. Zoo-like visits by villagers as a way to generate money exploited those held inside. These first tourists were not there for research or humanitarian purposes. In addition to entertainment, the tours served as a form of general deterrence. People went inside to experience firsthand what would happen to them if they were caught engaging in criminal behavior. The very conditions used to scare people then are what modern day oversight agencies are designed to prevent.

Perhaps the first recorded fact-finding prison tour was by Alexis de Tocqueville and his friend Gustave de Beaumont, who were sent by the French government in 1831 to investigate and then report their findings about how American penitentiaries delivered punishment. During their 9 months traveling through a young United States (comprised of 24 states and a handful of territories), they toured Sing Sing Penitentiary in New York where the Auburn model was used. There, inmates worked together during the day but were not permitted to speak to each other. They worked in silence and walked the prison halls in lockstep. Tocqueville and Beaumont also toured Eastern State Penitentiary in Philadelphia, designed by Quakers who believed penance would cure criminality. Under the Pennsylvania model, inmates were housed in their own single cells for the duration of their sentence. The solitary confinement conditions were the origins of today's super-max prisons wherein inmates live under 23-hour lockdown, are not permitted contact with any other inmates, and engage in minimal interaction with prison staff. Designed to provide inmates with maximum time to reflect on their criminal behavior and ask for forgiveness, this model was described by Tocqueville as both "the mildest and most terrible ever invented" (Damrosch, 2010, p. 123). His explorations of American society were published in his well-known work *Democracy in America*.

A decade later, Charles Dickens's travels from England to North America were published in *American Notes* (1842/2004). In his description of his visit to Eastern State Penitentiary, he concluded that the "slow and daily tampering with the mysteries of the brain to be immeasurably worse than any torture of the body" (p. 111). He wrote with great certainty that it would be "better to have hanged him at the beginning [of his sentence] than bring him to this pass" as any released man would return to society "unhealthy and diseased" (p. 121). He left the prison convinced that the silent system of New York was a more humane and less damaging alternative.

The tradition of visiting prisons to inspect conditions continues to this day. Prison monitoring, or oversight, is seen as a way to protect the civil rights of prisoners and ensure that legal standards of humane treatment are upheld. Getting tough on crime, which includes the war on drugs and mandatory minimum sentences, such as *three-strike laws*, has resulted in prisons becoming increasingly dangerous places for inmates (and staff). Mass incarceration and the ensuing overcrowding, coupled with decreasing prison programming including educational and vocational programs, has created potentially volatile conditions inside prisons across the country. Overcrowding has been associated with increased physical and sexual violence, gang activity, and the spread of disease. Being forced to house increasing numbers of people with fewer resources creates conditions that are ideal for misconduct on the part of prison officials. Exposing what occurs in prisons, then, is crucial for public accountability and reducing the likelihood of human rights violations. However, gaining access to prisons remains one of the biggest challenges in meeting these objectives. Prison officials accustomed to operating free from public scrutiny are often apprehensive about opening their gates to the wondering eyes of outsiders.

Today, the United States has three independent prison oversight agencies: the Correctional Association of New York established in 1844, the Pennsylvania Prison Society founded in 1787, and the John Howard Association of Illinois established in 1901. Each is organized differently, has varying degrees of power to bring about change in the facilities they monitor, and provide a variety of programs and services. Some offer direct assistance to clients, such as support groups for the families of inmates, while others are policy focused and work to bring about change through research, report writing, and political action. However, they share a key characteristic that makes them unique organizations: They each have access to prisons and are able to see things and talk to people that others cannot.

❖ MY POSITION WITH THE AGENCY

I worked for a prison oversight agency, spending nearly 4 years as the associate director of a project that monitored the state's prisons for men. The organization has an office located in a major city far from most of the state's prisons, where staff members also worked on the agency's other projects, including one that monitored conditions in juvenile facilities and one that focused on changing drug law policies in the state. Working as an advocate for the rights of prison inmates is not a socially valued position. Most of society has nothing but disdain for offenders—much of it based on media images. Facility administrators and security staff often regarded us as *inmate lovers*—a term meant to be derogatory. To the state's department of corrections central headquarters, we were generally considered bothersome pests.

Facility administrators and staff always knew when we would be visiting. We had to submit the list of prisons that we wanted to visit 6 months to a year prior to being granted permission. We toured approximately one prison each month. It was not always easy to coordinate a date between the prison administration and my agency's staff. While the project was devoted solely to prison monitoring, the executive director oversaw the agency's other projects and was not always available to spend time away to make a visit. As in many states, the facilities we visited were often located in remote parts of the state. It could take 2 days to conduct a visit—1 day of travel and 1 day of visit. The travel was only one part of what made the work difficult.

❖ THE WORK

The tours (visits) were full-day affairs and coordinated entirely according to a previously agreed-upon schedule. We might begin at 8 a.m. and leave at 3 or 4 p.m. We generally went to the same areas in each prison we visited: at least one housing unit; the special housing unit if there was one; a program such as a GED class or maybe a life skills course, such as anger management; and any unique programs such as the factory in the facility where license plates and state-use goods were made and puppy programs in which inmates train dogs to become service or working canines. Each year, we focused on a special issue. When we were concentrating on mental health services in order to write a comprehensive report about receiving mental health care inside the state prisons, we would be sure to schedule a visit to the mental health unit. Once there, we interviewed inmate patients, mental health staff members, and security staff members assigned to the unit. When we were studying the general working conditions of the security staff, I would facilitate a focus group with correction officers (COs) at each facility we visited. I asked about their safety, including if they thought staffing levels were appropriate (i.e., if posts go unfilled), thought that staff members were required to do excessive overtime (once on a shift, if too many call in sick for the next shift, officers can be forced to remain for another unplanned 8-hour shift), felt that they had the support of administrators (if officers have the tools needed to adequately perform their jobs, such as training in identifying mental illness in inmates and the opportunity to train in special tactics such as cell extraction), and used methods to mediate their on-the-job stress. The information we gathered was then written into a report that went to the commissioner of the Department of Corrections and the top administrator at the visited facility and was made available to the public through the agency's website.

The research reports that we wrote under the auspices of the visiting project were designed to add to the existing literature about what works in corrections. Our work combined qualitative and quantitative research methods. By being inside the prisons and experiencing firsthand the phenomena we were studying, we were conducting what could be described as miniethnographies. We also had numbers to support our findings. For example, the size of the mental health services caseload was used to support our argument that more facilities specific to mental health care were needed. Our inquiries led to other conclusions. For example, we found that receiving medication in a prison setting was not therapeutic and the ability of the mental health care workers to be effective was stymied by the priority of prison security. We were constantly reminded that the staff of the office of mental health worked in the house of corrections. Also, when studying working conditions we learned about the strain caused by the racial differences among security staff members at some facilities. Some staff wondered, Would a CO of a different race "have your back" and immediately help in an emergency, or would that person delay coming to your assistance for 10 to 15 seconds—time that could make the difference between life and death?

While the director of the visiting program and I were responsible for achieving the research goals of the project, we were only part of the ensemble that conducted the prison visits. The group always included the program director, me, the executive director of the agency, and a handful of others. Sometimes, we might take two or three of the agency's board members, sometimes a doctor or other specialist. We wanted enough people to be able to split up at times during the day to see more areas, but we did not want so many as to make the group unmanageable. The board members were wealthy people who literally allowed the agency to exist, so if one of them insisted on accompanying the project director and me to a certain area, we would have to accommodate him (the board of directors was composed of mostly men). Bringing what we believed to be too many people into a given area of the prison could be problematic in a number of ways. We found that staff members and inmates were generally more willing to open up and talk to one or two of us. Board members might take time asking about things that we deemed unimportant because we had our own agenda of questions requiring answers. The gender makeup of the group visiting a given area also mattered. There were times when the program director, another female, and I felt that bringing a male member of the group would change the dynamics in such a way that people would not feel free to speak. We were also obviously younger than the members of the board of directors, and we found people sometimes felt more comfortable talking to someone closer to them in age.

The size and makeup of the group was particularly important when visiting an area with restricted access, such as a special housing unit (SHU) where inmates were on 23-hour lockdown. Security staff was generally uncomfortable with too many people walking around the most secure areas. We were told that this was for our own safety and general security purposes, but these inmates were also the most psychologically compromised men and were living under restrictions that went beyond those of the general prison population. Here were men whose possessions were limited to one or two sets of clothing, basic hygiene items, one pillow, one blanket, and one or two books. There were no pictures on the walls and no TVs, and you could see that the isolation took a toll on them. The conditions also made our work more challenging. In these units with solid metal doors, we had to talk through the *feed-up slot*, the small door that opened to allow food to be passed through; we would kneel on the floor and do our best to hear the answers to our questions above the din of the unit. The monotony of life in these places sometimes led to a commotion when we arrived on the unit. Because we wanted to maintain the inmates' confidentiality when speaking with them about their living conditions, we did not want to yell back and forth through the doors.

When we visited the facility that housed the state's death row inmates, the size of the group became an issue. In addition to practical matters, these visits also demonstrated a principle of our work: Inmates are not fish in a fishbowl to be looked at or examined—they are people. However, at the time, I was adamant about getting to go to death row. How could I not? It was a once in a lifetime opportunity to enter one of the most restricted areas in any prison in the state. I was ultimately included in a four-member group to visit death row. More than anything, I remember the men's unwillingness to talk with us. These men were fighting legal battles to save their lives and get off death row; they were not interested in talking with us about their extraterrible living conditions. The camera on the wall across from their cells meant that they were subject to 24-hour surveillance—an intrusive compromise to their dignity. They were watched even while going to the bathroom. The lights on death row, one large fluorescent fixture on the ceiling of each cell, were never shut off. Being helplessly subject to 24-hour illumination took a toll on their mental health. These were understandably angry men. While each had been convicted of homicide, there were thousands of men convicted of taking another's life who were fortunate enough (in the eyes of these death row inmates) to be living under the conditions of the general population in a maximum-security prison. The crimes committed by the men on death row were not necessarily more heinous than others' but due to extralegal factors, such as where the trial took place (a disproportionate number of the men on death row were tried in a county known to be politically conservative) and the quality of their defense, they were on death row while other killers were not.

My ambition was to be able to say that I visited death row; the uniqueness and status I believed it would provide me as a budding criminologist blinded me to the very reason I did this job. People in prison are human beings. I feel that we have all done something wrong and nearly all of us have broken laws; people in prison happen to have been caught, and as a society, it is wrong for us to never allow them to move beyond their lives' worst acts.

I think one of the most surprising things I learned from visiting prisons came from interacting with men serving life sentences. Prior to sitting down with my first group of lifers, I was expecting to meet a group of angry men; why would they not be mad—mad at the system, mad at themselves, mad at the rules that governed their lives. Instead, the men I met were uplifting and full of hope. I sat among a group of men who appeared to be in better spirits than I was. I was awestruck by their inner strength; they all had a sense of optimism about their futures. They believed they could have their sentences commuted or otherwise reduced. I learned that to live in prison you must have hope; without hope, there is no reason to continue to live. I do not think that I would be as strong as these men.

There was one other facility that I desperately wanted access to: the state's super-max prison. Everyone inside lived under 23-hour lockdown in addition to other restrictions, not only in terms of their possessions but also even in terms of their meals and the number of showers they could take each week. Although they were officially permitted 1 hour of yard or recreation time each day, many of them did not take it. Some did not want to bother to go through the process of being shackled at the hands, legs, and waist (referred to as being hog-tied) to leave their cell for what at that point would be less than a full hour, just to go out to be put in another cage—essentially an outdoor dog run. Their recreation time would be spent in a rectangular-shaped area created with a 20-foot high chain-link fence. There were no balls or sports equipment. They could run or walk in short circles or do push-ups or sit-ups.

I was surprised when neither the executive director of the agency nor any member of the board of directors was interested in visiting this facility. As a result, the visiting group consisted of three females: the program director, me, and the director of the women's prison project. Never had I been on a visit with just three females. It is important to remember that working in the criminal justice system, particularly inside prisons, is a male-dominated environment. The administration and staff's attempt to intimidate who they thought were three naive, young women began when we entered the prison and were asked by the warden, or top administrator, if we had brought our raincoats. We had to admit that we did not understand his reference. We were then told that we were about to come into contact with many chronic "throwers." *Throwing* was the name conferred on the phenomenon of throwing a concoction of various bodily fluids, such as urine, semen, and feces, on a staff person passing by a cell. While some known throwers were housed in areas with solid metal doors, which minimized but did not completely protect staff from being thrown upon (throwing could also happen when food was passed through the feed-up slot), the facility did not have enough of these types of cells. Some throwers were locked in traditional cells with bars, but the security staff had placed large sheets of Plexiglas over most of the front of the cells to minimize the threat of being thrown upon.

I was confident that we were not in jeopardy—I never felt threatened in any prison at any point during the time I spent inside. In fact, I felt prison was a lot safer than where I lived in Brooklyn at the time; no one in prison had a gun, and there was a high level of control and scrutiny of behavior that was impossible on a city street. The vast majority of men I have met in prison have been nothing but respectful. Even though they were fully aware that we were not going to come in and make prison a hotel, they were grateful to know someone was spending their time and effort to get inside and ask them about how they were living.

The visit to this super-max prison was unique in only one way: The things I saw and the inmates with whom I interacted made me ask myself if I could continue this type of work. The men I met were all too thin. One of the punishments in this super-max, and in other prisons, is being put on a diet of *the loaf*—a nutritionally complete but unappetizing blended and baked mix of vegetables, grains, and protein that could be served to an inmate three times a day for up to 5 days. Those on this diet were supposed to be medically monitored and receive a regular diet for 2 days before they could be returned to the regimen of the loaf. Most of the men also appeared pale—even the men of color looked pallid.

The memory of an interaction I had with one man locked inside this facility has stayed with me to this day. He was a Vietnam War veteran and was actively hallucinating while I attempted to have a conversation with him. My prior experiences working with people with chronic mental illness taught me to recognize symptoms and behaviors of serious mental illness. This man was holding a conversation with someone not present in this reality; he was responding to stimuli not in this reality. I asked the CO who was escorting me to tell me a little bit about this man, and he disclosed the inmate's status as a veteran. Being sent to a super-max or living under super-max conditions is further punishment for not adhering to the conditions of punishment. Someone unwilling or unable to conform to imprisonment receives this type of sentence; it is referred to it as *prison within prison*. Super-max is where a prisoner goes when maximum-security prison does not control his behavior. This man was obviously unable to follow prison rules due to his mental illness. Hearing what amounts to an uncontrollable radio in your head will distract you from listening to those immediately around you; this is how schizophrenia is often described. However, prison is not designed to accommodate people with chronic mental illness. Prison is designed to punish people who break the rules of society. But what if some break society's rules because they are distracted or preoccupied by something like voices in their heads that they cannot silence? They could be sent to prison lacking the capacity to follow its rules; violating rules in the general population could then lead to more secure confinement and ultimately to a super-max prison.

Super-max conditions raise an important question: Does an inmate bring maladaptive, rule-breaking behavior with him, or do the conditions of confinement encourage maladaptive behavior? It is a sort of chicken and egg conundrum. The question is particularly striking when one considers the escalation of the severity of conditions from general population to super-max. Prison administrators and staff argue that people end up in super-max *because* they do not follow prison rules. On the other side are those of us who argue that mental illness can prevent a person from being capable of following prison rules. Today's policies dictate that the end result of being unable to follow prison rules is increasingly restrictive conditions. Research consistently shows these conditions only exacerbate mental illness. Making mental illness worse, not better, fuels the cycle of increasingly maladaptive behavior. Once sentenced to a super-max, one must earn his way out. This can be done by demonstrating good or conforming behavior. But if serious persistent mental illness prevents one from conforming to these rules, the result is the ineffectual cycle that has become super-max punishment in America today.

Another memory of an interaction with an inmate has stayed with me. We never asked why a person was in prison. We were not there to determine their guilt or innocence or provide them with legal advice. Questions about their crimes distracted from our mission to find out about their living conditions and could upset them. I broke this rule only once and quickly regretted it. Visiting a 23-hour locked down unit in a facility, I came across a young man who seemed too young not only to be in an adult facility but also to have broken rules or exhibited such unruly behavior that required him to be locked in the SHU. Kneeling on the floor and talking to him through the feed-up slot, I told him that he looked too young to be there and asked what he had done to get himself incarcerated in the first place. He immediately began to cry and told me he had been driving drunk, and the passenger in the car, his best friend, had been killed. He was convicted of involuntary manslaughter. I felt horrible: Not only was he in an adult maximum-security prison—locked in the SHU—but I reminded him also of the tragic event that he had to live with. His regret was obvious, and there was nothing I could do to help him cope with a burden that he would bare for the rest of his life. I had to move on to talk to other inmates in the unit and was forced to leave this young man crying on the floor of his cell. I never asked another person about his conviction. The fact that I remember this particular interaction, of the hundreds if not thousands that I have had with people inside, reflects the effect it had on me and my regret to this day.

❖ EXPERIENCING RACE, CLASS, GENDER, AND AGING IN PRISON

Poor Minorities

Groups based on race and class, which are inexorably linked in this country, are more easily caught up in the criminal justice system. There is a shamefully large racial disparity in our nation's prison population. The extralegal factors of race and class play a large role in who are punished and how. Too many times, I stood looking out at a prison yard or in the mess hall at a sea of black and brown faces. I have a hard time not believing that our criminal justice policies have created a new type of enslavement. Some argue that our capitalist economy does not have the capacity to employ everyone and that something needs to be done with the surplus of workers. Some of the people who comprise this surplus literally disappear behind the prison walls and do not get counted in the national unemployment rate.

Moving beyond economics, the disproportionate incarceration of poor people of color also has interpersonal ramifications. The racial composition of prisons plays a large role in the nature of the relationships between inmates and staff. Most of the prisons in the state in which I worked are in remote, rural communities with almost exclusively white populations. The first time that many of the residents in these communities regularly interacted with people of color took place inside prison. The only people of color they may know are those being punished for committing crimes against society. The racial dynamics inside most prisons do not foster positive interactions or opportunities to learn about and from people different from oneself. Rather, these racial dynamics create strain and contribute to continued tensions.

Women

While most of my time was spent inside prisons for men, I did spend a limited amount of time inside prisons that incarcerate women. The first time I walked into a women's prison, I immediately sensed a lack of tension that is nearly always present inside male facilities. Violence still occurs in women's prisons, but women experience prison differently than men. Growing up, females are socialized differently than men, so not surprisingly, the process of *prisonization* (being socialized according to the demands of the prison environment) is different for women.

Women face unique struggles when serving time. Perhaps most significantly, women must often deal with the loss of their children and may be more harshly affected by family separation. One result of differential socialization is that women form what are called *play families* in which a more senior inmate takes a newly incarcerated woman under her wing to show her the way and protect her, thereby developing a type of support system. Also, it is more socially acceptable for women to express their feelings, and rates of some mental health problems, such as depression, are significantly higher in women's prisons. Despite the lower levels of violence inside women's prisons, I have met many COs who say that they prefer working with men rather than women because men are less likely to show their emotions. When working with men, they say, the rules are more formal, while when working with women, their emotions can make enforcing rules and regulations more difficult.

Aging Prisoners

My work also brought me into contact with some older prisoners. One of the collateral consequences of locking people up for longer periods of time, especially for life, is that people are growing old inside prison. In many ways, aging inside is no different from aging outside: Older persons tend to require more medical care, accommodations such as more time to perform tasks, and acknowledgment of limitations, such as being less able to climb to the top of a bunk bed. Also similar to the outside, older people in prison are more vulnerable to victimization because of physical limitations and dependence on others. One significant difference is that the costs of medical care and security for the aging are higher in prison than in the community. Aging is more expensive in prison.

As this country's economic downslide continues, politicians at both the federal and state levels of government have started to rethink their enthusiasm for harsh penalties. A life sentence is expensive, and the three-strike laws that became increasingly popular in the 1990s are now being recognized as too expensive to continue. Especially since the U.S. Supreme Court decided that a person's third felony need not be violent or serious, these laws have helped fill prisons beyond their capacity. We are beginning to see state leaders reevaluate policies, but a significant amount of damage has already been done; we have created an enormous and ever-aging prison population that we now need to provide with care and services.

❖ CONCLUSION

The most difficult aspect of the work is what ultimately led me to leave my job. The project produced reports that were disseminated by the organization and sent to the state department of correctional services' central office, but our findings and recommendations were just that—recommendations. Neither the state nor the administration of any facility we visited was obligated to make any of the changes that we proposed. The limitation of our power was frustrating. We could go inside prisons and poke around and ask questions, but this was the extent of our authority. I struggled with knowing about the significant flaws of the system and viewing them firsthand but not having the ability to make changes that we believed would improve conditions, limit injustices, and reduce people's pain and suffering. I asked myself, What was I accomplishing? Who was I helping?

There are two general approaches to creating change in a system, one is from the inside, and the other is from the outside. The visiting project held the unique position of being both inside and outside, yet I was not seeing improvement. But that is the nature of a bureaucratic system—it is not designed to change. Change in a bureaucracy occurs slowly over time. The stability of a bureaucracy is generally considered one of its strengths. Today, it is through teaching college students that I hope to influence the future of how this country approaches punishment. I believe that the next generation of voters and criminal justice system workers are the most likely agents of change. If my teaching can educate and enlighten those who carry the future in their hands, then maybe I can help make change more possible.

While some people undoubtedly need to be separated from society, many do not. In my opinion, prisons have proven themselves to be an expensive and largely failed experiment. I learned more about the realities of prison life from working in the field than in any class that I took. I also learned how one mistake can change a person's life. Walking out the prison doors at the end of the day and leaving behind all the men I met was always difficult. But it has made me appreciate my liberty and freedom in ways I would not have otherwise. I will be eternally grateful for the opportunity to work with and learn from all of the people I met inside prison.

❖ REFERENCES

Damrosch, L. (2010). *Tocqueville's discovery of America*. New York: Farrar, Straus & Giroux.
Dickens, C. (2004). *American notes*. New York: Penguin Books. (Original work published 1842)

❖ RECOMMENDED READINGS

Damrosch, L. (2010). *Tocqueville's discovery of America*. New York: Farrar, Straus & Giroux.
Dickens, C. (2004). *American notes*. New York: Penguin Books. (Original work published 1842)
Pollock, J. M. (2004). *Prisons and prison life: Costs and consequences*. Los Angeles: Roxbury.

DISCUSSION QUESTIONS

1. Should there be more or less oversight/monitoring of U.S. prisons? Assuming that prison oversight is required, should it be done by governmental or private agencies, or both? Should the public be allowed to visit prisons? Explain your answers to each question.

2. What kind of major impacts did the author's experiences in corrections have on her? Imagine that you had the same experiences. How do you think the events and conditions that the author witnessed would have affected you?

3. Think of a significant change that should be made in or to the correctional system. If you had to make it, would you work inside or outside the system, or some combination of both? Describe the actions that you would take.

9

Learning Corrections

Linking Experience and Research

Lucien X. Lombardo

Editor's Introduction: Professor Lombardo taught prisoners at New York's historically significant Auburn Prison. Working from 1969 to 1977, he experienced the "pendulum swing" from an emphasis on rehabilitation to punishment during the 1970s. He makes important connections between his experiences and scholarship while offering insights to today's generation of corrections workers, who are also experiencing major social changes. Lombardo found it difficult to educate prisoners against institutional pressure to adopt security as the primary purpose of his position. He believes that a dominant way of thinking among correctional authorities stands in the way of solving important problems. Lombardo recommends using new perspectives in corrections, including those from academia, that maintain human beings as the focus of decision making.

❖ INTRODUCTION

> *As I approached the front gate for my first day of prison work,*
> *readying myself for the winding journey into the prison in which*
> *I'd be locked up for eight hours a day, I recalled a former football*
> *coach talking about his experiences as a substitute teacher in the*
> *prison one summer. He said he could never get used to the doors*
> *slamming shut behind him. Being locked in bothered him so much*
> *he never went back. How will I react? (Lombardo, 1969)*

Like many who entered the field of corrections before the 1970s, my experiences started before there was an academic field called *criminal justice*. I had absolutely no knowledge of "corrections" when I started work as a teacher in the Osborne School of Auburn Prison. In addition, the prison system at the time provided no training. This was a new world, one I would strive to understand, and I would have to do it on my own. I had an undergraduate degree in Spanish Linguistics, a master's degree in Latin American Studies, and a provisional teaching license for social studies and languages. My teaching credentials enabled me to get a position teaching high school Spanish and fifth and eighth grade English to prisoners in a correctional institution in my hometown, Auburn, New York, in August 1969. I stayed in this position until 1977.

I started to experience correctional institutions during a time of dynamic changes in the relationships between prisoners and the institutions in which they lived. The late 1960s and 1970s was a period of examination and dramatic change in the criminal justice and correctional institutions. Following years of sometimes not so benign neglect, the 1960s saw the civil rights revolution (including prisoners' rights), anti–Vietnam War protests, waves of urban violence, and political assassinations. Crime and all aspects of the criminal justice response to it were at the center of societal concern and political life. In the mid-1960s, the President's Commission on Law Enforcement and the Administration of Justice issued its report *The Challenge of Crime in a Free Society* and its accompanying Task Force Reports. The experiences described in this essay took place during this time of change.

In 2009, Senator Jim Webb of Virginia introduced legislation (S. 714), the National Criminal Justice Commission Act, "to look at every aspect of our criminal justice system with an eye toward reshaping the process from top to bottom." Thus, my experiences at Auburn Prison following and during a critical period of criminal justice reform are likely to have relevance as we undergo another period of examining and reforming the criminal justice and correctional system.

In November 1970, Auburn Prison experienced a 1-day riot and takeover of the prison yard. Stemming from reprisals against prisoners stemming from symbolic protests related to Black Solidarity Day, the riot preceded the infamous Attica rebellion by 1 year. These events and the political and legal reactions that surrounded them formed the background for my own institutional experiences. (For a description of my experiences of the Attica Riot, see "Attica Remembered" at http://www.odu.edu/~llombard/resources/collected_papers/3.pdf.)

As I attempted to understand the prison life of prisoners and staff as well as my own experiences, a chance meeting with Donald J. Newman of the School of Criminal Justice, University at Albany, State University of New York (SUNY), led me to return to graduate school to see what I could learn. From 1972 to 1974, I took an educational leave of absence from my prison teaching position to pursue graduate study in Criminal Justice at the School of Criminal Justice at SUNY, Albany. My years at SUNY provided me an opportunity to learn many new perspectives, to engage in discussion and study of proposals to reform many aspects of criminal justice administration especially in the area of sentencing and corrections, and to test much of the informal study of the prison world that I did on my own after I started my prison teaching career. This essay describes my experiences of learning about prison life particularly in the years before I pursued graduate study in criminal justice. It describes my attempts to understand what I was observing, hearing, and experiencing in relation to my students (the prisoners), the world they inhabited (the prison), and the place where I worked (the prison as an organization).

❖ AUBURN CORRECTIONAL FACILITY

The workplace where my understanding of correctional institutions began was Auburn Prison as it was called when I started. Soon afterward, as part of the enormous changes that were taking place in the correctional institutions field, it became Auburn Correctional Facility in 1970. The renaming was part of an emphasis on corrections rather than imprisonment that was taking place in New York and around the country. Auburn Correctional Facility was part of the new Department of Correctional Services, which envisioned an integrated correctional institutions and parole. Auburn was and is a maximum security prison in central New York State.

As I was to learn, Auburn Prison had historic significance. It was the prison where the *Auburn*, or "congregate," *system* had its start in the early 1800s; it was studied by Alexis de Tocqueville and Gustave de Beaumont in 1831 as part of their efforts to inform postrevolution France about the prison and democratic experiments taking place in the young United States. (De Tocqueville was also the author of *Democracy in America*.) De Tocqueville and de Beaumont described the Auburn System (separate cells, congregate labor, silent system, use of flogging) as a model prison in their 1833 book, *On the Penitentiary System in the United States and Its Application in France*, making the Auburn system known throughout Europe. Auburn Prison was the site of the first purposeful electrocution (using the electric chair for the death penalty) in 1890; and it was the prison of Thomas Mott Osborne and the Mutual Welfare League, a form of prisoner participation in decision making, or prisoner democracy. In the late 1920s, it was the site of a major prison riot that was the subject of prize-winning reporting. Housing between 1,500 and 1,600 prisoners in single cells, it was an institution that experienced little turnover in either the prisoner population or correctional staff during the time I worked there.

While Auburn is a prison with a long and storied history, it is also a prison where programming and change were important. Prison industries were complemented with a school program that served over half the institutional population. From Adult Basic Education through high school and college programming, the institution has had from its beginnings an educational mission. Community programs from Junior Chamber of Commerce programs to Dale Carnegie and community groups representing African Americans, Hispanics, and Native Americans would enter the prison and interact with prisoners on a regular basis. As I was to learn, when the Department of Corrections wanted to institute a new policy, Auburn was the place where it was first tried out. Though it was a maximum security prison, Auburn had a relatively relaxed atmosphere. One of my early prisoner students described it in 1970:

> I remember when I was on the bus coming up from New York City: a street wise young black man going to the rural white sticks. I heard so much about the hostility of the white hacks toward us blacks. All the way up I was building up my defenses, preparing myself for the hostility. However, when I get to Auburn and we march from the bus and start going through procedures, this white guard who was with us says: "How ya doin'? Everything OK?" I couldn't believe it. I was ready to fight everything and there was nothing to fight. Auburn really throws you off balance.

❖ HOW TO UNDERSTAND THE PRISON WORLD

Almost as soon as I started working at Auburn Prison, I started my informal study of the prison world. As I encountered this isolated world within a world, this informal study helped me understand my experience and the dynamics of the prison world. We often hear that it is the experience that matters and that academic understanding reflects an ivory tower perspective. However, my experience has taught me that I could not have understood or functioned well within the correctional institutional world without insights from scholars that helped me understand the meanings and dynamics of my correctional experience.

Though the prison world that I entered in 1969 seemed to be one of dramatic change, one of the first principles that I learned concerned *the stability of the prison world*. Weeks after I started as a prison teacher, I visited Auburn's public library to see what I could learn. One of the first books I encountered was *Report of Gershom Powers, Agent and Keeper of the State Prison, at Auburn: Made to the Legislature, Jan. 7, 1828*. As I read this report I was startled by how little had changed in the 160 years since it was written.

This report described much of what I was seeing: prisoners in uniforms lining up in the yard to march to their various assignments (though it was not the lockstep march of Elam Lynds, one of Auburn's early keepers, or wardens). On my first day of work, I along with other new employees met with the PK as he was known, the Principle Keeper (in today's language, Deputy Superintendent for Security). *Keeper* was a term from the early 1800s. There were also descriptions of the new *congregate prison labor* system, which mirrored the prison industries of 1969 where prisoners made license plates and furniture, and packed tobacco, which was shipped to prisoners throughout the state.

This 1828 report also contained discussions of issues that were of importance in 1969. Concern was expressed for prisoners suffering mental breakdowns from isolation cells (the Pennsylvania model); it described prisoners suffering from substance abuse withdrawal from alcohol and even more dramatically from tobacco. It described the low level of education of prisoners and the institution's attempt to enlist local seminarians as teachers in an informal school program; it provided a discussion of problems related to abuse of force by prison staff and the difficulties of deciding how much force was appropriate in a specific case. It seemed that every prison issue that was being debated in the late 1960s and early 1970s was present in the nature of the institution and its inhabitants and workers at the time of Auburn's founding.

A second book that I encountered in my informal study of the prison world was Thomas Mott Osborne's *Within Prison Walls* (1914). This personal narrative of 1 week's voluntary confinement in Auburn Prison by one of the leading prison reformers of the early 1900s introduced me to a second principle important in understanding the prison: *Prisoners are people not images and stereotypes.* Just as Osborne described architecture of the prison world, his encounters with unreasonable staff and sympathetic staff, his observations of violence, the routine of prison counts and order, the life in the workshops, so he was describing what I was encountering in discussions with my prisoner students and staff. However, his interactions with and descriptions of the human reactions of prisoners to their separation from their families and communities and attempts to make due in a world of deprivation showed how stereotypical "criminal" images failed to reflect the humanness of the prisoner's life. The dedication of Osborne's book captures this spirit:

> This little volume is dedicated to OUR BROTHERS IN GRAY and especially those who during my short stay among them in Auburn Prison, won my lasting gratitude and affection by their courtesy, sympathy, and understanding. (p. vi)

This view was reinforced when expressed in August of 1970 (3 months before the 1970 riot at Auburn) by the past president of the local correctional officers' union in an article in the local newspaper, *Auburn Citizen Advertiser* (August 29, 1970). After reports of increases in the number of officers being assaulted by inmates surfaced, this former union leader stated,

> There have been several occasions where I personally have overheard officers talking to an inmate as though he were some kind of animal, and there were just as many occasions where a little less brute force should have, and could have, been used to control a difficult situation.
>
> I feel, as I am sure a great many of my fellow officers do, that a man is a human being whether he be inside or outside of these walls, and that if we expect to be respected and looked up to for guidance, then this respect should be returned.
>
> A man serving a term in prison is being punished for a crime, and to make this time more difficult would be to destroy everything our institutions are meant to stand for. ("Guard Decries Brutality," 1970, p. 2)

After learning about the principles of stability and humanness from the materials available in the community library at Auburn and seeing these concerns mirrored in contemporary (1969–1972) debates about the purposes and processes of corrections, I pursued other perspectives. One lesson that I learned quickly in my workplace was that those who did prison work did not often understand why they were doing what they were doing. After working for a few months I asked a fellow teacher with 25 years' experience why we did something a certain way. The question seemed to stump him. After 2 minutes of silence, all he could say was "I don't know!" This baffled me.

As I searched for an answer, I encountered Erving Goffman's (1961) *Asylums: Essays on the Social Situation of Mental Patients and Other Inmates.* As a neophyte to the prison world, I found this book was a revelation. In this book, the prison world as it was being described in the prisoner and political rhetoric of the late 1960s and early 1970s found explanation. The *concept of prison as a total institution* and the *ritualistic processes* through which total institutions, such as correctional institutions, operate on both inmates and staff became clear. According to Goffman, prisoners (inmates of all types) were dehumanized to fit the roles defined for them by the institutions. The world of the total institution was controlled and regularized and all facets of life were dictated by the institutional regime: the constant counts, the rules, the paper trails of reports of structured behaviors, identities, and interactions of both prisoners and staff within and across their groups.

While the concept of the total institution defined the *formal world* of prisoner and staff identities and their interactions, Goffman also pointed out that there were *informal worlds* of both staff and prisoners where individual prisoners and staff would reach accommodations that allowed each to maintain a degree of humanness and autonomy within the total institution. Thus, what I was seeing in my students and the staff of the prison (and in myself) was not unique to us as individuals but was part of the life of correctional institutions of all types. Understanding this allowed me to use this knowledge as I worked with my prisoner students and staff. This insight proved valuable for understanding my own interactions with the prison and those of prisoners and other staff.

Finally, I discovered Donald Cressey's book *The Prison: Studies in Institutional Organization and Change* (1961). During these early years, I felt that there were many *contradictory goals and messages* that were part of the corrections. Security demanded that prisoners be seen as potentially dangerous and not trustworthy or indeed worthy of respect. Yet as a teacher, processes of education demanded that a certain degree of trust and mutual respect be shown if the teacher–student connection was to be enhanced. While these contradictions were confusing, the various studies described in Cressey's book let me see that what I was experiencing was normal and that these were simply contradictions inherent in the complex nature of correctional organizations and work. These contradictory perspectives (security or custody and treatment) cannot be maximally achieved in the same institution, yet they were both part of the institution in which I worked (a high-programming maximum security institution).

❖ SOME KEY LEARNING EXPERIENCES

As I started my work as a prison teacher, some key experiences led me to reflect certain dimensions of my role and the institution within which I worked.

Visit With the "PK" on First Day of Work

Field notes, August: Even though I had filled out all my forms and had my picture taken (like the prisoners), I had to meet with the man in charge of security, the PK (later I learned this meant Principle Keeper) before I went to the school to start teaching. This visit is mandatory for all new employees. Since I was a teacher and not a guard (whose responsibility was security), I didn't understand what this had to do with me. Being new to prison life, I had no idea security in prison was such a fragile thing. Six of us who were starting today were sent into the room and stood around a large table.

Two people stood out. One was a rather short fellow about 45 years old dressed in civilian clothes. He looked at me, shrugged his shoulders, and laughed. He said this place was just like the army, hurry-up-and-wait. This turned out to be my boss, the academic supervisor in the school. He was returning to Auburn after an initial period as a new supervisor at another prison. The other was a 6 foot 3 inch tall, and a well-built, 220 pounds in a sergeant's uniform. No chuckles from him; he appeared to be as cold as an iceberg. He gave the impression that he didn't want to be here.

As we stood there, the PK came in and sat behind his desk. He looked through us as we stood. After the sergeant, who worked in the PK's office, introduced him, the PK started his speech. He reminded me of a football coach giving a pep talk. We were welcomed to the team. We were expected to do a proper job, a good job. He emphasized that we were going to be working in a maximum-security prison and that maximum security meant MAXIMUM security. Everyone in the institution is responsible for security. This meant teachers, sergeants, supervisors, clerks, secretaries, everyone. The PK pointed out that the men we would be working with were convicted of crimes. They were convicts. Many were dangerous. He said they would try to use us to gain any advantage they could for themselves. "Never do a favor for a convict," he emphasized. If we did, we'd be in the criminal's back pocket forever. He'd have a hold over us. He could and would use us. The PK warned us never to bring anything into the institution or take anything out. (After he said this, I noticed that my new supervisor and the experienced sergeant were both carrying their lunches; they were bringing something in. This is confusing.) Everything and everything "out of the ordinary" was to be reported to his office. But, what, I thought to myself, was ordinary? I'd been in the institution for three and one-half hours as an employee—trying to figure out what was "normal" was going to be fun. The PK told us we'd be tested by everyone in the institution and that we'd better not fail the tests. Failure could mean our jobs. (When he said *everyone*, did he mean employees as well as inmates? I am not sure.) Finally, the PK lectured us on the use and abuse of sick time. He told us to come to work when sick and not to abuse the "privilege" of sick time. Absence means one place in security may be uncovered. Replacements never know the job as well as the regular man.

How Did I Understand This Experience?

This first experience as a corrections employee left me a bit confused. My feeling at the time was that the PK was speaking to us (the employees starting at Auburn that day) as if we were children. "Do everything I tell you children, or I'll throw you right out of here," was what I heard. I started to wonder about the conflicts between my role as teacher and my role in security. My sense of self was somewhat taken aback by all of this. I felt competent enough to be trusted, but I was given no clue that I was. I felt that I wasn't trusted and that no one in the prison trusted anyone. I felt controlled, or at least, I felt attempts by the system to control me. *Their* judgment was to be substituted for *my* judgment. Do what *they* say, and you are OK. I resented this straight off. I didn't know what all of these feeling would mean in day-to-day practice, especially in a prison. But I did feel, after only 4 hours, that I had to somehow "beat the system" if I were to be an effective teacher. I did not know how the system worked or, indeed, if there was a system. I felt that battle lines were being drawn between my own sense of self and the workings of the prison. I had the feeling that this was someplace where I could work. But I knew at this early date that I could never see myself as part of the prison.

Later, I would come to an understanding that my attempts to "study the prison" to learn about the institution and those who lived and worked in it were probably a coping strategy where I continued to study as I had done as a student in school most of my life.

Professional Corrections Conference, September 1970

Field notes, September: I went to a conference sponsored by the New York State Probation and Parole Association. This was my first contact outside of Auburn Prison with correctional professionals. The previous months have seen discussions on the press and political arena of increased violence in prisons around the state, criticisms of judges and parole boards that decided the fate of many with their sentencing and release decisions, delays and excessive bail in court proceedings, lack of caring on the part of governor and legislators, and lack of community support and money for programs. At the conference legislators, members of corrections commissions, judges, and members of the parole board discussed these same problems. At my table were the vocational education supervisor from my school at Auburn and a former Auburn teacher who was now directing an education program at a nearby reform school for girls.

> The director of the reform school program says, "It's as bad here as it is at Auburn. Nobody cares. The state doesn't care; the commissioners don't care; nobody does. Just cover yourself, make the time go by and be happy! You can't do any more. They don't want you to. If you try, they won't let you. Books, they're a joke, 10 to 15 years old, falling apart and not very useful. Supplies are always in short supply no matter what you do. We've got a good staff, but what the hell can they do? You know how it is. Right now, I can't get out of here. They're starting to pay better and I'm getting stuck. I hate the feeling but it's true."
>
> A black woman in the audience rises to make a point. "But senator, you talk about community corrections as if it's such a great thing. I've been trying to run a group home for girls for years, and they won't give me a license. They say I've got to have a licensed counselor on my staff. But to tell you the truth, I don't have any

staff, just me and my husband. We care about these kids and have helped many on our own. But as soon as word gets out that kids are staying with us, your people, I mean the state's people come around and close us up. You say you want people to care to help out, to let kids and prisoners know the community cares. But you keep saying, 'Do it by our rules, our way!' Why don't you give us a chance? Why don't you make it easier for people to get involved?" (Lombardo, 1970)

How Did I Understand What Happened at This Conference?

I started to see that the problems I had experienced during my first year as a correction's professional were not unique. Perhaps it was the same all across corrections. Here were people who ran the programs, people in charge, and people with power. All of them were criticizing "the system" for failing, all of them knowing where and why corrections failed, all of them seemingly not powerful enough or not caring enough to change it. But maybe it was not power or caring that made a difference. Maybe it was the way they looked at the problem. These correctional professionals were saying the same things I have heard inmates say over and over again. They all complained about being dehumanized, manipulated, and lied to by others in power who had promised changes.

The black woman who spoke received a huge ovation. A state senator responded, "Licensing regulations are important because they see to it that all homes are run by professionally trained competent people. I'm sure once you can assure the state that your program meets the minimum requirements, your program will be licensed" (Lombardo, 1970). But the senator had missed her point. Caring, not professional training, was her yardstick. She spoke of people. The senator spoke of the "state" wanting to help; she spoke of people. The senator could not speak of people. Knowing his abstractions were failing, he still sought to remedy the situation through abstractions.

Post-Attica Activism (Letter to the Commissioner)

Following the prison experience known as Attica in September of 1971, correctional professionals in the state of New York and around the country were searching for answers to the problems posed by our correctional institutions and the violence that was filling them. In December 1971, the Deputy Commissioner of the New York State Department of Corrections proposed the development of a maximum-maximum security (maxi-maxi) facility (the equivalent of today's super maximum security prisons). As a member of the correctional profession, I found this proposal took any idea of corrections out of corrections. I could not help it. At this point, I could not help but decide to take a more activist role and express my concerns to Commissioner Russell Oswald, who had become commissioner at the same time that I had started my teaching career in corrections. I believed he would listen. On December 19, I wrote a letter to Commissioner Oswald. Here are some excerpts:

> One would think that men occupying authoritative positions in corrections would possess a more in-depth understanding of the problems with which they deal. The issues involved in the legal and correctional mechanism have, for the most part, been complicated by the politization of prison populations and the racial issue. However, my faith in correctional administrators is severely shaken when I hear such contradictory statements as the following attributed to Deputy Commissioner Butler: "The last decade has brought in a whole new breed of inmates. Frankly we are at a loss to know how to handle them." This is followed by: "What we need is a place that is very, very, very secure. Where so-called political prisoners, inciters, anarchists, and whatever else they are, who don't want to be part of our program, can get involved in a program geared especially to them."
>
> . . .
>
> Does Mr. Butler actually expect that a maxi-maxi facility will have maximum security with maximum program? What kind of program can the state have in light of the observation that "we don't know how to handle them"?
>
> . . .
>
> Why do correctional personnel refuse to take a new perspective? It appears that the correctional apparatus is permeated with people steeped in the tradition of "let's create a program to help people we don't understand live in a society we don't understand. But while we do this, let's run these programs in a manner that will limit their effectiveness."
>
> . . .
>
> We create the expectations of corrections in the inmates. They honestly believe in it. They expect us, corrections professionals, to correct them. We may say to ourselves that only the inmate himself can correct his behavior, while at the same time, we prevent him from doing so. We create the expectation that public interest and support will help. However, I do not believe we can honestly expect people to be that interested. ("Deputy Commissioner Calls for Maxi-Maxi Prison," 1971, p. 1)

Understanding the Experiences in Corrections

Knowing that Commissioner Oswald was quite busy with post-Attica investigations, I never expected to receive a reply to my letter. Venting my frustrations and synthesizing what I had learned from my informal study of prisons and applying that learning to our current correctional chaos provided a positive feeling. However, in March of 1972, the Director of Correctional Education for the state was visiting our school and asked to see me. As we walked through the prison yard, he told me that the commissioner appreciated my letter and the perspectives it represented. He said that while he agreed with much of what I had written, there were many political and administrative realities that made the work of corrections very difficult. He said that the commissioner expressed his appreciation to me as a thoughtful employee.

❖ SUMMARY

In reflecting on my early experiences in the field of corrections, there are a number of lessons that I would draw from my personal experience. First, there is a strong link between the academic study of corrections and the effectiveness of correctional personnel. Understanding forces that shape correctional work and the people involved in the process gives one insights into how to move one's day-to-day activities in the directions improving the correctional system for all involved. Second, it is important to understand that although corrections and prisons are incredibly stable institutions, they are always in a state of change, sometimes dramatic change (as in the 1960s and 1970s), sometimes less drastic (as from 1990 to 2010). As correctional professionals, we should be aware of these changes and attempt to harness them in positive ways at whatever level we work. Third, it is important to understand the broad political context within which corrections policy and administration operates. It is not a satisfactory answer to say "I don't know" when asked why we do things the way we do. Politicians, administrators, and all correctional personnel should be able to give positive and responsive answers to the public and each other. It is important for correctional personnel to ask questions! Finally, it is important to remember at all times that corrections and prisons are human enterprises. They are attempts to help people cope with problems in nonhurtful ways using their most important tool, people.

❖ REFERENCES

Auburn Prison, & Powers, G. (1828). *Report of Gershom Powers, agent and keeper of the state prison, at Auburn: Made to the legislature, Jan. 7, 1828*. Albany, NY: Croswell & Van Benthuysen.

Cressey, D. (1961). *The prison: Studies in institutional organization and change.* New York: Holt, Rinehart & Winston.

Deputy Commissioner Calls for Maxi-Maxi Prison. (1971, December 13). *Auburn Citizen Advertiser*, p. 1.

Goffman, E. (1961). *Asylums: Essays on the social situation of mental patients and other inmates.* Garden City, NJ: Anchor Books.

Guard Decries Brutality. (1970, August 29). *Auburn Citizen Advertiser*, p. 2.

Lombardo, L. X. (1969, August). [Field notes]. Unpublished raw data.

Lombardo, L. X. (1970, September). [Field notes]. Unpublished raw data.

Osborne, T. M. (1914). *Within Prison Walls.* New York: D. Appleton.

❖ RECOMMENDED READINGS

Christianson, S. (2000). *With liberty for some: 500 Years of imprisonment in America.* Boston: Northeastern University Press.

Lombardo, L. X. (1989). *Guards imprisoned: Correctional officers at work* (2nd ed.). Cincinnati, OH: Anderson.

Rhodes, L. (2004). *Total confinement: Madness and reason in the maximum security prison.* Berkeley: University of California Press.

Toch, H. (1977). *Living in prison: The ecology of survival.* New York: Free Press.

DISCUSSION QUESTIONS

1. Which principles and concepts did the author use to "understand the prison world," and what are the published sources associated with each? How do these principles and concepts help create an understanding of corrections?

2. The author approached his work not just as a person paid to perform tasks but as a person *studying* the social institution within which he worked and in his essay identifies some "key learning experiences." Should everyone approach their work this way, kind of like a social scientist? Will you? Why or why not?

3. What was the author's basic argument in his "Letter to the Commissioner"? Think of a current major law or social policy issue. Regarding this issue, would you like to see changes or things kept the same? If you were to write a letter asking a law or policymaker to take your stand on the issue, what would you say?

10

Corrections

Experiences in State Parole

Tiffiney Barfield-Cottledge

Editor's Introduction: Professor Barfield-Cottledge was a state parole officer who focused much of her energy on helping ex-prisoners reenter the community. Lengthy incarceration leaves the ex-prisoner with fewer resources and disrupted ties to the community, which makes transitioning back to society difficult. Successful reentry depends on meeting needs such as education, employment, housing, and health care. Failing to successfully integrate into the community can lead to re-offending. Barfield-Cottledge points out some of the particular reentry difficulties faced by women and racial and ethnic minorities due to social inequality. She also discusses the challenges of reintegrating sex offenders. Barfield-Cottledge emphasizes the importance of having resources with which to offset the strain faced by ex-prisoners during reentry.

❖ INTRODUCTION

Corrections have experienced significant gains since the Middle Ages when violators of social and religious norms were beaten, tortured, and publicly executed. During the 18th century, theorists began to examine criminal behavior to better understand individual choices to commit crime as well as society's ability to identify and create preventive measures that significantly reduce criminal and delinquent behavior. During this same period, criminal behavior was thought to be the result of free will and individuals' ability to weigh the costs and benefits of committing crime in their pursuit of pleasure and avoidance of pain (Akers & Sellers, 2009). Specifically, Beccaria posited that to deter crime, punishment must be certain, swift, severe, public, and proportionate to the crime committed.

Corrections in America have emerged from 18th-century torture and a later emphasis on rehabilitation to become more punitive in nature than ever. This evolution or cycle, as Thomas J. Bernard refers to it, is largely the result of continued prevalence in criminal behavior despite social control mechanisms both formal (police, laws, and punishment) and informal (family, school, church) designed to prevent and reduce crime and delinquency. Still, punishment is not the only function of modern corrections. While corrections are primarily a punitive system, state parole requires additional efforts toward transitioning newly released prisoners.

In this essay, I discuss my professional experiences while working in Texas as a state parole officer. Specifically, I highlight my experiences working with diverse populations and a variety of social services, drawing connections throughout the essay between my experiences and theory and research on crime and corrections.

❖ EMPLOYMENT BACKGROUND

Texas State Parole

In Texas, the Texas Department of Criminal Justice oversees the functions of the State Parole Division, and the Texas Board of Pardons and Paroles serves as the body that makes decisions about which prisoners will be released on state parole supervision. This board also determines conditions of parole supervision as well as conditions that lead to parole revocation. Parole is revoked when the terms of the parole certificate are violated. In making these decisions, factors identified with empirical research are used to decide which offenders are more likely to persist in criminal behavior over the life course. As such, factors considered in decisions to approve parole supervision mimic those taken into account at the sentencing phase of corrections and include offender age, history of parole releases and revocations, prior incarcerations, employment history, and the nature and extent of the current conviction offense.

According to Petersilia (2003), 93% of all prisoners are eventually released back into society, and approximately 80% are released to parole supervision. As a measure of the significance of Texas state parole, in 2009 the Texas State Board of Pardons and Parole reviewed 76,607 cases for release on parole supervision and of those 23,182 were approved. The paroled populations comprised both serious and nonserious convicted offenders: violent aggravated nonsexual assaults (n = 2,513), violent aggravated sexual assaults (n = 795), violent nonaggravated nonsexual assaults (n = 2,802), and nonaggravated sexual assaults (n = 461), with nonviolent releases (n = 16,611) constituting the largest group of parolees (Texas Board of Pardons and Patrols: http://www.tdcj.state.tx.us/bpp).

Parole Supervision: The Job

In January of 1995, I began working as a Texas State Parole Officer for the Texas Department of Criminal Justice. Upon receiving the call from human resources with the notification to "hire," I was informed that I would be attending 2 weeks of training in Austin, Texas. This training was designed to provide entry level parole officers with knowledge and materials covering state policies and functions of parole officers as well as safety (physical defense and mace). Within the scope of this training, facilitators also covered parole supervision (home visits), chronology documentation of compliance with release requirements, access to the secure Texas-wide corrections databases, and the wealth of resources available to assist parolees with their successful reentry.

In this position, I maintained and supervised between 70 and 100 persons released from prison (parolees). While there are many divisions in pardons and parole, I worked for the field operations section of the Texas state parole. As a parole officer, I was largely responsible for supervising parolees' reentry into society. As such, I also investigated release plans for residential placement and employment prior to the offender's release, as well as developed supervision plans based on offender needs and stipulations of the parole agreement. Learning the techniques and functions of the job, rules and regulations, and state policies took some time but once learned were like second nature to me.

The Parole Officer I position that I held is the entry level position for parole officers with no experience and requires a bachelor's degree. I did not go right into state parole on graduating from college, however. In fact, it was about 6 months after completing my BS degree in criminal justice and working in a law firm when I realized that I wanted to work in corrections and subsequently applied for the state parole officer position. It took an additional 6 months to be approved and hired into the position. During these 6 months while waiting to hear back from parole, I enrolled in graduate school and later obtained my master's degree in counseling which I believe had a significant impact on how I supervised, referred, and ultimately communicated with parolees on my caseload. By January of 1996, I had earned promotion to State Parole Officer II, which is the standard promotion after successfully completing 1 year of service in parole.

As a state parole officer, I had several responsibilities. However, the major responsibilities honed in on supervision, largely dictated by the standard of promoting societal safety, which focused on knowing where parolees lived and worked. One of my major supervision responsibilities was that I verified home, or residential, placements. While maintaining caseloads, new parolees became eligible for parole daily. Once these eligibilities surfaced, it was my job to verify that if approved by the parole board to be released, a person had a documented approved place to live on release from prison. Even after release and initial verification, monthly home visits were conducted. In addition, mandatory office visits and employment and education referrals as well as verification of attendance in alcohol and/or drug treatment programs were instrumental when calculating propensity toward successful societal reentry. Parolees were required to come in to their locally assigned parole office monthly. During these visits, I would meet with the parolee to discuss updates, transitions, and needs and depending on the stipulations of parole, conduct urinalyses to test for drug use. It was also my responsibility to notify the state office of parole violations (which could lead to parole revocation). These notifications were sent to the warrants department, which would then investigate the allegations, issue pre-revocation warrants, assist law enforcement in the apprehension of offenders, and arrange extradition of offenders arrested in other states.

Documentation of every aspect of supervision for each parolee on the caseload was the highest level of accountability for a parole officer.

Files had to be maintained in a transparent manner to ensure that any state official reading the files would know not only the whereabouts and employment status of the parolee but also referrals and last point of contact and verification dates. Typical supervision or regular parole supervision would consist of monthly visitation and verification.

For a great majority of the time that I worked as a parole officer, I also worked as a counselor at what was initially a nonprofit counseling agency that eventually emerged into a partial hospital. At this agency, I was responsible for leading and facilitating individual and group sessions with adult populations, many of whom were either on probation or parole and/or had a history of criminal activity. During this time, I was able to recognize a gap between the needs of parolees and the available services that impacted successful reentry into society.

❖ EXPERIENCES: MY CASELOAD

My caseload was quite diverse in that parolees had convictions that included serious violent crimes, nonviolent crimes, and drug offenses. However, the large majority of parolees on my caseload was convicted of drug crimes or affiliated drug offenses. Parole caseloads also vary based on race, or ethnicity, and gender. My parole caseload comprised all racial and ethnic groups, but minorities constituted the majority. The largest group comprised African Americans, with Hispanics being a close second and Caucasians representing the smallest. Males continue to constitute the majority of convicted criminals and as such the majority of those on parole supervision. My caseload was no different. Females, however, did make up a significantly smaller group on my caseload. Although the very nature of the term *parole* may signify adult populations, I had several parolees on my caseload who were *minors waived to adult court* (treated as adults). Thus, the age of a parolee could range from 17 years old to a much older age depending on sentence length and time left to serve at the time of parole. In the following sections, I discuss some important issues that emerged as I worked on my caseload: working with females and racial and ethnic minorities, sex offenders, neighborhood characteristics, and community resources (education, employment, treatment, and family).

Working With Females

Females in my caseload typically had been convicted of theft, welfare fraud, prostitution, and/or drug related offenses. While females commit many of the same offenses as their male counterparts, they experience different stressors upon release back into society. For females in my caseload, the vast majority of the issues faced upon release from prison mimicked those of males. However, differences included dealing with victimization (such as intimate partner abuse), pregnancies, the loss of children while incarcerated, single parenting, day care, and fractured family structures as the result of child placement with other family members or in the foster care system.

I recall one specific case involving an African American woman who presented with a *dirty urinalysis* (tested positive) for marijuana. She was thus in violation of her parole agreement. In contrast to a male in her situation, she faced more social consequences than just possible parole revocation because she was pregnant. I had to make decisions that ultimately affected this female's success or failure as a paroled person. The resources available were significant here as there was an opportunity to refer her to an in-patient rehabilitation facility. This was vital as the unintended consequences of having a baby addicted to drugs at birth yield developmental, educational, and even legal ramifications.

Working With Racial and Ethnic Minorities

Though society has evolved in some areas of equality, the fact remains that underrepresented populations of people suffer strain and may thus be more predisposed to commit certain crimes. Racial and ethnic minorities suffer disproportionately in the areas of educational and employment attainment when compared to their white counterparts (Gabbidon, 2010; Petersilia, 2003). Research also shows that when compared to nonminorities, minority groups differ in recidivism rates. The unintended consequences of being a convicted felon disproportionately affect minority populations in their ability to secure and retain employment (Petersilia, 2003). In his study of social differences among both criminal and noncriminal persons, Pager (2007) found that African Americans suffer disproportionately more social problems when compared to their white criminal counterparts. Specifically, his findings suggest that white criminals are more successful at getting jobs than blacks with no criminal records (Western, Kling, & Weiman, 2001). Additionally, minority groups have greater health and medical needs associated with HIV and AIDS.

Educational, employment, and health problems were also prevalent among parolees on my caseload and in many cases acted as barriers to successful reentry without future criminal incidents. Likewise, for minorities on my caseload, one of the most significant barriers to successful reentry was substance use or abuse. This is not to say that I did not have my fair share of parolees who sold drugs but to highlight that drug use and abuse were more prevalently exposed under parole supervision. Petersilia's (2003) finding that about 75% of parolees have substance abuse histories and therefore require specialized treatment supervision accurately portrays my caseload. In fact, the majority of my caseload parolees was required to attend Alcoholics Anonymous (AA) and/or Narcotics Anonymous (NA) meetings and submit to random urinalyses.

Having knowledge of criminological theory, as well as a counseling background, had a significant impact on how I did my job, particularly with populations who, as William Julius Wilson (1987) would suggest, are "truly disadvantaged" as the result of limited knowledge about and access to available legitimate resources. I add that I too demonstrated diligence in the manner in which I persisted in my efforts to persuade and seek resources specific to the individual needs of parolees. There were several times when parolees would come into my office and state, "I could not find a job." Knowing the truth about employment opportunities for minorities, especially minority males, allowed me to use compassion and exhibit humane treatment toward them instead of quickly going to the extreme by charging a violation. This is not to suggest that parolees did not lie about seeking employment but to highlight the fact-finding nature of parole supervision. Although finding a job was a parole requirement, it was my job to verify employment attempts and make referrals to employment projects and any additional training likely to increase parolees' opportunities of finding and retaining employment.

Sex Offenders

My caseload included persons convicted of sex crimes. While sex offender populations are typically assigned to specialized programs that include therapy and residential placement, it was not uncommon for sex offenders to be on regular-supervision caseloads. The majority of sex offenders on my caseload were middle-aged white males. The sex offenders on my caseload were meticulous, orderly, and always on time. In short, they were compliant. They did not raise any red flags until they disappeared altogether and without notice. Sex offenders on parole had special transitional challenges that not only included finding places to live and employment but also involved safety concerns as a result of the sex offender registry (some citizens may be motivated to attack them). As with other serious offender populations, there were variations among the sex offenders, including specific types of sex offenses committed (statutory rape, rape or sexual assault, child molestation, etc.).

The Rehabilitation Programs Division of Texas's state parole was and still is responsible for ensuring that specialized caseload populations are placed in programs geared toward their successful completion of parole as well as their successful reentry into society. Specifically, the Sex Offender Education Program and Sex Offender Treatment Program are programs that assist sex offender populations. The consensus in the literature is that the treatment of sexual offenders should begin early and continue. Likewise, harsher punishments also continue to surface as a deterrence mechanism. Treatment can significantly account for variations in deterrence when conducted at early stages of development.

Neighborhood Characteristics

While working in state parole, I noticed that there were many functions deemed as vital in the monitoring of prisoners released into society, including face-to-face contact with them in their neighborhoods. Home visits and establishing relationships with family members and vendors (service providers) were a part of keeping track of parolees, which served as a twofold effort not only to protect society from victimization but also to help create needed opportunities for parolees' success. Ensuring the safety of society and successful reentry for convicted felons go hand in hand. In addition to requiring parolees to come into the office, then, I conducted monthly field visits to verify residence, employment, and attendance at required programs.

I was responsible for supervising parolees who were released to live in certain zip code areas in Texas. The specific areas comprised neighborhood characteristics described as socially disorganized in accordance with Shaw and McKay's social disorganization theory (Akers & Sellers, 2009). For example, in these neighborhoods, parolees had limited employment opportunities, police presence decreased political power, and there were several abandoned homes. Throughout my experiences, I found that returning to the same or similar disorganized neighborhoods presented a challenge for parolee transition. In one case, a Hispanic male came in one day for his monthly office visit and presented his life situation and expressed a desire for a better future for his family. The occasion was that he found out that he was having a baby girl. He decided to get married, liked his job at an auto parts store, and even considered for the first time in his life opportunities to move up into a management position. During this visit, he also decided to move outside of the city away from the negative influences in his life. He eventually successfully completed his parole.

The Importance of Community Resources

Verification of residential placement is vital to supervising parolees upon their release from prison but more important are skills, knowledge, and access to resources that increase the likelihood of successful reentry. According to Agnew's (1992) general strain theory, individuals commit crime as the result of the presence of a negative stimulus, the removal of a positive stimulus, or the realization that desired life goals are not likely going to be met, and/or some combination of these three variables. Although differences certainly existed, all parolees on my caseload suffered from some form of strain that impeded their ability to successfully complete their parole supervision. As such, social resources saturated parole offices throughout the state of Texas in attempts to decrease recidivism rates.

Educational attainment is one of the most significant factors related to criminal and delinquent behavior. Societies all over the world heavily invest in targeting underrepresented populations thereby increasing the likelihood of educational attainment for these groups in which the convicted belong. During the time that I worked for state parole, the link between educational attainment and propensity to continue a life of crime was a major focus of the Texas Department of Criminal Justice Parole Division, which partnered with education service providers to offer general educational development (GED) courses to newly released persons. Similar to national statistics on prison-based populations, most persons on my caseload comprised minority males with minimal education. Specifically, education levels ranged from noncompletion of high school, completion of high school, and some college level courses. While educational levels differed, many parolees had taken advantage of GED services while incarcerated. As such, it is easy to measure one of the most impactful assets of corrections addressing a significant environmental factor necessary upon reentry. When newly released persons had not participated in GED services, inclusion of this and/or a vocational training stipulation was included on the parole certificate.

Many parolees on my caseload were required, depending on the parole certificate agreement, to participate in social skill building programs designed to increase their chances of a successful transition back into society. One of the greatest rewards about working for state parole in the 1990s was experiencing the push for resources for such programs and the collaborative efforts with employers to hire convicted persons. This effort was realized through Project Re-Integration of Offenders, or Project RIO, a program overseen by the Texas Workforce Commission designed to assist parolees in finding and retaining employment. The Texas Workforce Commission also works with inmate populations to provide them with skills and training while incarcerated that will enable them to take advantage of employment opportunities immediately upon release. This employment program was created to decrease high recidivism rates by providing otherwise unskilled persons with employment opportunities.

In addition to minimum education levels and underemployment, significant numbers of parolees also suffered from alcohol and/or drug addiction. Parolees were required per their parole certificate (as a condition of release) to attend AA and/or NA meetings as well as provide random urinalyses at the time of their scheduled office visits. I conducted monthly and random urinalyses on parolees with histories of drug use and/or abuse or drug related convictions including drug trafficking, possession, and distribution. In addition, however, I identified several resources to help them keep from recidivating (committing future crime) and required parolees to attend drug rehabilitation programs and support groups within their surrounding communities.

To further meet the needs of parolees, in addition to parole supervision, our office building housed additional state funded social work and counseling programs that pursued a collaborative initiative to reduce recidivism. Included in these programs were AA and NA, state social workers, GED personnel, and a broad spectrum of social service providers. These resources assisted parolees in meeting their personal, educational, and environmental needs upon their release, assisting them in achieving a smoother transition back into society. Crime rates in America have always fluctuated somewhat, and while they have decreased in the past few years, the recidivism rates of persons released from prison remain high. While they were not the majority of my particular caseload, plenty of the parolees I supervised did recidivate.

My experiences also taught me how important family bonds can be to parolee reentry (assuming that the bonds are with people who are good influences). Travis Hirschi (1969) argued that persons with strong bonds to family, community, and the larger society (attachment to parents, commitment to and involvement in conventional activities, and belief in conventional morality) are not likely to commit crime while persons with weak bonds are more likely to commit crime. I recall one parolee in particular, a Hispanic male, who had been on parole for years and was approved to visit the office and verify his home and employment every 6 months. Prior to the end of my tenure with state parole, he was successfully discharged from parole and moved back to Mexico to be with his family, including his grandchildren and great grandchildren of whom he talked about regularly. Thinking back, I see how his attachment to his family, albeit later in his life, acted as a significant social control mechanism and likely stimulated his successful discharge.

❖ CONCLUSION

Working with adults released from prison who suffered from lack of resources and opportunity even after they had paid their "debt" to society made me realize two things: (1) People who go to prison will likely be released back into society, and (2) society will benefit from decreased recidivism and victimizations if this population of people is afforded the skills necessary to be successful. As I mentioned earlier, the state of Texas aggressively sought to provide parolees with employment and educational services to assist with their successful reentry. In Texas, parolees' needs were met through resources provided by social work programs housed in my parole office building and included counseling services, assistance with transportation (bus line cards), and residential or halfway house placement.

The truth of the matter, however, is that as a parole officer, I could do everything "right" and still have a parolee who goes out and commits another crime. Thousands of convicted criminals are released from prison daily and recidivism rates, particularly for minorities, continue to be a major societal concern. Several criminological theories offer plausible explanations as to why people commit crime, including those focusing on social processes, such as social control. Although social processes are significant in the success of all human viability, the social process related to informal mechanisms of control, such as those having to do with education, employment, neighborhoods, and family, have been largely ignored when examining the reentry success of parolees. Likewise, it is important to realize the extent of the depth of resources required to assist newly released persons from prison back into society. Parolees and other released prisoners can be reintegrated into society and steered away from re-offending, but it takes a large number of resources such as those providing assistance with education, employment, and housing.

Working as a parole officer certainly impacted my life and ultimately my pursuit of increased knowledge about the criminal justice system and its affected populations. As my knowledge grew, I realized that society is composed of people from all ethnic and social backgrounds who have been either directly or indirectly impacted by the corrections arm of the system. I also learned that these effects far surpass the everyday traffic stop offense and extend into contact like arrest, prosecution, conviction, and ultimately societal reentry. As a collage, my experiences in state parole and counseling helped me to hone in on my passion for crime deterrence and later interests in explanations of adolescent crime and delinquency persistence. Although they largely amount to a cycle of monthly verifications, the functions of a state parole are a necessary cycle holding parolees accountable for the agreed upon stipulations of their early reentry to society.

❖ REFERENCES

Agnew, R. (1992). Foundation for a general strain theory of crime and delinquency. *Criminology, 30,* 47–87.

Akers, R. L., & Sellers, C. S. (2009). *Criminological theories: Introduction, evaluation, and application* (5th ed.). New York: Oxford University Press.

Gabbidon, S. L. (2010). *Race, ethnicity, crime, and justice: An international dilemma.* Thousand Oaks, CA: Sage.

Hirschi, T. (1969). *Causes of delinquency.* Berkeley: University of California Press.

Pager, D. (2007). *Marked: Race, crime, and finding work in an era of mass incarceration.* Chicago: University of Chicago Press.

Petersilia, J. (2003). *When prisoners come home: Parole and prisoner reentry.* New York: Oxford University Press.

Western, B., Kling, J., & Weiman, D. (2001). The labor market consequences of incarceration. *Crime and Delinquency, 47,* 410–428.

Wilson, W. J. (1987). *The truly disadvantaged: The inner city, the underclass, and public policy.* Chicago: University of Chicago Press.

❖ RECOMMENDED READINGS

Agnew, R. (1992). Foundation for a general strain theory of crime and delinquency. *Criminology, 30,* 47–87.

Akers, R. L., & Sellers, C. S. (2009). *Criminological theories: Introduction, evaluation, and application* (5th ed.). New York: Oxford University Press.

Gabbidon, S. L. (2010). *Race, ethnicity, crime, and justice: An international dilemma.* Thousand Oaks, CA: Sage.

Hanser, R. D. (2010). *Community corrections.* Thousand Oaks, CA: Sage.

Lior, G., & Hung-En, S. (2010). *Rethinking corrections: Rehabilitation, reentry, and reintegration.* Thousand Oaks, CA: Sage.

Stanko, W., Gillespie, W., & Crews, G. A. (2004). *Living in prison: A history of the correctional system with an insider's view.* Westport, CT: Greenwood Press.

DISCUSSION QUESTIONS

1. Do you think that if you had enough resources, you could keep released prisoners from re-offending? Why or why not? What resources would you need?

2. Do you believe that by helping persons convicted of crimes, you are helping society? If so, exactly how does helping them help society, in which specific ways? If not, then why doesn't helping them help society? What would be the consequences of not helping them?

3. Do you think that released prisoners and community-sanctioned persons should all be treated the same, having the same requirements and receiving the same services, or differently according to their particular situations, including membership in a minority group? Explain or justify your answer, including an accounting for fairness and equity.

11

An Attempt to Change Disproportionate Minority Contact by Working in Youth Corrections

Robert J. Durán

Editor's Introduction: Professor Durán was a youth worker at a private residential treatment facility and a youth security officer at a state juvenile correctional facility. Like most correctional environments, both places held a disproportionate number of racial and ethnic minorities. Durán approached youth work with a sense of social justice. Employing a sociological imagination, he places his experiences in the context of societal-level inequality, including his descriptive analysis of instances of staff discrimination against minority youth

(Continued)

(Continued)

that he witnessed. As he found out, working toward social change from within a social system like corrections is very difficult. Durán points out, however, that correctional employees can make a difference by refusing to tolerate racism and discrimination.

❖ INTRODUCTION: MY BACKGROUND

In this chapter, I explain my experiences as a Chicano and having the opportunity to work within the criminal justice system while pursuing advanced degrees devoted toward the study of crime. My goal was to find solutions for crime in my neighborhood and explore why my family and friends were seen as part of the problem. This pursuit led me to comprehend larger societal issues of race and ethnicity, specifically disproportionate minority contact (DMC). DMC is an area of inequality studies that focuses on racial and ethnic disparities in the juvenile justice system (Pope, Lovell, & Hsia, 2002). DMC research involves the collection of juvenile justice data to determine whether youth of color (blacks, Latinos, and Native Americans) are more likely than white youth to be arrested, placed on probation, and sent to secure confinement. Working within the criminal justice system gave me the opportunity to see the lived reality of higher numbers of blacks and Latinos experiencing differential treatment. My education gave me the knowledge and research tools to explain why this was occurring and how inequality could be corrected. Criminal justice employment offered me mainstream legitimacy. Growing up, I often felt targeted for misbehavior, and now I was enforcing the law.

Working within the criminal justice system exposed me to the unethical behavior of a small number of staff members who remained protected by a *code of silence*: a term used to describe the withholding of vital information to demonstrate loyalty and to protect the group to which an individual belongs (Maas, 1973). In the realm of criminal justice, the unwritten employee perspective was that humans make mistakes; therefore, staff should support one another. Such a belief system and code of conduct led to many problems that I'd like to explore in this essay. I hope my story can help others see the importance of working within the criminal justice system for "hands-on" knowledge, to encourage advanced education teachers to make sense of these experiences, and finally the combination of the two in order to create a better system for changing behaviors and improving the lives of our future leaders.

Having grown up in a working class social environment, I was interested in providing protection for my family and friends. Physical confrontations were a possibility, and thus, accomplishing the goal of legal protection was a challenge for many residents. The racial, economic, ethnic, and religious prejudices of residents within the state of Utah resulted in differential opportunities and treatment for individuals who did not fit the white, blond, blue-eyed, and Mormon profile of the majority group. When I was a teenager, the groups providing protection were occasionally involved in gangs, and this only enhanced opposition by criminal justice agencies who perceived the entire community as criminal. This stereotype was defined as "ecological contamination" by Werthman and Piliavin (1967). These researchers argued that people living within a community were often treated as possessing the same attributes as the small number of individuals who were criminally involved (see Rodriguez, 1997, for more on this topic). I wanted to change the differential treatment by the criminal justice system and work to provide a more fair and respectful relationship (see Ruiz, 1997). Attending college was the first step in accomplishing this goal because it allowed me opportunity, academic credentials, and mainstream respectability regardless of my lack of mainstream social capital.

While first attending college, I originally did not know what I wanted to major in. I liked working with people, but making money was something that appeared very desirable. My schooling first focused on business management at a small technical university. My minor was accounting. I wanted to use my degree to start a lowrider shop where I could fix up customized cars. This school was really helpful at increasing my academic skills but horrible when it came time to transferring credits toward a bachelor's degree: None of the credits were accepted.

While attending Weber State University I found a class that really caught my attention: sociology. Schaefer (2000, p. 3) defines sociology as "the systematic study of social behavior and human groups." To understand social behavior, sociologists rely on the sociological imagination. C. Wright Mills (2000, p. 5) described the concept as follows:

> The sociological imagination enables its possessor to understand the larger historical scene in terms of its meaning for the inner life and the external career of a variety of individuals. It enables him to take into account how individuals, in the welter of their daily experience, often become falsely conscious of their social positions.

Mills argued that the sociological imagination is the most fruitful form of self-consciousness in distinguishing between troubles within the character of the individual and those of the nature of society and in linking personal problems to larger social issues. Sociology included broad issues beyond crime, so it really supplemented my minors in criminal justice and psychology. The stratification of society includes class and racial and ethnic inequality. I was curious to explore how these concepts could have real consequences in impacting persons' life chances.

My previous jobs were in fast food and manufacturing. Gaining entrance into the criminal justice social world required for me a mixture of education and experience. To gain this experience, I began working in volunteer and part-time positions. I was maintaining full-time school, work, and family, and so finding the extra time required giving up the social life of my younger days. This was beneficial for me because it kept me out of much of the "drama" that my friends continued to experience while hanging out in the neighborhood. I was busy trying to raise two young children with my high school sweetheart. My first volunteer job involved helping second graders at a low-income school learn to read. The students made me smile with their curiosity and enthusiasm. Helping youth perceived as unworthy to accomplish their goals had become my calling. This position led to working with Child and Family Services as a youth mentor and then as a Deputy Juvenile Probation Officer. Each of these experiences could be the narrative of this article, but I'd like to focus on my employment as a youth worker for two different juvenile correction facilities (1999–2000 and 2005). I hope by sharing these experiences I will be able to encourage new employees to continue critical thinking and speak out when observing staff misconduct.

❖ OVERVIEW OF THE FACILITIES

Youth correction facilities in Utah and Colorado are primarily composed of different levels of housing based upon the seriousness of the offense and offender history. When most youth are committed to a facility, several less serious alternatives have been tried to correct the behavior in the past. Serious offenses do not always follow this pattern, and some cases get transferred to adult court. For example, in Utah, a juvenile court hearing has several options including (1) release; (2) detention or work camp; (3) Division of Child and Family Services custody; (4) juvenile court programs—probation, state supervision, and restitution, or fine; (5) juvenile justice system custody; and (6) transfer to adult court. The juvenile justice system commitment facilities in Utah consist of an Observation and Assessment (O&A) unit (90-day placement when I was employed but now 45 days), community programs (usually group homes), and secure care (the length of stay can range from 1 year all the way until someone turns 21).

Working in youth corrections for the state of Utah required a bachelor's degree whereas a private facility required only a few years of college. In Colorado, a few years of college were required. Both facilities encouraged prior experience. Therefore, my first opportunity to work within youth corrections in Utah was at a private facility. The pay and benefits were not as good as those paid by the state, but it allowed me the opportunity to work with at-risk youth. I was hired as a youth worker at an O&A unit. The entire facility housed a detention center and secure housing. The O&A unit could hold up to 18 youth at one time, and it was mixed gender. Both boys and girls between the ages of 12 and 18 were housed here to determine future placement. The acts of delinquency varied from sex offenses, assaults, property offenses, and drug and alcohol abuse to other minor level offenses. The youth lived in individual rooms separated by one large day room. Their day was spent primarily within the unit or at school. Breakfast, lunch, and dinner were in the kitchen connected to the day room. At least one staff member monitored the day room at all times. Between the hours of 7 a.m. and 10 p.m., there were usually three to five staffers working.

The program was run on a very strict schedule: wake up, eat, shower, go to school, free time, peer groups, activities, mentoring, and bedtime. There were no surprises in the routine. Behavior was constantly monitored by staff with a plus and minus system. Misbehavior could earn a minus, which if accumulated throughout the week resulted in reduced privileges. No minuses earned additional privileges such as leadership roles, off-campus activities, and more free time. The youth evaluated their behavior during a peer group held Monday through Friday. A staff member guided the group as the youth gave each other feedback for reducing minuses and maintaining good behavior. It was very impressive to hear and see the impact of constructive feedback from peers on how to do well within the program. The staff provided the structure and the youth fit within the framework and achieved positive results. Other services offered included skill building groups, recreation, community service, counseling, and treatment plans. Each staff member was assigned one to three youth as *goal kids*. Staff met with goal kids weekly to evaluate behavior and discuss how to accomplish objectives. Before our goal kids went to court, various agencies involved in the welfare of the youth met to determine the best placement. When the youth went to court, the judge asked an O&A staff member for a housing recommendation.

At the second facility in Colorado, I worked as a Youth Security Officer. It was a 240-bed residential correctional facility considered to house the "most serious and violent delinquent youth" according to the Office of Juvenile Justice and Delinquency Prevention. The process of getting hired at this facility took longer than in Utah and required an application, common-sense test, and interview. I applied for the job in August of 2004, hired on in January 2005, and began training in February. The entire process took around 6 months, which would be overwhelming for someone needing an immediate job. The position was with the state of Colorado, and it offered better pay and benefits. The pay range at the time was $2,877 to $4,170 a month. The Colorado Department of Human Services, Division of Youth Corrections ad read as follows:

> The position provides corrective, cognitive, emotional, and behavioral experiences within a structured secure program. . . . Specific responsibilities include: control movement of youth in the unit or agency; control behavior in individual or group settings; maintain constant visual observation of youth in custody; record observation of behavior [in] Daily Observations, Shift Logs, Incident Reports in automated and non-automated systems, or on other reports as necessary. . . . This employee will interact with parents, professional visitors, and law enforcement agents as necessary in person, or by telephone. Will ensure access to and/or reasonable care for all hygiene needs, medical needs, and meal service. . . . Will conduct clothed and unclothed searches to prevent contraband entry and will conduct searches of property and areas to include internal and external perimeter searches. (p. 2)

The unit where I worked included a variety of adjudications for delinquent acts including sexual, property, violent, and drug and alcohol offenses. The facility was originally created in 1881 as the State Industrial School for boys and had grown to include a 15-acre campus of a variety of buildings with youth between the ages of 16 and 21 years of age. The unit was very different from the O&A unit in Utah because of its numbers of youth and size of the building and campus. The building consisted of three pods each housing from 15 to 22 youth for a total size of around 60 youth. The units were separated by thick plated glass windows. The control room was located in the center of the building and controlled the entrance and movement within the unit. Speakers allowed for monitoring of audible behavior. Within the main day room and/or control center were three isolation rooms. Each pod included a day room, individual rooms, and an upstairs. Each pod had a clinical group leader. The clinical group leader ran individual therapy groups based on the offense and evaluated staff. Each shift had a supervisor, and the entire unit had a manager. Most youth shared a room with another individual unless they had been found to commit a sex offense. Therefore, this unit was about the size of three to four O&A units. The program followed a *normative culture* structure, which was similar to the pluses and minus system of behavior. According to the Colorado Department of Human Services Division of Youth Corrections, normative culture is "a behavior management program that is based on juveniles holding members of the peer community accountable for behaviors that violate the facility 'norms'" (2005, p. 1). The facility was surrounded by a 25-foot curved fence, which was constantly monitored by video cameras and car patrol. The youth ate in different buildings, and recreation was usually on the main field or gym. Leading youth between buildings required strict silence, hands in pockets, and walking in a single line. The daily routine included school, free time, and moving to and from eating rooms. The facility followed a strict schedule, and so the routine was very well-known by the youth. Extracurricular activities for positive youth included track and field, basketball, football, debate team, and movies.

❖ MY EXPERIENCES

In this section, I describe what it was like to work in two different youth correction facilities. I draw from memories of lived experiences, a diary, and notes taken while working in both facilities. I separate this section based on my employment during undergraduate school and later graduate school. I think this is important because of (1) the type of facility: short-term versus long-term; (2) different state strategies (Utah and Colorado); and (3) my increasing educational and ethical consciousness during graduate school.

Undergraduate

Working in youth corrections was completely different than what I imagined. When I started I was only 5 to 10 years older than the youth. I can clearly recall my first day. The supervisor was giving me a tour of the facility and had to go in to a meeting. He asked me to stand at the desk for a minute. While waiting, four staff members passed by, and one asked, "What are you doing here?" I felt embarrassed, like I didn't fit in. I was dressed professionally, but I had a "tail" (long hair in the back) and an Old English tattoo running down the inside of my forearm. I replied, "I work here now." He looked at me rudely then walked off with the other three staff members who looked more curious than hostile. I later observed this staff member, who I will call Tim, carry the same negative and hostile behavior toward many youth in the facility. Tim was previously a police officer in Texas and carried a superior demeanor. The other staff members I came to know were great. The supervisor was really energetic and everyone reinforced and supported one another. This is where I learned the value of structure and how clear guidelines were helpful for youth and the overall unit. I felt sort of out of place with the staff, so I was working hard to fit in. My rapport with the youth was excellent. Several of the youth were those I knew while working as a deputy probation officer. The supervisor and other staff members began to teach me the expectations for the job. They advised me to not allow youth to split staff: Support one another and if in disagreement, talk about it away from the youth. They also stressed to be very careful with all interactions with females housed in the facility to prevent any allegations of misconduct and that safety and security is the most important thing to maintain at all times. The longer I worked at the facility, the more patterns I learned for explaining and confronting negative behavior.

The youth did their best to adjust to life away from family and friends. They wanted to go home. Some of the kids didn't receive visits whereas others had a lot of family support. The youth housed at the facility, like in the surrounding county, were primarily white. There was, however, a higher proportion of minorities housed within the facility. In my unit, seven of the nine staff members were white, along with one Tongan and one Chicano, me. Most of the staff members at the facility were Mormon with ties to a small town in Utah. With the exception of Tim, I considered my colleagues friends. We worked together to encourage the youth to make better decisions. I handled the day-to-day management of activities, bathroom breaks, lunches, dinners, cleanup, and treatment groups. I later came to learn through experience that having a mixed gender unit brought with it many challenges of flirting, dating, and trying to impress one another. I really enjoyed working with kids to help them accomplish their goals.

For some reason, Tim constantly gave me a hard time. I did not like how he interacted with most of the kids of color. He seemed to give them a harder time, including one youth who had been adjudicated delinquent for the charge of statutory rape. He was 16, and she was 15. The two had consensual sex, but the parents filed charges. He was black, and she was white. Another youth was forced to strip naked in the bathroom because Tim accused him of hiding contraband. The young boy cried as I stood there observing Tim direct verbal threats. Tim maintained a good relationship with the other white staffers. Some of them seemed to admire his behavior; thus, I never complained to supervisors about how he treated me or many of the youth. I put up with it, and the youth had no choice. This is something I continue to regret to this day.

As it turned out, the facility was going through some downsizing, and Tim was let go. I was the most recently hired and was required to switch to graveyard shift for a period of time. Working graveyards, going to school after my shift, and managing the day-to-day schedule of my family was tremendously difficult. I wasn't getting much sleep. Fortunately, it lasted only for 2 or 3 months. On the graveyard shift, two staff members conducted bed checks every 15 minutes to make sure everyone was in the room and sleeping OK, and youth on suicide watch were checked every 5 minutes.

Overall, I enjoyed working as a youth worker at this O&A unit. I really liked working to help encourage youth to succeed. I liked how the staff worked closely together to create a supportive environment. I didn't like Tim and how he continually abused his authority. For the most part, restraints were rare. Verbal de-escalation was essential although we were trained in pressure points. When I applied for graduate school, I was also going through the process to work in Youth Corrections for the state of Utah, which would have included better pay and better benefits. I wanted to work in the city where I grew up. This area was perceived as having more hard-core and gang involved youth. I wanted to work more with this population as it matched my background. I wanted to help them accomplish their dreams. When I was accepted to the University of Colorado to begin pursuing my doctorate, I resigned from my position in youth corrections to pursue the potential benefits that might exist with school.

Graduate Years

Graduate school was difficult, and each year I wanted to quit. I wanted to work directly with individuals considered to be criminals. I didn't want to talk about it. I wanted to provide motivation and encourage alternatives. School seemed too much like an ivory tower and did not relate to my lived experience (see Acuña, 1998; see also Ladner, 1973).

I enjoyed mentoring students, but Boulder, Colorado, and the students who attended the university were very different from the culture and people of my background. Many of these young adults were rich and from educationally privileged backgrounds. I wondered whether a doctorate degree could still help me to accomplish my goals. I decided to go back to working within youth corrections, and I considered leaving academia. I was at the all-but-dissertation (ABD) stage, so I had already finished all of my comprehensive exams. My doctoral chair was really worried about whether I would finish or give it all up. I too didn't know what I would end up doing.

The training for my new position lasted 2 weeks. It began early in the morning and lasted all day. The trainees came from a variety of backgrounds. The first week focused on policies and the second week was devoted to continuum of force and pressure points. When my first shift began, I felt like a rookie learning many things from scratch. The facility had several rules that were new, and I was expected to hold youth accountable at all times. Whereas at the Utah facility there were 4 to 6 staff interacting with 15 to 18 youth at one time, I was now placed in a pod of one staff member per 15 to 21 youth. Each staff member was required to run the pod. The other staffers primarily rotated, stayed in the control room, or ran the visits or other errands that were needed. The only time a staff member was not in a pod was when the entire pod was on lockdown, and all doors were locked. This lower staff-to-youth ratio brought increased challenges. It was more difficult to catch everything, and horseplay was very common. The youth learned that being aggressive could prevent bullying from other youth. I had to constantly monitor and challenge several things such as noise level, language, and movement within the pod. The staff member ensured that all doors were locked when the youth were in the day room. Television time was limited to certain hours on the weekends and after 9 p.m. on weekdays for the youth who were at higher levels of positive behavior. There were limits on how many phone calls were allowed each week. Recreation time was only for youth who were positive and not for those on the Juvenile Disciplinary Program. The youth on the disciplinary program were under several rules, were closely watched, and required a positive youth to escort them around the unit. Eating included many additional rules. Youth needed to ask before dumping food trays, and only level 2 and higher youth could get extra juice. No sharing of food, talking between tables, or looking out windows was allowed, and tables needed to be wiped before leaving.

Overall, I felt overwhelmed by a structure that overcontrolled without enough staff support to make it consistent. Some staff members enforced the rules strictly and others loosely. There were far too many youth per staff member. The youth felt too little structure to guide their behavior. The staff who had worked at the facility for a long time told me that things were worse in the past; there was about 80 youth per 1 staff member. A lawsuit in the early 1990s led to many changes and improvements. I liked many of the youth, but I struggled to show them a better alternative within a structure that was working against me. At least 8 out of every 10 youth in the facility were Latino, black, or Native American.

I came to encounter a staff member who was very similar to Tim from O&A. I will call him Bill. Bill and I started off getting along well. We talked about boxing. My first and last names are associated with one of the most famous boxers in history, and so the conversation is one I've been having all my life. A few of the youth in the facility who were Latino began telling me on my first day that this staff member was racist and abusive. Not wanting to divide staff, I listened and said that we have been getting along. A young Latino who was about to be released told me to be careful. A black staff member who was working overhead the conversation and told me he concurred with this youth's overall assessment of Bill. I was placed primarily on the back-end shift, which was Thursday, Friday, Saturday; then, I worked on the front-end shift on Sunday. Bill was the supervisor of the front-end shift, so we worked together only 1 day a week. The front-end staff was all white, and the back-end staff included 3 black staff members. I was the only Chicano employee, and this matched my experience with O&A. There were a total of 15 staffers who worked in this unit including myself. Two were female and 4 were from ethnic minority groups. I made good friends with the majority of staff members; Bill later became the exception. The longer I worked at the facility, the more I noticed a much different presence every time Bill worked. He had the youth locked in their rooms more. He was more verbally aggressive. Youth were afraid of him, and he seemed to like this. He was also very active whenever a youth needed to be restrained. In fact, probably half of the staff members were really pumped up and excited whenever there was going to be a restraint. I found this kind of strange because I primarily used verbal de-escalation, and I was overall very good at this technique. I could calm down even some of the most upset youth, and I took pride in this skill.

Bill was my supervisor, but we began to disagree on tactics after a restraint that he became involved in. It all began on a Sunday morning. Bill came into the unit in a grumpy mood. All of the youth were still sleeping around 8:30 a.m., and breakfast was about to begin. Bill walked into a pod, and suddenly, one of the youth's buzzers went off. I was working at the control desk, and I asked, "Can I help you," through the intercom. I then heard a great deal of noise in the background. Two staff members ran into the pod to assist Bill. I heard cuffs applied; then, I saw Bill walk the youth, who I will call Mark, toward the isolation room with his arms far behind his back. Bill pushed Mark onto the metal bed and the other two staff members came to assist, but before they could apply the foot and arm restraints, Bill slammed Mark three to four times onto the metal bed. The other staff member came out and grabbed a mat to put under Mark. Bill then lifted up Mark's arms behind his back, and Mark began making coughing noises, as if he could not breathe. Another staff member arrived, who I will call Shirley, and she started going through the documenting process for placing a youth in a 3-point restraint in the isolation room. She then followed procedure and made a call to the unit manager. Bill reported that the youth hit him, and I asked, "Are you okay?" and he replied, "Yeah, I just need to cool off for a minute."

Mark had been in 3-point restraints for an hour and a half when I started to complain that we were violating policy. Shirley, who was friends with Bill, notified me that Mark had been spitting at the floor off and on for the first 39 minutes, which demonstrated lack of compliance. I walked into the isolation room, and asked Mark how he was doing. We had good rapport with one another, and he was just lying there during most of my checks. Mark told me that Bill was harassing him, so he responded negatively to the rude behavior. I told Mark to calm down and we would get him out of there soon, just be compliant. During another check—these occur every 15 minutes—Mark told me his wrists were hurting. I told Shirley that the handcuffs were very tight and maybe we should loosen them a little. She told me "handcuffs are not supposed to be comfortable and that Mark should have thought of that before assaulting staff." I agreed youth should not assault staff, but I said, "Handcuffs are for safety and security and not punishment." She asked if his hands were blue. I said no, and so she dismissed my comment. I told her I was not in agreement with the continued 3-point because Mark had been for the most part lying face first on the bed. There was no lack of compliance. Shirley told me that she thought Bill would leave him there all day. I told her that I would no longer sign his observation paper on the isolation room door. I mentioned that maybe I should call the unit manager, and she said that I should talk to Bill before taking such action.

I then walked into a pod while the youth were locked down and talked with Bill about removing Mark from the 3-point restraints. Bill replied that he could leave him like this because Mark was a threat to staff. I disagreed. It was under Bill's direction that Mark remained in 3-point. Bill did not want him to be released. To cool off, I walked the parents who had finished visiting several youth back to the main office. This allowed me some time to leave the building, collect my thoughts, and assess my evaluation of the situation. Bill and Shirley must have used their time in a similar manner because when I returned, Shirley told me they'd loosened Mark's handcuffs a little. I felt relieved that I had attained some progress. Shortly after, I was working in the pod where the dispute occurred when some of the youth whom I had a good relationship with told me that Bill started the confrontation. They said Bill grabbed Mark and slammed his head into the wall to make sure that he hurt him. They thought Mark should file a grievance. Later in the day, Mark was released from the 3-point restraints and continued to stay in isolation. This was my first conflict with Bill, and several more were to develop over the next several months.

Bill and I no longer really talked. He barked orders at me, and I confronted him about his demeaning behavior. I told Bill that I was not going to tolerate his abuse because I was not one of the youth. I told him I did not care if he was my supervisor because he was not above me. I was referring to his white male racial entitlement and his demeaning treatment of youth of color. I told Bill that he cannot treat youth or me as inferior and do whatever he wanted. A few days later, one of my goal kids was restrained by Bill, and his face had been dragged along the carpet. My goal kid called 9-1-1 afterward when he had phone privileges and filed a complaint. When I began my shift, I was briefed on the situation and realized that Bill's negative behavior needed to stop. All of Bill's attacks were directly targeted against black and brown youth. I tried to change Bill's behavior by talking with more senior staff but received no encouragement. I was told by the clinical manager to listen to my supervisor and was scolded for telling my supervisor that he is not above me. After receiving no help, I turned in my 2-week notice to resign my position. When word got out that I was leaving, several of the other staff members reported to me that they too were in disagreement with how Bill behaved and that they were not like this. The youth in the pods where I worked were upset that I was leaving because they related to me. My goal kids wanted me to continue hanging in there, but with full-time work, working on my dissertation, and teaching two classes, plus managing my family, I was falling apart from the stress. During undergraduate and graduate school, I relieved my stress through exercise and boxing, but lately my hectic schedule did not allow any time for these extracurricular activities.

I quit my job at a point when I did not have additional employment. I was not signed up to teach summer or fall classes. I wanted to leave academia, but even more, I really hated what was going on within the juvenile justice facility where I worked in Colorado. I took a huge risk in quitting, but everything worked out. I received a phone call a few weeks later notifying me that I had received the Society for the Study of Social Problems Race and Ethnicity Minority Graduate Scholarship for Scholarship and Activism. My final year of my dissertation was covered. I now had the time to finish my dissertation and enter the job market.

❖ CONCLUSION

After many years devoted to youth mentorship in a variety of programs (e.g., helping second graders read, Division of Child and Family Services, juvenile probation, and youth corrections), I became disillusioned with my ability to create change within the system. I had spent around 13 months working full-time in two different facilities: one in which I probably would have continued working had I not received the opportunity to attend graduate school and the second where I struggled daily. I benefited from a tremendous amount of hands-on knowledge that continues to inform my understanding and insight. I believe this insight can inform others about the difference between what is taught and what is practiced.

The quality of any youth correction facility is very dependent upon the structure of the program and the qualifications and personalities of the staff. Developing a structure that will help empower youth requires resources, training, and adequate supervision. Youth corrections alone is unable to challenge the inequalities that are present in wider society, such as racism and classism, but it can help youth make better decisions so that they are less likely to come under the radar of the criminal (adult) justice system. Preventing future misbehavior will require staff that does not mirror problematic behaviors present in the wider society.

What I learned about myself was that I am really against individuals who abuse their authority. Much abuse of power was directed at youth of color. Individuals such as Tim and Bill were often liked by their peers. They were leaders. They were aggressive. They felt superior. In their world, I was not welcome. More than likely, individuals such as Tim and Bill continue to work in the criminal justice system and sadly have supporters who do not confront and challenge. These individuals cause more problems and take away from everyone who is trying to make the best of the structure in place. I think the biggest lesson here is the importance of holding central the values and ethics I stood for when I started. Staff members need to be fair and provide positive mentorship to youth in order to help them pursue an alternative outcome in their lives. I was able to accomplish more through verbal de-escalation and rapport. I followed the golden rule of treating others like I wanted to be treated. I have no idea where the youth I mentored at both correctional facilities are now. Maybe one or more of these individuals will be in a college course reading this book. I hope they are doing well and realize that I really cared deeply about helping them to achieve a better life. Their day-to-day encouragement was important for me in continuing to give. I also miss the friendships created with staff from working together through stressful situations. I think we all tried to follow a model to demonstrate better alternatives. After leaving youth corrections, I continued to target the misbehavior of those in positions of authority. I made it my mission to no longer remain silenced when there is strong evidence that something is not right. Racism is present in many institutions, and it is sad to see certain kinds of individuals in positions of authority, especially because they can continue to abuse and still receive support from colleagues.

❖ REFERENCES

Acuña, R. (1998). *Sometimes there is no other side: Chicanos and the myth of equality.* Notre Dame, IN: University of Notre Dame Press.

Colorado Department of Human Services Division of Youth Corrections. (2005, June). *Policy 14.1.* Available at http://www.cdhs.state.co.us/dyc/PDFs/P-14-1.pdf

Ladner, J. A. (1973). *The death of white sociology.* New York: Random House.

Maas, P. (1973). *Serpico.* New York: Bantam Books.

Mills, C. W. (2000). *The sociological imagination.* New York: Oxford University.

Pope, C. E., Lovell R., & Hsia, H. M. (2002). *Disproportionate minority confinement: A review of the research literature from 1989 through 2001.* Washington, DC: Office of Juvenile Justice and Delinquency Prevention.

Rodriguez, R. (1997). *Justice: A question of race.* Tempe, AZ: Bilingual Press.

Ruiz, M. (1997). *Two badges: The lives of Mona Ruiz.* Houston, TX: Arte Público Press.

Werthman, C., & Piliavin, I. (1967). Gang members and the police. In D. Bordua (Ed.), *The police: Six sociological essays* (pp. 56–98). New York: John Wiley.

❖ RECOMMENDED READINGS

Acuña, R. (1998). *Sometimes there is no other side: Chicanos and the myth of equality.* Notre Dame, IN: University of Notre Dame Press.

Ladner, J. A. (1973). *The death of white sociology.* New York: Random House.

Maas, P. (1973). *Serpico.* New York: Bantam Books.

Mills, C. W. (2000). *The sociological imagination.* New York: Oxford University.

Rodriguez, R. (1997). *Justice: A question of race.* Tempe, AZ: Bilingual Press.

Ruiz, M. (1997). *Two badges: The lives of Mona Ruiz.* Houston, TX: Arte Público Press.

DISCUSSION QUESTIONS

1. Describe how elements in your personal background—your family, neighborhood(s) you grew up in, education, racial and ethnic identity, major personal experiences, beliefs and attitudes, et cetera— may impact how you approach your prospective job or career?

2. If you personally witnessed a coworker mistreat a person under correctional supervision (juvenile or adult, incarcerated or in the community), how would you react? Would it matter if the person was your friend? What if the person had more influence than you, such as a supervisor? What would be your concerns about reporting or not reporting this person?

3. Do you think that it is possible to reduce social inequality by working as a frontline employee in corrections? What kinds of actions can a worker take to improve equality? Would one even have the power to do so? Is it appropriate for one to be an "activist" in such a position, or should one "just do his or her job"? Explain.

12

Helping Residential Youth Pursue Their Interests

Good for Youth and the Youth Worker

Lee Michael Johnson

Introduction: Professor Johnson was a youth worker in a residential treatment facility. Providing another frontline perspective, he reflects on his past experiences helping residents pursue their creative interests. He discusses an art and recreation program and three youth with whom he worked closely. Based on personal experience and scholarly work on corrections programs, he argues that helping system-involved youth pursue their creative interests gives staff an important part to play in treatment and institutional management. Johnson reports enjoyable experiences working with youth with serious offending and victimization issues. He believes that by helping youth pursue their interests, he was able to establish rapport and build productive relationships with youth, manage behavior, improve workplace environment, and counteract stress.

As the essays in this book reveal, corrections is very serious and challenging work. Institutional youth work is no exception. Youth workers are expected to change troubled youth in a way that prevents them from harming others, with little resources and heavy institutional constraints. Success is hard come by while heartbreaks—including residents' victimization histories—are not. In addition to the systemwide problems that inhibit efforts to help troubled youth, they themselves often seem to be the biggest obstacles. Against this backdrop, I propose that working with residential youth is fun, rewarding work and that having fun counteracts the stressors present in youth work and helps to achieve important institutional goals.

From May 1994 through August 1996, I worked as a residential counselor for Family Resources, Inc., a private nonprofit agency that offers a variety of child, family, and community services in the Quad Cities area of Iowa and Illinois.[1] My position was entry-level; it required a bachelor's degree or significant progress toward one, as well as some kind of experience working with youth. I was hired while working on my bachelor's degree and after doing volunteer work with at-risk and offending youth. I had just transferred to a 4-year university immediately after receiving an associate's degree in social work. I was majoring in both sociology and psychology with a concentration in general human service work with young people. I graduated in the spring of 1996 and left the job at the end of summer to go away to graduate school. As my choice of undergraduate studies may suggest, I wanted to get a job "helping troubled kids." The responsibilities of my position consisted largely of the following: writing and implementing treatment programs for the residents; facilitating cognitive and social skill development groups; facilitating educational groups; planning and conducting social and recreational activities; cofacilitating coping groups focusing on surviving abuse; engaging in general milieu treatment—restorative living activities, safety and control of behavior, and role modeling; and performing administrative support duties.

❖ OVERVIEW OF THE WORKPLACE

Family Resources operates several residential youth treatment programs at the Wittenmyer Youth Center in Davenport, Iowa. These

---

[1] Many thanks to Cheryl Goodwin, President/CEO; Mary Macumber Schmidt, Vice President; Tiffany Hood, Lead Residential Counselor, Bridge House Program (and my daughter); and all of Family Resources, Inc.

programs treat children who are unable to live in a family situation and provide a high degree of supervision, safety, structure, and therapeutic services. The residential counselor's role at the center is "to provide behavioral management for problematic behaviors while focusing on assisting the young person in learning, applying, and realizing the motivations necessary to exhibit social skills and healthy emotional coping"[2] (Family Resources, Inc., 2010). I worked at the center, mostly in a program that treated 12- to 17-year-old behavior-disordered and delinquent boys with a broad range of offending and victimization issues. Some of the residents were at-risk children removed from bad homes, some were found by the court to be children in need of assistance, and a few were adjudicated delinquent. Most of them were found to be behavior-disordered, and several were diagnosed with Attention Deficit Hyperactivity Disorder and Oppositional Defiant Disorder; a few were diagnosed with psychiatric disorders. Several residents possessed lower than normal intellectual functioning abilities, a few were mildly mentally retarded, and some had special needs due to physical and/or learning disabilities.

At the time I was hired, the youth center campus housed three other programs for boys: two secure juvenile correctional programs for serious offenders (one with a special focus on those with substance abuse issues) and a *nonsecure* program for normally functioning moderate offenders ("nonsecure" meaning that the doors were not locked from the inside, although residents were required to remain inside unless permitted to leave the building or campus). The programs were located in separate buildings, commonly referred to as "cottages." The agency also operated a residential program for girls and one for small children (co-ed) at nearby off-campus sites. I occasionally worked in these other five programs as well.

An art and recreational center serving the various programs was also on campus. The center was located in an older building containing a gym and basketball court, weight room, and art rooms (as well as offices and meeting rooms). Also, a small softball field, outdoor basketball court, sand volleyball court, and vegetable and flower garden were located on campus, and a large public park and recreational facilities were within walking distance. In addition to arts and crafts, several recreational activities were offered—kickball, badminton, volleyball, "pick up" softball and basketball, cookouts, dances, et cetera. The co-ed softball team (which I coached) and boys' basketball team played in a league against teams from other facilities. Many of the residents did not

---

[2]Family Resources, Inc. (2010). Retrieved February 27, 2010: www.famres.org.

possess strong artistic and physical abilities, but the purpose of the programs was to explore and develop the diverse interests of participants in an effort to create therapeutic, educational, and productive environments, not to discern talent or create competition. However, the program could function to cultivate strong artistic or physical potential.

A few months after I was hired, art and recreation counselors visited programs on campus and asked for residential counselors' help in carrying out art and recreational activities. The art and recreation program had only a few staff members of its own and would not have been able to carry out its activities without the cooperation and participation of the staff and supervisors working in each of the other programs. I jumped at the chance to do something fun with the residents, perhaps for my own benefit as much as theirs. In our program, a few of us staffers participated heavily in these activities, acting as informal art and recreation liaisons.

Staff members could also do planned or spontaneous small-scale art and recreational activities in their own programs. Residents could draw, paint, write, and play music if an instrument was available, and they could be taken outside or to the gym to play. The outdoor basketball and volleyball courts happened to be located right behind the building that housed our program, so we could conveniently take our residents out to play. Residents not considered a safety risk could be taken off grounds for activities and events—to museums, art galleries, concerts, sporting events, volunteer projects, and the mall, just to name a few.

The ways in which staff could help residents pursue their interests were quite limited. We could not support activities that were expensive or threats to health and security, and many residents had trouble identifying things in which they were significantly interested. The arts seemed to be a bit of an exception. Several residents had creative interests, and it was feasible to support some artistic activities. Although I am neither skilled nor knowledgeable in the arts, I wanted to establish a productive rapport with youth, and helping them to pursue their creative interests seemed to be a good strategy.

❖ FRAMEWORK

In the next section, I describe situations that illustrate recreational art's usefulness and potential for residential youth work. My theory's application strategy is simple: I consider the resemblances between my experiences and the functions of art identified in art-in-corrections literature. Before proceeding to the analysis, I will identify these functions. A body of scholarship produced by teachers, artists, therapists and counselors, administrators, and researchers experienced in art-in-corrections shows that art has several possible uses (see Gussak & Virshup, 1997; Hanes, 2005; Kornfeld, 1997; Liebmann, 1994; and Williams, 2003, for example). In general, this work shows that art serves four important functions in corrections.

First, art is educational. While art's aesthetic value and cultural relevance make it an important academic subject, practicing art helps develop social, cognitive, vocational, and physical and mental health skills. Art inspires creative thinking—a problem-solving skill important in many different kinds of academic curricula and indeed life in general. Also, art makes education more fun, which piques students' interest in learning.

Second, art is therapeutic. Art improves mood, increases feelings of self-worth, relieves stress, and teaches healthy coping strategies. In particular, art helps institutionalized persons cope with confinement; producing art is a safe outlet for negative emotions and a diversion from destructive behavior. Further, art can help clients explore treatment issues, such as past traumatic experiences (victimization, for instance), substance abuse, and accountability for their offending.

Third, art is socially integrative. Art fosters mutually beneficial relationships with others in the community—potentially maintaining, repairing, and creating bonds with the community. It offers prosocial ways to have fun in contrast to destructive activities that may be done to produce some kind of enjoyment, such as substance abuse, vandalism, stealing, fighting, and bullying. Contributions to the community can be made through art by providing entertainment, creating valuable pieces of art and craft, or engaging in collaborative charity work.

Fourth, art improves institutional management. Art directly benefits both employees and residents by creating a higher institutional quality of life. Correctional environments are tough to live and work in. They severely restrict space and autonomy and can be very physically unpleasant. Creativity and recreation "humanize" these environments. A setting that is touched by opportunities for creative outlets and enjoyment, as well as aesthetically pleasing stimuli, give residents constructive alternatives to destructive behavior and improve the moods of residents and staff alike. Thus, creativity and recreation counter environmental stressors and reduce residents' tendencies to "act out" (i.e., break rules, refuse to follow directions, commit assaults, etc.). Therefore, relationships among residents and staff improve, the environment becomes more safe and secure, and the financial costs of environmental stress decrease.

❖ EXPERIENCES

The Art and Recreation Center

Participating in formal and informal art and recreation activities proved to be very beneficial in my job as a youth worker. The design and implementation of formal art programs was the domain of the art and recreation program. Its activities included painting, drawing, sculpture, and graphic arts. Art and recreation staff relied on youth workers from the various cottages for support, mainly to facilitate residents' participation in the program. When we were present during the art and recreation center's activities, we were there more to transport and monitor youth, maintain safety, help with minor tasks, and participate with youth when possible.

I do not believe that art and recreation staff conducted formal art therapy, but education was an obvious purpose of the program. Many of our residents had problems achieving academic success, sometimes due to learning disabilities. They had several types of educational needs in addition to basic cognitive and vocational skills—emotional self-management and social skills, for example. To have the same abilities and opportunities as youth not involved in the system, though, it was important that the residents did well in a variety of academic areas, including the arts and humanities. Rehabilitative education was a key part of their treatment. The center's art rooms looked quite a bit like your average older school art classrooms; they were designed to teach art skills, not just provide rewards for good behavior. However, the knowledge and skills that residents potentially acquired by participating in the program extended beyond artistic. Correctional art teachers maintain that learning art strengthens general cognitive, emotional, social, and behavioral abilities. Art education integrates knowledge, emotions, and manual skills, nurtures creative problem-solving abilities that apply to many life situations, and helps develop new and diverse ways of thinking.

The art rooms also demonstrated how art provides constructive activities, humanizes the environment, and improves quality of life. I think I enjoyed spending time at the center as much as the residents. It felt good to take residents to an environment that did not differ from that of a mainstream school or community center. The presence of art supplies and artistic creations had the effect of convincing us that we were in a fun place more than "an institution." Even residents with more severe behavioral problems behaved better in the art rooms. They were content, preoccupied with creating art. Students tended to get along well with each other and with staff. We felt less like adversaries in the art and recreation center. This effect may have extended beyond the art rooms, as our residents had to retain the privilege of going over there with good behavior. Art making was very important to many residents because it provided them with several benefits: a way to enjoy themselves, an outlet for creative expression, a break from their problems, and a way to make decorative items for themselves or friends and family members.

The art rooms also provided residents with opportunities to contribute to the community. One benefit of art programs is that participants can create publicly useful artwork. I recall one impressive project in which residents created several attractive silk-screened banners that were hung throughout the city to promote commerce and community identity. The youth in the programs typically came from low socioeconomic status homes, and because of their involvement with justice and/or social service agencies, lost a great deal of control over their daily lives. They likely did not have high degrees of social power and through their offending had presumably taken from the community. Thus, they may be viewed, perhaps even by themselves, as community liabilities. Being viewed as a liability is stigmatizing and will interfere with a system-involved child's self-confidence and ability to identify as a productive member of the community. According to interactionist, or labeling, theory, such a child is at risk of re-offending. In contrast, by creating art that significantly benefited the community, the residents became givers; they were acting as assets, not liabilities. It was refreshing to see the residents empowering themselves by participating in the silk-screening project. Further, it is worth noting that such philanthropy is respected, conventional behavior. As social bond theory argues, involvement in and commitment to conventional activities reduce the risk of offending. Hopefully, the honor that came with making a notable contribution to the community served as a reward that increased the participants' stake in conformity. At any rate, it was plain to see that the center's art rooms had a value extending well beyond the provision of time-occupying rewards for well-behaved residents.

Because I did not spend a great deal of time at the art and recreation building, most of my efforts to help interested residents pursue their artistic interests were informal, spontaneous, and one-on-one. I noticed that several residents liked to draw, paint, and write, and although I am certainly no expert on art, I noticed that some were very good. Next, I discuss my relationships with three youth with whom I worked closely. Two illustrate art's usefulness in frontline youth work while one illustrates its difficulty.

"Shane"

Sometimes, staff members worked in other cottages to help out when understaffed. I spent a great deal of time in the nonsecure program that housed normal functioning males with moderate delinquency issues such as shorter histories of property, drug, and less-serious assault offenses as well as chronic status offending. The program was viewed as a "last chance" for youth at significant risk of re-offending, meaning that doing poorly in the program or committing another offense would likely lead to secure detention. I worked in this program often enough to get to know some of its residents. I was spending some one-on-one time with one whom I will call Shane when I noticed his small sketches and drawings hanging up in his room. They were very good. They brightened up his room and made it look somewhat normal, more like a teenager's bedroom instead of a residential dorm room. I thought that they were interesting, so I initiated a discussion with him about his artistic interests. He was very interested in art but in more of the non-mainstream types. I thought of his work as having a "graffiti style" or maybe "tagger art," although I cannot say for sure that he was a graffiti artist. I never asked him about, nor did I investigate, his file for gang affiliation. I wanted to gain his trust and build rapport by engaging him as an individual rather than on the basis of any possible deviant peer group memberships.

I asked Shane to make a drawing for me. In exchange, I would give him enough poster boards and watercolor markers to keep himself busy for awhile. Providing residents with opportunities to engage in constructive activities instead of nonproductive or destructive behavior—both as a socialization strategy and a more immediate way to prevent misbehavior—is a major part of working with troubled youth. Art making is a good way to fill idle time, get children in the habit of engaging in socially acceptable behavior, and keep them preoccupied and out of trouble. Because he had a record of good behavior in the program, Shane earned the privilege of keeping items such as art supplies in his room. However, it was understood that the regular staff at his program would oversee his work to prevent expressions of gang affiliation, sex and violence, and "other inappropriate themes" (subject to staff discretion). I am uncomfortable with censorship, but this was firm policy. Open artistic expression offers several therapeutic benefits, while the suppression of creativity can lead to a feeling of being violated. Shane never complained to me that his creativity was being suppressed, nor did I hear complaints from staff or administrators about his work. As far as I know, he was granted an adequate degree of freedom of expression.

Shane eventually created a mural-style drawing for me. It was a very nice depiction of an urban neighborhood, with several people working, playing, or hanging out around a large apartment complex. They had varying shades and colors of skin, suggesting a multiracial and multiethnic neighborhood and possibly an embracement of multi-culturalism. I let him know how much I liked his work and thanked him for it. I look back quite fondly on my exchanges with Shane. He did not talk much or express many feelings, but I detected some mutual respect and appreciation between us. A quality-of-life benefit of art in corrections is that it helps build cooperative, mutually beneficial relationships between residents and staff. Certainly, it is better to interact with residents when they are productively enjoying themselves as opposed to acting out destructively; it is better to have a good time with them than have to control and discipline them. Staff and residents need each other really: Residents need staff to help them pursue their interests and grant them privileges while staff members need residents to be receptive to their efforts to manage behavior and give treatment. While I did not interact with Shane on a daily and long-term basis, it is worth pointing out that I never had a problem with him.

"JT"

Youth workers inevitably come across "characters" they will remember for quite a long time. JT, as I will call him, was one such person. JT was fun to be around and could be very cooperative, but although he wasn't violent, he was somewhat prone to disruptive behavior. His antics were often inappropriate and cost him privileges, but they were usually not the kind that created major crises. In fact, he sometimes tested my sense of decorum; while correcting him on the outside, I may have been laughing on the inside. He was quite the comedian, and his joking around was usually more untimely than hostile or insulting. If his humor was mean-spirited, it was because he was upset about something. Although his disruptive behavior was not excusable, JT (like several residents) had a rough childhood that warranted empathy, compassion, and understanding. I had a very good rapport with JT. In fact, he often told me that I was his favorite staff member. Of course, he said this to just about every staff member. Still, I was flattered. He was in the program for most of my time there, and I interacted with him frequently. He was even on the softball team that I coached. During one of our discussions he expressed an interest in art and claimed to be good at drawing. I responded to his claim by encouraging him to draw something when he got the chance. Unless deemed to be a safety risk, our residents had limited but fairly regular access to paper and pencils.

JT was right about his drawing ability. One day, he greeted me with a smile and handed me a black and white pencil sketch of a wizard that he created. I immediately liked it and told him that he did a great job on it. He said that I could keep it. I reached into my pocket, pulled out all the coins that I had, and gave them to him. It was less than a dollar (it was against policy to give residents significant amounts of money), but he responded with a surprised look on his face, as if he couldn't believe that someone "paid" him for something he drew. The recognition seemed to legitimize his effort to create it. At the time, he had no money and, unlike some of the other residents, was receiving none from family. Although residents could keep their money in "accounts" locked up in the office, they were not allowed to have more than $5 on them at a time. Thus, even small amounts of money were a big deal among the residents. After our transaction, JT thanked me profusely and then shyly went on his way. To this day, JT's wizard hangs in my living room.[3] It reminds me of the fantastic images of wizards, dragons, and warriors that adorned my favorite posters and hard rock and heavy metal album covers from the 1970s and early 1980s. However, I find the old wizard's somber, worrisome, weary facial expression to be curiously different from other popular images depicting mighty wizards exercising their magic powers.

Regardless of the amount, receiving money for his art meant that JT had entered into a mutually beneficial exchange with me: He creatively produced a desirable object and was appreciated for it, and I now proudly own it. His art making and search for my approval were prosocial behaviors worthy of validation. Though we should be careful not to associate good behavior with material gain too much, the exchange hopefully reinforced JT's prosocial behavior. Impressing me and the symbolic affirmation conveyed through "being paid" were likely more rewarding than the actual amount of money he received. Judging by his reaction, the exchange made JT feel pretty good about himself. The improvement of self-image (self- concept, esteem, confidence, and worth) is a well-recognized therapeutic benefit of art. If repeated as part of ongoing relationships, praise and material rewards for creative and intellectual work—any prosocial behavior really—can have a powerful impact on the development of behaviorally and mentally healthy self-identities. Perhaps giving him the money and

---

[3]Because the drawings were given to me as gifts, without permission to reproduce, I do not include them as figures.

expressing how impressed I was with the quality of his drawing sent the message to JT that he is a good artist.

I am not in the habit of making conclusions about someone's internal states on the basis of what they draw, but I can't help but wonder about the significance of the wizard's somber facial expression, especially considering that JT endured traumatic childhood experiences. He certainly carried with him negative feelings associated with memories of past events. So I wonder: While JT was very jovial on the outside, was/is he the wizard on the inside—cold, mysterious, and capable of incredible acts both good and bad? Some therapists point out that clients often use visual imagery to "say" what they cannot with words and that art helps generate self-insights—to learn more about oneself and bring suppressed thoughts and feelings to the surface (those connected to memories of traumatic experiences, for example). Revealing troublesome thoughts and feelings, in some way, can lead to a release of negative emotions, making one feel better and perhaps more capable of managing behavior. Yet it can be difficult to bring disturbing matters out in the open. One may be reluctant to openly and directly deal with them for a variety of reasons: embarrassment, guilt, shame, the appearance of vulnerability or weakness, other threats to self-identity, and lack of inner awareness. Using images separate from the person as expressions of troublesome thoughts and feelings creates a safer distance from which to confront and discuss them.

JT became interested in American Indians after he acquired a book on American Indian history. It included stories accompanied by photos and portraits of famous American Indian leaders. JT is white, but like most of the residents, he was economically disadvantaged and had experienced significant victimization. It was not unusual for our residents to relate to people that have historically endured widespread hardship and oppression, even if from different ethnic and racial backgrounds. These kinds of sentiments present treatment opportunities. Through art, one can explore the perspectives and experiences of others, including crime victims, and potentially understand their loss and suffering. In other words, art can help create empathy for others, which is a key element of treatment. Art provides a vivid and concrete way to see what life is like for other people and acquire empathy for them. Empathetic individuals understand how they have hurt others and are thus better prepared to take responsibility for their actions, make amends, and heal relationships with victims and the community. Further, taking the perspective of others is a key part of multicultural education. It helps develop an appreciation of and respect for diversity.

From his book, JT copied a famous portrait of Chief Joseph of the Nez Perce Tribe along with his famous quote: "From where the sun now stands, I will fight no more forever." It is my understanding that copying other works of art has educational value. It can improve manual dexterity, teach technique, and even help one develop a personal style, especially when one has little or no experience making a certain kind of art. He copied (not traced) the portrait very well, and added a little color of his own choosing. JT gave me this drawing as well. I believe that I gave him $2 for this one—not because it was more valuable than the wizard, but probably because I had more money on me at the time.

JT and I built a good relationship. Unlike with Shane, however, there were times when I had to confront JT for misbehavior. I was more likely to have problems with him because I spent more time around him and because he had a more volatile personality than more reserved residents like Shane. As I said before, JT had to deal with traumatic memories that caused him a great deal of distress. Sometimes, it seemed, he acted out with misbehavior as a way to deal with stress. Further, he had somewhat of a tendency to mishandle frustration. The program and the cottage had several rules limiting personal freedom, and like many residents, he rebelled against rules he thought to be unfair. Therefore, having a way to build a rapport with a resident like JT and manage his behavior was all the more important. While I used several other methods to build a cooperative relationship with JT, looking back, I think that supporting and sharing his interests made him more receptive to my authority. Maybe he listened to me only because I could provide him with privileges, but hopefully, he also listened to me because he trusted me and appreciated my support. The rewards to me included that it was fun being around him, I really liked his drawings, and I did not have to worry as much about him attempting to harm me. While JT and I had our clashes, they were not very severe or frequent. Without respecting and supporting his interests, our relationship likely would not have been as good.

"Will"

I do not mean to suggest that all of my attempts to encourage residents to participate in creative activities had great results. Sometimes, they initially responded to my offers of support favorably, expressing excitement about pursuing their interests, but in time lost interest or access to resources because privileges were taken away from them. I recall one resident in particular. Will, as I will call him, was very bright, creative, and energetic. Judging by some of his small drawings on notebook paper, he appeared to have some artistic ability. He was also one of the most unruly residents in the program. His staunch resistance to authority and interference with the functioning of the program tested even the most patient youth worker. He spent nearly all of his time in the program on restrictions and rarely earned privileges, which to him gave him more reasons to be defiant and disruptive. Still, Will was a likable young man. It was difficult to differentiate his anger, anxiety, and hostility from unbridled energy and passion, so it was easy to think, "If only his intelligence, energy, and spirit could be channeled into productive, socially acceptable behavior."

At one point, I offered Will a deal. If he improved his behavior and acquired permission from the program coordinator, I would buy him some art supplies. He readily accepted the deal (we "shook on it") and displayed excitement in telling me about all of the things he could draw. Unfortunately, he did not improve his behavior, and I was unable to give him art supplies. I do not recall that a successful strategy for changing or managing Will's behavior was ever constructed. Like a few other staff members, though, I had a pretty good rapport with him. He never became verbally or physically aggressive with me personally and sometimes paid me compliments about what I was like as a staff member and a person. Interacting with him was not a problem if we were one-on-one, especially if he was able to do something active. I recall that he particularly liked to talk while playing basketball by himself. I was not able to direct Will's behavior; he simply chose to be less disruptive around me. I can only hope that even though I was not able to provide him with art supplies, he appreciated the fact that I tried.

❖ CONCLUSION

Looking back on my experiences with recreational art activities at the agency, I find that they affirm art's usefulness in corrections work. My experiences at the art and recreation center and with Shane and JT allowed me to illustrate several of the recognized uses of art in corrections. I don't know how Shane, JT, and Will turned out as adults, just that Shane and JT left their programs under good circumstances and Will did not. Even if they turned out fine, I would not know enough to be able to claim that art helped reform them and keep them out of trouble with the law. However, my youth work experience taught me that art can improve the treatment environment and staff–resident relationships.

My youth work experience demonstrates that staff occupying more entry-level positions in youth corrections and services—residential and day-treatment counselors, correctional or detention officers, interns, volunteers, and so on—play an important part in art and recreation treatment. One does not have to be an expert in education, therapy, or art to be significantly involved in art and recreation activities. I myself have never been a therapist, licensed teacher, or artist. In fact, like other programs, art and recreation will probably not be very effective without the cooperation, support, and involvement of the frontline workers who spend the most time with residents. Formal art therapy and education must, of course, be delivered by qualified therapists and teachers, and the design and implementation of programs must be overseen by the appropriate administrative authorities. I stress that *one should never attempt to practice therapy and teach without the necessary qualifications.* However, specialists must deal with several cases, and administrators must oversee several operations. They are very limited in the amount of time that they can spend with residents. Thus, frontline youth workers are needed to administer treatment on an hour-to-hour, day-to-day basis. They are largely in charge of milieu therapy, the regular, daily environment, activities, and interactions that are also supposed to be rehabilitative. As with all treatment, it is important that youth workers work closely and cooperatively with experts in charge of art and recreation.

My work experience, combined with visits to several other programs over the years, gives me the impression that secure and nonsecure youth facilities *can be* gloomy environments (a few have actually been rather nice), in terms of both physical surroundings and social atmosphere. They often lack material and human resources, which has adverse psychological and behavioral effects on both staff and youth. Upon entering a facility, it would be no surprise to find residents and workers in bad moods and the interactions among them to be sluggish and routine. The look and feel of "such an institution" lacks energy. At times, the environment can turn hostile, when residents become verbally and/or physically violent toward themselves, other residents, or staff. It is hard to imagine how the kind of changes that are expected of troubled youth can take place in this kind of environment.

Working with juveniles in placement is very difficult. Most youth workers have a genuine desire to improve the lives of children and, in so doing, contribute to society. Unfortunately, threats to staff morale seem to be ever present. Many times, youth do not respond favorably to efforts to help them. Maintaining appropriate behavior within institutional settings is difficult, and intervention strategies that are proven to be highly effective at reducing recidivism are hard to find. Trying to improve the lives of young people with tragic backgrounds and behavior problems, with few resources but several barriers, places a great deal of stress on the youth worker. It is difficult though not impossible for one to remain upbeat and avoid becoming jaded and pessimistic under these conditions. Youth workers often experience sadness, anger, frustration, and indifference upon perceiving a pervasive failure in treating youth. In time, the daily fatigue can lead to burnout. Some youth workers may come to believe that treatment does not work and will thus abandon their goals of helping youth and the community.

To create and maintain a rehabilitative environment, then, administrators and staff must pay a great deal of attention to their institutional quality of life. Youth workers who are themselves emotionally and physically healthy while at work are better able to help children. It takes strength to remain optimistic about rehabilitation, and youth workers need help in maintaining this strength. Despite hardships, it is also a reality that working with placed juveniles can be invigorating, enjoyable, rewarding, and effective. Creative and recreational activities will not by themselves transform a harsh work environment into a pleasant one, but they can go a long way in making it more pleasant. Activities that are fun, creative, energetic, educational, and constructive brighten up the setting and create an atmosphere that is psychologically and behaviorally healthy for both staff and residents. Such an environment reduces hostility in staff–youth relations and is more conducive to treatment. Engaging in activities appealing to residents offers youth workers opportunities to enjoy themselves as well. Those enjoying themselves at work are more likely to remain optimistic about treatment and rehabilitation.

While facilitating the pursuit of creative interests is helpful in work with offenders, one may wonder if it can actually help reduce crime. Do the benefits of the arts culminate into reduced re-offending? This question has yet to be sufficiently researched, but hypothetically, art can be used to counter criminality if it is included in groups of services tailored to individuals' needs. Art gives a boost to education, therapy, community involvement, and institutional management in corrections. It seems that the more educational, therapeutic, reintegrative, and humanizing corrections becomes, the more effective it will be in steering system-involved persons away from re-offending. Before we can determine whether or not art reduces re-offending, art components in correctional programs must be given a chance—they must be properly constructed, carried out, and evaluated with research. Like any other type of treatment, the cooperation and assistance of staff, the frontline workers, are needed to make art and recreational programming in corrections work.

In this essay, I use art as a convenient example of an area of interest that serves as a focal point for developing healthy, productive relationships with residential youth. However, it could have been any area of interest (technology, academics, sports, exercise . . .). The main point of this essay is that helping youth to pursue their diverse interests is an effective way to help treat youth, create a better environment, and make work in juvenile corrections more fulfilling.

❖ REFERENCES

Family Resources, Inc. (2010). *Residential treatment*. Retrieved February 27, 2010, from www.famres.org

Gussak, D., & Virshup, E. (Eds.). (1997). *Drawing time: Art therapy in prisons and other correctional settings*. Chicago: Magnolia Street.

Hanes, M. J. (2005). Behind steel doors: Images from the walls of a county jail. *Art Therapy: Journal of the American Art Therapy Association, 22*(1), 44–48.

Kornfeld, P. (1997). *Cellblock visions: Prison art in America*. Princeton, NJ: Princeton University Press.

Liebmann, M. (Ed.). (1994). *Art therapy with offenders*. Bristol, PA: Jessica Kingsley.

Williams, R. M. (Ed.). (2003). *Teaching the arts behind bars*. Boston, MA: Northeastern University Press.

❖ RECOMMENDED READINGS

Gussak, D., & Virshup, E. (Eds.). (1997). *Drawing time: Art therapy in prisons and other correctional settings*. Chicago: Magnolia Street.

Hanes, M. J. (2005). Behind steel doors: Images from the walls of a county jail. *Art Therapy: Journal of the American Art Therapy Association, 22*(1), 44–48.

Kornfeld, P. (1997). *Cellblock visions: Prison art in America*. Princeton, NJ: Princeton University Press.

Liebmann, M. (Ed.). (1994). *Art therapy with offenders*. Bristol, PA: Jessica Kingsley.

Williams, R. M. (Ed.). (2003). *Teaching the arts behind bars*. Boston, MA: Northeastern University Press.

DISCUSSION QUESTIONS

1. The author built rapport with youth through a shared interest in art. What other kinds of interests would you explore to build rapport

with youth? What kinds of activities would you like to engage in, and what would you hope to accomplish with youth in your care?

2. Do the activities and applied concepts identified in this essay apply to relationships with youth in other types of environments—at school, in the community, and even at home? Do they apply to youth that are at low risk of behavior problems? Explain your answers.

3. This essay has implications regarding how staff should deal with working in a stressful environment. What are they? Describe them. (Look for more than just "coping strategies.")

13

Experiencing the Parallels Between Juvenile and Adult Community Corrections

Cassandra L. Reyes

Editor's Introduction: Professor Reyes held multiple positions in juvenile and adult probation and parole, putting her in a good position to find similarities between juvenile and adult community corrections. Reyes offers insights useful for both adult and juvenile community corrections officers. For example, she identifies important safety issues that probation and parole officers should be concerned with. Also, she noticed that her interactions with probationers and parolees and their families exposed some of the factors and processes identified in social learning theories. Reyes's accounts show that instead of just being agents of control and punishment, probation and parole officers provide a wide variety of important services intended to prevent criminality, including those directed at meeting clients' needs.

Since John Augustus became known as the American father of probation and Alexander Maconochie developed the basis for parole in the 19th century (Abadinsky, 2003), millions of people within the United States have been under probation and parole supervision. Recently, according to the Bureau of Justice Statistics (2010) at year-end 2009, 7,225,800 people in the United States were on probation, in jail or prison, or on parole. Approximately 69.5% (5,018,900) of these individuals were being supervised within the community (Bureau of Justice Statistics, 2010). However, according to the United States Bureau of Labor Statistics (2010), in May 2009, there were only 92,910 probation officers and other correctional treatment specialists, including parole officers, within the United States. This means that on average, each probation or parole officer would have been supervising about 54 people. But is offender supervision the only duty of a probation or parole officer? The answer is no. This chapter will focus on various duties of probation and parole officers based on my 9 years of experience between 1994 and 2003 within an East Coast State.[1]

My experience as a probation and parole officer-bilingual began in January 1994 when I was hired provisionally as a probation officer-bilingual for the Western County Criminal Division in Little City, East Coast State. During the summer of 1995, I transferred to the Western County Probation Division, Juvenile Probation Unit, where I began supervising juvenile probationers. In September 1997, I transferred to the East Coast State Department of Corrections and became a supervising adult parole officer-bilingual. In July 1999, I transferred to the East Coast State Juvenile Justice Commission (JJC) as a senior parole officer-bilingual and supervised juvenile parolees. After I left East Coast State JJC in January 2000, I took a brief hiatus from governmental work. In April 2000, I returned to the judiciary and worked as a probation officer-bilingual for the Western County Family Court. I was employed in this capacity until the end of April 2003, when I resigned to pursue my graduate studies. Throughout this experience, I learned many duties of both a probation and parole officer. In addition, I realized that these responsibilities were similar whether I was working with juveniles or adults.

❖ MY JOURNEY AS A PROBATION AND PAROLE OFFICER-BILINGUAL

My journey as a probation and parole officer-bilingual has revealed many parallels between the juveniles and adults who have encountered

---

[1]Pseudonyms were used to disguise the identity of the locations discussed.

the criminal justice system including community corrections. The beginning of my expedition as a probation and parole officer-bilingual began when I was hired provisionally by the Western County Criminal Division in January 1994. As in many probation departments, one of the job requirements was that I had a bachelor's degree. My bachelor's degree included a double major of criminology and Spanish, the latter proving to be beneficial to my career prospects. Because there was no civil service list at the time of my appointment, I was hired provisionally until I took the civil service examination through the East Coast State Civil Service Commission later that year. In addition to the regular probation officer examination, as a bilingual officer, I needed to pass a test called the Bilingual Communicative Ability Test (BICAT), which evaluates the applicant's ability to translate and transliterate from Spanish to English and vice versa. Successfully passing both examinations allowed my employment to become permanent.

While I was employed in the Western County Criminal Division, I had the opportunity to work with a number of criminal court judges, including the presiding judge. My main duty was to write Presentence Investigations (PSI), which reflects what Adler, Mueller, and Laufer (2009) and Mutchnick (2010) describe as a function performed by probation officers. Additionally, I wrote Pre-trial Intervention (PTI) reports. To complete the PSIs, I would first interview the newly convicted offenders in both English and Spanish. Then, the answers were combined with other information garnered through an investigation such as arrest history, juvenile records, and verification of the offender's responses. Once the information was collected, the PSI was written and presented to the judge prior to sentencing so that the judge would have more well-rounded information to make a decision on the outcome of the case. The process was similar with the PTI reports; however, the individuals were not convicted.

After working for the criminal division for over a year and a half, I wanted to experience the supervision responsibility of a probation officer and requested a transfer to juvenile probation. In addition, writing PSIs and PTI reports gave me a greater understanding of the steps taken to sentence an offender to incarceration, community corrections, and alternative sanctions. This knowledge helped prepare me for the transition into supervision. Because I was a certified bilingual (Spanish and English) officer, I had a caseload of approximately 75 bilingual and nonbilingual male juvenile offenders who lived in Little City. Generally, they were considered bilingual and placed under my supervision if they spoke only Spanish, if their family members spoke only Spanish, or if they spoke both Spanish and English. The majority of the juveniles I supervised was on probation for drug-related offenses and/or had issues with illegal drug usage. It was while working in this capacity that I learned the more traditional duties of a probation officer. As part of enforcing the juveniles' probation conditions, my responsibilities included keeping track of the juveniles' school records to ensure that they were attending school, if applicable; maintaining contact with their parents or guardians to discuss rules of the home; performing home and school visits; and in-office reporting with the juveniles. Finally, if a juvenile violated his conditions of probation and a bench warrant was issued for his arrest, I would have to arrest the juvenile and return him to court. These duties proved trying at times, which I will discuss later under "Reflections on My Experiences"; however, they prepared me for the next stage of my career in community corrections, adult parole.

I had worked in juvenile probation for a little over 2 years when I took the civil service examination to become a parole officer-bilingual, which not only allowed me to attend the East Coast State Parole Officers' Academy but also gave me the opportunity to return to Little City to work. This was important to me because I was familiar with Little City's neighborhoods as well as other law enforcement agencies, such as the Western County Sheriff's Department. I was excited to take this next step because the salary was higher, and I could carry more weapons for protection, such as a .40 caliber Smith & Wesson 4053 semi-automatic pistol. While I worked for Juvenile Probation, the only equipment I carried was my set of handcuffs but no other form of protection.

After the psychological and physical preemployment examinations were completed, all of the newly hired parole officer recruits attended the East Coast State Parole Officers' Training in Small Town, East Coast State. The academy was housed on the grounds of a former juvenile detention facility, so we lived in barrack-like settings. The paramilitary 9-week academy was composed of classroom lectures, physical training, defensive tactics, and training on our various pieces of equipment. The training was certified under the East Coast State Police Training Commission and provided us with a strong foundation to properly perform our jobs upon graduation. After graduation, we returned to our parole district offices and began our 16-month probationary period to become senior parole officers.

My previous experience in juvenile probation, coupled with the academy training proved to be a good foundation as I began to supervise my caseload of approximately 75 bilingual adult parolees who lived all over Little City. Like the juvenile probationers I supervised, the vast majority of parolees under my supervision had been incarcerated in jail or prison for drug-related offenses and had issues with either drug and/or alcohol abuse. However, I did have two individuals who were convicted of aggravated manslaughter. In my opinion, many people turned to drug dealing activities due to the high rate of poverty within Little City. When I asked them about these decisions, I was often told that they could make substantially more money more quickly than by working at a legitimate job for minimum wage. Although I did not condone this behavior, this really opened my eyes to the struggles that many people were facing. This lifestyle reminded me of the differential association and social learning theories that I'd learned in my undergraduate studies, as the parolees were continuing the behavior learned within their physical and social environments.

My duties in adult parole were relatively similar to those in juvenile probation. One of the main differences was that I no longer needed to deal with the parolees' parents or guardians. These individuals were adults thus making the supervision more streamlined. In addition to in-office reporting, random urine monitoring, home visits, and arrests, I performed work visits and made sure that the individuals were attending Narcotics Anonymous or Alcoholics Anonymous meetings if mandated by their conditions of parole. Additionally, I performed pre-parole investigations in which I would meet with individuals while they were still incarcerated to formulate a release plan with them. This plan would entail an investigation of their proposed housing upon release. One stipulation that became difficult to address was ensuring that there were no other persons living within a residence who were in negative contact with the law, due to criminality issues within Little City. This became especially problematic when there were generations, for example, fathers and sons, who were on parole or probation living together. Furthermore, when individuals were being released, they were returning to the environment that fueled their criminal activity thus creating a means for recidivistic contact with law enforcement by allowing the cycle to continue (see Harm & Phillips, 2001; Petersilia, 2003). This cycle was realized when I would see my former juvenile probationers now under adult parole supervision.

I worked in adult parole for approximately 2 years and had been promoted to senior parole officer-bilingual before applying for and receiving a lateral transfer to East Coast State JJC. Once I transitioned into JJC, I was reissued the same equipment that I carried in adult parole (24-inch Armament Systems and Procedures, Inc. [ASP] baton, handcuffs, Oleoresin Capsicum pepper spray, and Smith & Wesson 4053 pistol with two extra bullet magazines); in addition, I was given a state car to take home and a pager because I was on call 24 hours a day.

This new position provided the opportunity to supervise individuals in other parts of East Coast State. I was given a smaller caseload of approximately 30 juvenile parolees; however, they lived in three southern counties in East Coast State. Although the caseload was smaller, the responsibilities remained fairly the same as in adult parole, but the individuals lived farther apart. In addition to being on call 24 hours a day, 7 days a week, I also conducted curfew checks on the juveniles. Finally, I regularly attended Multi-Disciplinary Team (MDT) meetings to discuss and monitor the juveniles' progress. These MDT meetings included participants from academic institutions, child and family services, psychological and psychiatric services, and parole. The MDT meetings reflected previous research on programs that focus on the prevention of delinquency and aggression (see Farrington & Welsh, 2002; Gottfredson, Wilson, & Najaka, 2002; Sauder, 2000; Welsh & Farrington, 2007) by using a collaboration of school, community, and therapeutic-based programs. However, in the MDT meetings, two vital pieces were missing from the equation, the juvenile and his or her family. Because I left after only a short time, it is unknown if the MDT meetings had an impact on the juveniles' delinquent behavior as suggested by the literature. Even though I enjoyed working in this position, I resigned in February 2000 due to personal reasons.

After a brief hiatus from working for state government, I returned in May of 2000 as a probation officer-bilingual in the Western County Family Court Division. Within this division, I executed other duties not typically considered to be the responsibility of a probation officer. I was afforded the opportunity to conduct proceedings in child custody, visitation, and paternity matters; perform investigations for juvenile pre-disposition reports; and interview applicants in Spanish and English for temporary domestic violence restraining orders and dismissals. The child custody, visitation, and paternity proceedings entailed mediation between the involved parties to create court orders that were in the best interests of the children in the cases. These orders were then signed by family court judges.

The juvenile Pre-Disposition Reports (PDRs) were very similar to the adult presentence investigations mentioned earlier; however, they were presented to the judges prior to the disposition hearings instead of the sentencing hearings in criminal court. In addition to information included in PSIs, if the juveniles were in school, academic records including grades, attendance, and disciplinary issues were included in the PDR. If a juvenile passed a General Educational Development Test, (GED), this was incorporated into the school information. The juveniles and parents or guardians were interviewed to ascertain the information needed for the PDRs. Then, as with the PSIs, this would be verified through official sources.

My final assignment in family court was in the domestic violence unit. In my opinion, this was my most stressful placement and could lead to the highest rate of burnout for employees. Much like recidivism with criminal behavior, domestic violence follows a cyclical path, leading the survivors and defendants to the court time and time again. During my tenure there, I witnessed many of the same men and women returning to the court for temporary restraining orders or dismissals of temporary or final restraining orders. As a domestic violence survivor, I found it hard to watch the appellants returning to court, although I understood the cycle all too well. I worked in Family Court until the end of April 2003, when I resigned to pursue my graduate studies.

My journey as a probation and parole officer-bilingual has shown numerous similarities between juvenile and adult community corrections. Although the criminal justice system often treats individuals according to their age, the responsibilities are frequently parallel for those employed in juvenile and adult community corrections. Understanding this likeness could help individuals seeking careers in the criminal justice system and working with people both below and above the legal age of 18.

❖ REFLECTIONS ON MY EXPERIENCES

Over my 9-year career as a probation and parole officer-bilingual, I have encountered many situations that I will never forget. I can use these experiences as examples in my criminal justice courses to bring the "real world" into the classroom. Now, I will discuss some examples of experiences from my journey as a probation and parole officer-bilingual that have impacted me in regard to officer safety and cooperation with offenders' families.

Safety and Cooperation

I would often be mindful of my surroundings before working in probation and parole, but there were several instances that brought thoughts of officer safety to the forefront. The first memorable situation happened during my interview with an arsonist while I was working in Western County Criminal Division. He was clearly angry at the world because of his conviction, and he told me that he was HIV positive and not afraid of anything. As mentioned, he was very angry during our interview. He repeatedly told me that he would burn down my house when he was released from prison. At the time, my maiden name was Bullers, and I was the only known Bullers listed in the area phone books. I immediately asked the phone company not to list my phone number, and I became more aware of my surroundings. I did not live in fear of this man; however, I did not want to take any chances that he would look for me after his release.

The second experience stemmed from an interview with a known mobster indicted under the Racketeer Influenced & Corrupt Organizations Act (RICO). During the court proceedings leading up to his conviction, I was told by my supervisor that his PSI had to be perfect because it was a high profile case for our county. After the defendant was convicted, I asked him the standard interview questions for the PSI; however, at that time, our judges also used an additional questionnaire that asked about an individual's ability to read and write in English. The defendant was very offended and angrily explained to me that he was a 65-year-old educated man who of course could read and write in English. To try and defuse the situation, I simply reminded him that the judge wanted the questions answered and assumptions could not be made on an individual's ability to understand the English language. Although I knew I was only doing my job, I did not want to aggravate a person with known mafia connections.

The next situation occurred directly following an arrest of a male juvenile who had violated his probation. I was assisted by the Little City Police Department (LCPD) with his arrest at his home in East Little City. One of the male LCPD officers performed the pat-down search of the juvenile before we transported him to the court house to appear in front of the judge. I escorted the juvenile down a hallway attached to the garage, known as the *sally port*, to the elevators. There were no cameras or other people in the hallway. Once we exited the elevator on the second floor, where Family Court was housed, the juvenile was again searched by a Western County Sheriff's Officer. He was found to be in possession of a razor blade, which was kept in the watch pocket (the small pocket above another pocket on the front of his jeans). To this day, I am thankful that I had a good relationship with my juveniles, this one in particular, because it is conceivable that he could have cut me with the blade during our commute and walk to the second floor. One thing that I learned from this experience is that it is necessary to treat all people, regardless of their past criminal or delinquent behavior, with respect. It may save a life someday.

The final two events surrounding officer safety happened while I was working in adult parole. While I was in the East Coast State Parole Officers' Academy, an incident occurred in a nearby big city in which a parole officer shot a parolee. The parole officer encountered the parolee in a room hiding behind a mattress that was standing on its side. The officer thought that the individual had a gun in his hand and shot him. I do not know the outcome of the shooting, but it affected me during my first arrest after graduating from the academy. Within a month of being "on the street" after the academy, I volunteered to go on an arrest of an adult parolee who was known to resist arrest and assault officers. My partner and I searched the home of the individual, which led us down to a dark basement. Because we were aware of the parolee's combative tendencies, we were accompanied by LCPD officers. As we descended the basement stairs, we could see a number of boxes and other items piled all over the floor. Back behind the stairs, there was what appeared to be a full or queen-sized mattress standing on its side. The LCPD officers found the parolee hiding behind the mattress and drew their pistols; we followed suit. The scenario of the big city parole officer kept playing in my head as the episode was occurring. Thankfully, the parolee was taken into custody without confrontation. This situation taught me to be even more aware of my surroundings and be prepared for the unexpected.

The last memorable situation regarding officer safety entailed one of my parolees who was a drug dealer and known Ñeta. Ñetas were originally a gang founded in the prisons in Puerto Rico that expanded to the streets. They were known to live in Little City, as did the Latin Kings. I had a good rapport with this parolee. He regularly worked, was present for announced home visits, reported to the office as required, paid his fines, and did not have any issues with drug usage. He even called me when he received a citation for a moving violation, which would not technically be a violation of his parole conditions. In addition, he called me when he was arrested with another parolee for drugs by the Western County Park Police. Because he had not been convicted of the drug offense, I did not initiate parole violation proceedings. However, my supervisor disagreed. As a result, the parolee was arrested for a parole violation, and I had to defend the violation at a revocation hearing. The parolee was subsequently sentenced to serve a *hit*, which meant he served the remainder of his parole time in prison.

I ran into him upon his release from prison in North Little City. As usual, I was conducting home visits by myself. He was still angry from serving additional time, and he was not alone; he was with three other men. Because we once had a good relationship, I was able to talk my way out of any potential harm from the situation. This lesson reaffirmed that respect is a crucial element in survival in potentially explosive situations.

These situations regarding officer safety were valuable lessons and have impacted my life. It is important to be aware of one's safety at all times, regardless of the age of the offender involved. Therefore, officer safety should always be contemplated when choosing a career in juvenile or adult community corrections. However, my experiences with familial cooperation are just as crucial to professional development, especially for those seeking careers in juvenile justice.

The first event that I remember in regard to familial cooperation was from my time as a juvenile probation officer, an event related to random urine monitoring. On my caseload, I had a 16-year-old juvenile known to smoke marijuana. As with standard conditions of probation, he was to be subjected to random urine monitoring, which usually occurred during office visits. I had a good relationship with his mother who called me when her son was en route to reporting. She told me that a 10-year-old neighbor told her that her son bought this child's urine from him. He then placed the urine in a 35 mm film container and taped it to his leg to keep it at body temperature. I thanked her for the information and prepared for the juvenile's visit. When he arrived at the office, I asked a male Western County Sheriff's Officer to search the juvenile in the restroom. The film container was found on his person, and he was subsequently charged for hindering his own prosecution in addition to a violation of probation due to his random urine test that was positive for marijuana. During this situation, I learned that it is important to maintain a good relationship with the families of the juveniles in addition to the juveniles themselves.

As mentioned earlier, one of my duties as a juvenile parole officer-bilingual was to enforce the juveniles' curfews. Randomly, I would stop at a parolee's home in the middle of the night, sometimes as late as 2:00 a.m., to ensure that the juvenile was at home. The parents and guardians appeared to be happy that I would be diligent in monitoring their children's curfews and did not complain about the late hours. It seemed that this practice helped to keep the juveniles home at night and not out in the street committing new offenses. This relationship with the parents and guardians helped to maintain open communication about issues impacting the juveniles' lives at home. Some parents and guardians thanked me and said that they were relieved to have extra support in the supervision of their children.

In juvenile probation and parole it is crucial to have a good relationship with the juvenile and his or her family, but this rapport can be abused by parents who are frustrated when their children do not obey their rules and ask the officer to help enforce them. But in my experience, for the most part, this partnership is beneficial for the juveniles, their families, and community corrections. When offenders with their families and community corrections authorities work together, the collaborative effort appears to alleviate some further delinquent behavior as suggested by the literature.

Relevant Theory

As mentioned earlier, two criminological theories are prevalent when I reflect on my experiences as a probation and parole officer-bilingual: differential association and social learning theories. These closely related theories provide some perspectives on why individuals will recidivate in criminal behavior as well as continue to live in situations in which domestic violence abounds.

Sutherland and Cressey's (1970, pp. 75–76) differential association theory is composed of nine propositions, which help to explain how behavior is learned and continued:

1. Criminal behavior is learned.

2. Criminal behavior is learned in interaction with other persons in the process of communication.

3. The principal part of the learning of criminal behavior occurs within intimate personal groups.

4. When criminal behavior is learned, the learning includes (a) techniques of committing the crime, which sometimes are very complicated, sometimes are very simple; [and] (b) the specific direction of motives, drives, rationalizations, and attitudes.

5. The specific direction of motives and drives is learned from definitions of legal codes as favorable and unfavorable.

6. A person becomes delinquent because of an excess of definitions favorable to violation of the law over definitions unfavorable to violations of law. This is the principle of differential association.

7. Differential associations may vary in frequency, duration, priority, and intensity.

8. The process of learning criminal behavior by association with criminal and anti-criminal patterns involves all the mechanisms that are involved in any other learning.

9. While criminal behavior is an expression of general needs and values, it is not explained by those general needs and values since noncriminal behavior is an expression of the same needs and values.

A parolee who is released from prison, for example, is often released back into the environment where his or her intimate peer group is engaging in criminal behavior. A justification for drug dealing prevailing in this setting would reflect a definition (easy and fast money) that is favorable to a violation of the law in comparison to one (working at a legitimate minimum wage job) that is unfavorable to a law violation. This would be especially true if those criminal intimate peer groups are together frequently and for long periods of time. The individuals involved in these actions learn from each other and continue to behave in a manner that contradicts the law.

Like differential association theory, Akers's social learning theory has a similar premise in regard to criminal behavior and domestic violence. Akers (1977) expanded on Sutherland and Cressey's differential association theory. For example, he added that people model criminal conduct through imitation, and he indicated that the definitions and imitation will lead individuals into their initial criminal behavior (Lilly, Cullen, & Ball, 2007). This perspective can explain criminal behavior, such as drug dealing, but it can also account for the impact of domestic violence situations. For example, a child can experience and learn abusive behavior at the hands of his or her parents and repeat the behavior as an adult. On the other hand, if a survivor has learned from his or her family that violence is a form of love, he or she may remain in an abusive relationship. The imitation and understanding of violence from both viewpoints allows the cycle of violence to continue.

Several empirical studies have shown support for both differential association and social learning theories in regard to criminal behavior (see Akers, 1998, 2000; Akers & Jensen, 2003, 2006; Akers, Krohn, Lanza-Kaduce, & Radosevich, 1979; Akers & Sellers, 2009; Haynie, 2002; Warr & Stafford, 1991). These studies show that peer relationships appear to be a strong basis for learned and continued delinquent and criminal behavior. Although the studies provided do not specifically relate to parolees' recidivism rates or the commission of interpersonal violence, it may be reasonable to expect that they can be extended to these two areas of criminal behavior.

❖ CONCLUSION

As I reflect on the experiences of my past career, I know that I have gained more knowledge than I could have learned in a lecture or book. I have learned that it is important to maintain a good rapport with individuals under supervision. Related to rapport, respect is important to establish with everyone one may encounter; it could be key to survival in a dangerous world. In addition, I discovered that one can never be fully prepared for the unexpected. I also realized that each of the situations I endured has made me more adaptable to whatever life may bring my way. Although I am no longer working in community corrections, I will take these lessons with me throughout life.

Throughout this chapter, I have presented some of the challenges faced by probation and parole officers. One of the biggest challenges is to prevent recidivism, to participate in intervention activities intended to prevent re-offending. Welsh and Farrington (2007) provide some suggestions for the possible prevention of delinquent behavior, which could be beneficial with regard to domestic violence and other criminal behavior. They proposed that early intervention programs that include the individual, his or her family, his or her school, and the community could be successful in curtailing future delinquent and aggressive behavior. This also is reflected by Sauder (2000), who insisted that intervention at an early age helps to change childhood behavior, which has an impact on future violence and is easier to manage than adolescent behavior. It is possible that if early intervention is introduced in areas where criminal behavior is abundant, criminal recidivism and even domestic violence could be reduced.

❖ REFERENCES

Abadinsky, H. (2003). *Probation and parole: Theory and practice* (8th ed.). Upper Saddle River, NJ: Pearson Education.

Adler, F., Mueller, G. O., & Laufer, W. S. (2009). *Criminal justice: An introduction* (5th ed.). New York: McGraw-Hill.

Akers, R. L. (1977). *Deviant behavior: A social learning approach* (2nd ed.). Belmont, CA: Wadsworth.

Akers, R. L. (1998). *Social learning and social structure: A general theory of crime and deviance.* Boston: Northeastern University Press.

Akers, R. L. (2000). *Criminological theories: Introduction, evaluation, and application* (3rd ed.). Los Angeles: Roxbury.

Akers, R. L., & Jensen, G. F. (Eds.). (2003). *Social learning theory and the explanation of crime: A guide for a new century.* New Brunswick, NJ: Transaction.

Akers, R. L., & Jensen, G. F. (2006). The empirical status of social learning theory of crime and deviance. In F. T. Cullen, J. P. Wright, & K. R. Blevins (Eds.), *Taking stock: The status of criminological theory* (pp. 37–76). New Brunswick, NJ: Transaction.

Akers, R. L., Krohn, M. D., Lanza-Kaduce, L., & Radosevich, M. (1979). Social learning and deviant behavior: A specific test of a general theory. *American Sociological Review, 44,* 636–655.

Akers, R. L., & Sellers, C. S. (2009). *Criminological theories: Introduction, evaluation, and application* (5th ed.). New York: Oxford University Press.

Bureau of Justice Statistics. (2010). *Correctional populations in the United States, 2009.* Retrieved January 22, 2011, from http://bjs.ojp.usdoj.gov/content/pub/pdf/cpus09.pdf

Farrington, D. P., & Welsh, B. C. (2002). Family-based crime prevention. In L. W. Sherman, D. P. Farrington, B. C. Welsh, & D. L. MacKenzie (Eds.), *Evidence-based crime prevention* (pp. 22–55). New York: Routledge.

Gottfredson, D. C., Wilson, D. B., & Najaka, S. S. (2002). School-based crime prevention. In L. W. Sherman, D. P. Farrington, B. C. Welsh, & D. L. MacKenzie (Eds.), *Evidence-based crime prevention* (pp. 56–164). New York: Routledge.

Harm, N. J., & Phillips, S. D. (2001). You can't go home again: Women and criminal recidivism. *Journal of Offender Rehabilitation, 32*(3), 3–21.

Haynie, D. (2002). Friendship networks and delinquency: The relative nature of peer delinquency. *Journal of Quantitative Criminology, 18*(2), 99–134.

Lilly, J. R., Cullen, F. T., & Ball, R. A. (2007). *Criminological theory: Context and consequences* (4th ed.). Thousand Oaks, CA: Sage.

Mutchnick, R. (2010). *Criminal justice interactive companion text.* Boston: Prentice Hall.

Petersilia, J. (2003). *When prisoners come home: Parole and prisoner reentry.* New York: Oxford University Press.

Sauder, J. G. (2000). Enacting and enforcing felony animal cruelty laws to prevent violence against humans. *Animal Law, 6,* 1–21.

Sutherland, E. H., & Cressey, D. R. (1970). *Criminology* (8th ed.). Philadelphia: J. B. Lippincott.

United States Bureau of Labor Statistics. (2010). *Occupational employment and wages, May 2009: 21-1092 Probation officers and correctional treatment specialists.* Retrieved January 22, 2011, from http://www.bls.gov/oes/current/oes211092.htm#(1).

Warr, M., & Stafford, M. (1991). The influence of delinquent peers: What they think or what they do? *Criminology, 29*(4), 851–866.

Welsh, B. C., & Farrington, D. P. (2007). Save children from a life of a crime. *Criminology and Public Policy, 46*(4), 871–880.

❖ RECOMMENDED READINGS

Akers, R. L., & Jensen, G. F. (Eds.). (2003). *Social learning theory and the explanation of crime: A guide for a new century.* New Brunswick, NJ: Transaction.

Akers, R. L., & Sellers, C. S. (2009). *Criminological theories: Introduction, evaluation, and application* (5th ed.). New York: Oxford University Press.

Harm, N. J., & Phillips, S. D. (2001). You can't go home again: Women and criminal recidivism. *Journal of Offender Rehabilitation, 32*(3), 3–21.

Petersilia, J. (2003). *When prisoners come home: Parole and prisoner reentry.* New York: Oxford University Press.

Sauder, J. G. (2000). Enacting and enforcing felony animal cruelty laws to prevent violence against humans. *Animal Law, 6,* 1–21.

Sherman, L. W., Farrington, D. P., Welsh, B. C., & MacKenzie, D. L. (Eds.). (2002). *Evidence-based crime prevention.* New York: Routledge.

Welsh, B. C., & Farrington, D. P. (2007). Save children from a life of a crime. *Criminology and Public Policy, 46*(4), 871–880.

DISCUSSION QUESTIONS

1. When you think of the titles of probation and parole officer, what are the job duties that come to mind? Although these two positions are traditionally equated with supervision, what are some other functions that these officers may perform?

2. Why is it important to maintain a good rapport and respect with those under supervision and their families?

3. What conditions of probation or parole would you suggest be mandatory for everyone under either form of supervision? What would be some possible suggestions to reduce criminal and delinquent behavior through probation and parole?

14

Working With Minority Youth in Residential Treatment

Everette B. Penn

Editor's Introduction: Professor Penn was a child care worker in a residential treatment facility for youth offenders. He addresses the issues of disproportionate minority contact (DMC), socioeconomic disadvantages of minority youth, and subcultures of violence and describes how his practical experiences have gone hand-in-hand with his scholarly studies both as a student and a professor. Penn addresses the social and historical context in which DMC developed. Throughout U.S. history and the creation of the juvenile justice system, the concept of adolescence was not developed with minority youth in mind, and the belief that youth offenders are children in need of help was not extended to minorities. Professor Penn raises concern about the inclusion of race and ethnicity as indicators of youth's potential to be rehabilitated in current justice processes.

❖ INTRODUCTION

I attended Indiana University of Pennsylvania (IUP) during the 1990s for my doctoral studies in criminology. IUP is located in a rural area of western Pennsylvania, which was in stark contrast to the urban and culturally diverse environment of Washington, DC, in which I was raised and worked as a criminal investigator for the District of Columbia's Public Defender's Office. It was my time in Washington, DC, as a criminal investigator that motivated me to pursue doctorial studies in criminology. As an investigator, I constantly saw young black men involved in drug and violent offenses.

Once in the doctoral program, I developed a special interest in juvenile delinquency and justice as I desired to understand origins of criminal behavior and how our justice system responds, especially to minority youth. This led me to seek work as a child care worker in a group home for adjudicated youth in western Pennsylvania. The company that employed me owned several homes. These homes primarily served boys aged 10 to 16, as well as sexual offenders and girls. As a male, I did not work in the girls' home and spent a limited time in the sexual offenders' home. The great majority of my experience came from supervising adjudicated boys aged 10 to 16. Their offenses ranged from shoplifting to assault. The group home housed from 8 to 12 boys. It was a two-story house that blended well into the community. It had no identifiable signs that it was a group home for delinquent boys. The only characteristic that upon careful review may have provided a clue to its nature was a 12-passenger van in the driveway. The concept was simple: By blending into the community, the boys would be integrated and accepted more easily. Thus, the boys attended school in the community, played in the parks, and shopped at the local mall while supervised by members of the staff.

The leadership structure of the company that operated the group home where I worked was led by an executive director. The nonprofit company was able to receive grants and other programs unavailable to for-profit companies. This benefit provided food, medical care, and other goods and services from government agencies in the community. I did not see much of the executive director, as the company had five homes in the area. Daily, I did see the house manager. I remember him being a rather tough, stocky man who had recently left the U.S. Army. When he came in, he demanded respect from the boys as he was the disciplinarian of the group home. If there was a resident who would not follow directions, the house manager would straighten him out through words, punishment, or extra duties. There were times the house manager and I did not get along as he was very much into punishment, cursing, and breaking down a person. I was familiar with this process as I was a member of the U.S. Army and had attended basic training programs that have drill sergeants who follow this philosophy. Our differences probably stemmed from my being a doctoral student of criminology. As I learned more and more about the principles of juvenile justice, I became more removed from the drill sergeant practices. I remember having a talk with him one evening after he had yelled and threatened a resident who would not follow directions. He sarcastically called me "Professor" and stated that once I spent "more time in the *real world* I would understand."

To this day, I still remember those words and have tried to craft a career that combines the findings of research along with the practicalities of implementation. In this essay, I provide through the lens of my real world experiences theoretical concepts and issues related to juvenile justice corrections and minorities' involvement in the juvenile justice system.

❖ JUVENILE JUSTICE AND RESIDENTIAL PLACEMENT

The juvenile justice system and the adult criminal justice system have several similarities. Each system identifies and apprehends suspects, examines evidence, and executes judgment. But unlike the adult system, the juvenile justice system has a twofold philosophy that dates back to the late 1800s. Today, over 100 years later, the two-pronged belief of prevention and rehabilitation guides the juvenile justice worker and the entire system.

The first juvenile justice court was established in 1899 in Cook County, Illinois. The establishment of the court anchored the legal concept of *parens patriae*. This concept allows the state to serve as the surrogate parent in both law and administrative structure (Albanese, 1993). Thus, if both parents are unwilling to assert their rights, the state steps in. The Chicago Bar Association further defined that the state must step in and exercise guardianship over a child found under such adverse social or individual conditions that crime was a likely outcome. Under this belief, the actions of the juvenile court were to promote rehabilitation and prevention of delinquent and criminal acts. This was a departure from the prevailing classical thought of deterrence and punishment; rather, the juvenile justice system was created to intervene and treat young persons, in most cases, those who had not reached their 18th birthday.

This new system had its first challenge in 1905 with the case of *Commonwealth v. Fisher*. The question arose for the Pennsylvania Supreme Court: Is Pennsylvania's juvenile court unconstitutional? In other words, was it legal to have a process to adjudicate a child and commit the child to a house of refuge for the purpose of rehabilitation and prevention of future delinquency under the doctrine of parens patriae? The answer from the court was as follows:

> The act is but an exercise by the state of its supreme power over the welfare of its children, a power under which it can take a child from its father and let it go where it will, without committing it to any guardianship or any institution. (*Commonwealth v. Fisher*, 1905)

Thus, the creation of a juvenile court and placement of children by the court had been established by the *Fisher* decision. By 1945, all states had a juvenile justice system (Albanese, 1993). The placement of juveniles required a place that provided psychological intervention, access to schools, employment, health care, cultural events, and effective treatment programming. The overall intent was to modify delinquent causing risk factors so that the juvenile could be returned to his or her own biological parents and home environment.

Subsequent court cases established the rights of juveniles and created a due process system in which juveniles had rights similar to adult offenders, except for the right of a trial by jury (*Kent v. United States*, 1966; In *re Gault*, 1967; In *re Winship*, 1970; *Mckeiver v. Pennsylvania*, 1971; and *Breed v. Jones*, 1975). Although juvenile delinquency is down since its peak in the mid-1990s (Springer & Roberts, 2011), there are still thousands of youth every year who are placed in juvenile facilities. When a youth is placed in the custody of the state after being adjudicated, there are two choices for placement. The first is a secure facility, usually for the more serious offenses that were not waived to the adult court, and the second is placement in a residential treatment facility. The American Correctional Association (ACA) defines a *residential treatment center* (RTC) as a nonsecure residential program emphasizing family-style living in a home atmosphere. Program goals are similar to those for large residential programs: normal group living, school attendance, securing employment, working with parents to resolve problems, and general participation in the community. Although group homes usually house youth who are court committed, they also house abused or neglected youth who are placed by social agencies. Small group homes serve 8 to 12 youth. Their ages range from 10 to 17, with the typical concentration from 13 to 16 (American Correctional Association, 1994, p xiii).

❖ WORKING WITH YOUTH

A Residential Treatment Center

The American Correctional Association, which provided the preceding definition, is an organization of over 20,000 correctional professionals throughout the United States. It was established in 1870 and is the oldest professional correctional organization. For several years, when I was in the field as a child care worker, I belonged to ACA and found its training, publications, and contacts very beneficial to my career. ACA has a committee of juvenile residential facility experts who publish the *Standards for Juvenile Residential Facilities* (1994). This document sets accreditation criteria in the areas of administration and management, physical plant, facility operations, facility services, and juvenile services. Accreditation standards of and site visits by ACA are voluntary, but the minimal standards for each RTC are established in state codes. In Pennsylvania, it is PA Code 3810.

I refer to Pennsylvania because this is the state where I did my dissertation, appropriately called *Juvenile Residential Treatment Centers: Organizational Structure, Treatment Standards and Success Rates* (Penn, 2000). My research purpose was to examine the private sector's involvement in providing services for wayward youth. I saw that the government regulations and guidance provided was vague thus leaving day-to-day operations and procedures in the hands of the RTC staff. After surveying over 100 RTCs through a questionnaire sent to the manager of the facility, I determined that several elements lead to success (i.e., graduation or completion of the juvenile's court appointed time in the RTC). These elements included education level of the direct child care worker, direct child care workers' participation in management decisions, high amounts of training by employees, and time elapsed before the completion of the Individual Service Plan for each resident (Penn, 2000). Although my findings are rather dated, what is clear is the importance of a trained and well-prepared staff, especially the child care worker who is focused on the needs and rehabilitation of the child. Pennsylvania defines a child care worker as an employee of a facility whose responsibilities include care and supervision of children in daily program activities, such as meals, chores, personal grooming, study, and leisure time (PA Code 3819.4).

The Routine

Managing a RTC or group home requires a very important decision to be made about the personnel of the facility. Two models are employed. The first is the family management model and the second is shift work. The basic personnel issue is how to staff a facility 24 hours a day in order to provide the proper supervision over the juveniles. The family management model solves that problem by employing a couple to serve as "cottage parents" for the youth. This couple is usually provided housing, food, medical care, and a small salary for their compensation. In return, they run their house as if they are the parents of the juveniles assigned to the house. They often receive a day or two off during the week. During that time relief child care workers provide supervision.

The second model consists of shift workers who usually provide coverage over an 8- to 10-hour time span. This shift work model was how my RTC was staffed. My usual shift was from 2:00 p.m. to 11:00 p.m. On arriving at the group home at 2:00 p.m., none of the youth were there. At 2:00 p.m., there was a staff worker who had stayed in the home during the day in case there was an emergency with any of the boys. This staff member also prepared administrative reports and did some light cleaning around the house. When I arrived, I was briefed by this staff member who told me about any issues with the boys, the house, or in the community that I might face that evening. I would prepare the house for the evening's activities because by 3:30 p.m., they would start arriving "home" usually by school bus. At 3:00 p.m. my coworker for the evening would arrive. The company that employed me maintained a practice of two child care workers when the residents were awake.

By 4:00 p.m., all residents would be in the house. There were usually 8 to 12 in the group home. The practice was for the youth to remove their shoes upon entering the home. The shoes were locked in a closet. We told them it was not only to keep the place clean, which it did, but also it deterred running—the locks on the doors were to keep people outside from entering rather than to stop our youth from leaving the facility. Additionally, we had red tape on the floor of every doorway. A youth had to ask permission to cross over any piece of red tape. This allowed us to have control over the movement of all our youth. From 4:00 p.m. to 6:00 p.m. usually consisted of free time for the youth. Sometimes, we would take them to the local park to play sports, or when the weather was inclement, we would have them read, start their homework, watch television, or play video games. The students were very competitive with the video games, and every so often, we staff members would let a resident win in order to raise his spirits.

Chores were assigned weekly to include food preparation, bathroom cleaning, dishwashing, trash collection, and other chores. At 6:00 p.m., dinner was served family style on a large picnic table. Dinner usually consisted of macaroni with hamburger, green vegetables, salad, bread, dessert, and milk or water. During dinner, we would hold an informal group session in which we talked about the boys' day and presented them with questions about the choices they made and how they handled situations. At any time, the house manager could call a group meeting. When he did, it was usually because there was something wrong. Rarely did he compliment the boys. He would address issues such as suspension from school, lack of a clean or orderly house, and other issues that required attention. During the group meeting, all would sit at the picnic table. It was somewhat like a group counseling session as the boys would respond and provide confirmation that each one understood the lesson being taught. Often, the house manager would have one-on-one sessions with individuals who needed extra attention.

We completed dinner and cleaning the kitchen by 7:00 p.m. From 7:00 p.m. to 8:00 p.m. was the study hour for homework or quiet reading. At 8:00 p.m., everyone went upstairs to prepare for bed. There were two bathrooms, and the boys were given a very short amount of time to take their showers. Each was issued soap and other toiletries that had to be accounted for after their shower time. By 10:00 p.m., everyone was in bed, and the lights were off in the home. At night, if a child needed to use the restroom he had to knock on the headboard of the bed and wait for the child care worker to grant him permission to leave his bed. When we suspected boys were getting out of their bed at night, we placed baby powder on the floor to leave a trail of footprints to answer our suspicion.

Throughout the evening, my coworker and I had a clipboard with a form on which we marked the movements of each boy hourly. We also provided and subtracted points based on their behavior. These points were very important to the boys because they were revealed usually on Thursday evening and provided the outcome for the youth's weekend. Depending on the points earned during the week, a child might have privileges such as going home Saturday night or attending the group home's Saturday recreation activity (usually consisting of bowling, pizza, swimming pool, or some other fun activity). Those with low points were often relegated to the home for the weekend and had to take care of the most disliked chores for house clean up on Saturday morning.

From 10:00 p.m. to 11:00 p.m., my coworker and I would tally all points and write up the numerous reports required by the agency that ran the group home. I would leave at 11:00 p.m., and my coworker was relieved at 12:00 a.m. by the night worker who supervised the home until 8:00 a.m. His job was to make sure the home was safe at night, wake the boys at 6:30 in the morning, and serve them breakfast. He was joined by the day worker at 6:00 a.m. Thus, there were always two child care workers any time the youth were awake.

Although the group home in which I worked was located in rural western Pennsylvania, which had a small minority population, there was a significant number of racial minority youth in the group home. Throughout the country, the issue of minority youth (specifically blacks and Latinos) being disproportionately involved in the justice system has gained national attention. I address the social and historical context of the issue below.

Minority Youth

As a child care worker who was also pursuing a PhD in criminology, I saw a disproportionate number of minority youth as compared to the general population numbers in western Pennsylvania. This issue of disproportionate minority confinement (DMC) has been addressed at the national level.

In 1974, the Office of Juvenile Justice and Delinquency Prevention was founded, and the federal Juvenile Justice and Delinquency Prevention Act (JJDPA) was established. Among other mandates, it required states—in order to receive federal funds—to meet standards regarding the deinstitutionalization of status offenders, removal of less serious offenders from facilities, and separate facilities for juveniles held in adult facilities. By 1992, the issue of DMC became a major issue of discussion and policy. It was in that year that the DMC mandate required all states to investigate and reduce the problem of DMC among youth in juvenile and adult institutions (Penn, 2006). The intent of the mandate was threefold: Each state was to identify the problem, assess it, and create programs to intervene. DMC is measured by the DMC Index. A DMC Index Score is the percentage of *confined juvenile population minority* divided by the percentage of *overall juvenile population minority*. If the index value is more than one, then it indicates DMC (minority overrepresentation). A number of one indicates proportional representation while less than one would indicate minority underrepresentation.

When I reflect on disproportional minority youth in the juvenile justice system as a whole and in the group home specifically, I cannot help but think about the sociohistorical foundations that laid the foundations for the numbers we see today. I believe it is very important for every justice system worker to understand the sociohistorical foundation as it counters the notion that DMC occurred in a vacuum without any historical or social precedence. This approach looks at the history of African Americans pre- and post-emancipation in order to understand how the criminal and juvenile justice systems were driving forces that created DMC in the juvenile justice system.

In the 1400s, before the modern day juvenile justice movement of the 1800s, children were viewed as "little adults" often receiving the same punishment and work conditions afforded to the hardworking adults. A reason for this lack of child nurturing was the high mortality rates for infants and children. By the 1600s, children began receiving the title of "potential adults" as mortality rates declined. It was also during this time that children were seen as malleable or claylike human souls who must be shaped and molded and formed into law-abiding, God-fearing adults (Ward, 2001). By 1800, the term *adolescence* emerges as the gap between child and adult. What remained constant is a theme that children and adolescents need to be molded and guided before they became adults whose ways could not be changed. At first glance at the subject, the essence of molding, guiding, and directing children moves well into the theme of rehabilitation, which is the foundation of the juvenile justice system's founding in 1899. Ward (2001) along with Platt (1969) present other thoughts about a so-called benign—blind to color, gender, and class—system of juvenile justice in the United States. Ward states, "Evidence suggest rather unequivocally that, in the eyes of many nineteenth- and twentieth-century leaders and mainstream folks alike, black children have not been deemed especially 'malleable' in the first place nor worthy of the effort and investment" (p. 43). Thus, a story of child saving for black children appears very different from saving their white counterparts.

The focus of the difference stems from the differences in how white and black children were raised. White children were to mature into law-abiding adults whereas black children, marred by the reality of slavery, were to remain childlike regardless of age. A black child was raised to fit a subordinate status defined by the existing social order. The belief that African Americans were forever to be childlike continued into post-emancipation as they were viewed as less capable than whites because of their stagnant development and lack of education. There was a view that child saving was fruitless for African

American children because of their inability to make the transition to responsible adulthood. For example, white taxpayers refused to "waste" money on the needs of incorrigible young blacks: A bill to assist this population was defeated based on the belief that attempting to reform "a Negro" was futile. Governor Davis of Arkansas in 1905 provided a popular solution to the problem: The state would build a reform school where white boys would be taught useful occupations and "Negro boys" would perform the cleaning and other menial tasks to support the institution. DuBois found in 1901 that over 70% of southern prisoners were black. He noted that blacks were more easily convicted and received longer sentences. He pointed to the convict lease system as the reason for this practice. This system resembled slavery as it provided low cost human capital to a white, southern, agriculture-based economy (DuBois, 2002). In the north, the situation was one of neglect rather than malignance. New York was touted as being the first state to open a reformatory with a colored section in 1834. In 1849 Pennsylvania established a house of refuge for colored children. Before these establishments, black children were put into existing institutions such as almshouses, workhouses, and jails and prisons with adults where no efforts to rehabilitate existed.

Now that I am several years removed from working at the group home, I have often reflected on what I saw. I saw boys who were economically disadvantaged (Merton, 1938; Shaw & McKay, 1942) and who often had little ambition about the future and lacked self-control (Gottfredson & Hirschi, 1990; Hirsch, 1969). What I also saw was a subculture of violence deeply rooted in certain ways of rationalizing behavior and responses to whatever situations came its way (Anderson, 1994). An example was "John," a 13 year-old husky Latino boy who challenged directions given to him, especially to do chores around the house. On more than one occasion, we had to "take him down." As a child care worker, we were properly trained on how to put a resident on the ground for restraint without causing harm to him or ourselves. This response was used as a last result in the case of a resident causing violence to him or to others. After taking him down, we would take him to a room where one of us would sit with him until the house manager arrived. After the tense moments subsided and the boy would calm down, there was often good conversation about what the boy was feeling and why his actions became so explosive.

John told me how as a Latino boy he had to show his toughness because his brothers, uncles, and other males in his family taught him not to be a punk. He learned early that house work was for girls and that if anyone disrespected him, it was necessary for him to respond back with violence so that he would not be "dissed" again. Although he never mentioned his father, I did learn from reading his file that his father was killed in a knife fight. John looked at his future as a one-day-at-a-time journey that consisted of trying to be a citizen following the laws and rules of the general society when he was at school but never straying far from the "code of the streets" (Anderson, 1994) of violence and gaining respect.

As I was completing my dissertation I spent time as a Volunteer in Service to America (VISTA) in Fort Worth, Texas. The VISTA program allows persons to volunteer their time to develop neighborhoods and programs to better the environment in which the residents currently live. My neighborhood was an economically challenged area noted for gang activity, illegal immigrants, and crime. I worked with a local church, and together, we started an after-school program, summer camp, English as a Second Language classes, a resale shop, legal assistance, and daily meals for children. Initiating these programs involved the culling of resources inside and outside of the community. It involved finding networking and using my social capital to link those willing to donate with those in need of donations.

It was magical watching despair turn to hope when resources, human and material, were brought into this downtrodden community. Residents became more a part of the community and participated in programs. The church became the refuge in the community as people needed the services offered, but they also volunteered their own help in the way of cooking meals, providing babysitting services, and informing us about youth in trouble with the police or in school. Although I was a VISTA for less than a year, it provided the practical experience to support my understanding of the many theoretical terms I learned in my doctoral education. My practical experience reinforced my understanding of just how important environment, social capital, family bonds, and middle-class ways of life are to obtaining and maintaining law-abiding youth.

Another boy I remember was "Mike", a 12-year-old African American boy with a very small frame but a very large braggadocios presentation. In his opinion, he could take on any boy or man in a fight, have any girl or woman he wanted, and play sports and engage in other physical activities such as dancing better than anyone else. He presented an outward appearance of one never lacking self-esteem. His reason for being in the group home was partly parental neglect and partly delinquency—he stole items from a local store in response to peer pressure. Although he was not officially in a gang, his parental neglect, peer association, and social environment supported a path into eventual gang involvement. I was most sad for Mike on weekends, when other residents earned weekend home visits or had families visit them on Sundays. Mike had no family to go home to and not once did a family member visit him on a Sunday.

I departed from my position as a child care worker while Mike was still a resident. As a 12-year-old without a family support system, he had limited options for the future. Perhaps he stayed in the group home for several months longer than the usual 3 to 5 months; perhaps a caring, nurturing family member emerged to rear him; perhaps his biological parents came forward to resume their duties; or perhaps, sadly, he submitted to the lure of the gang. Mike's set of risk factors is not an isolated case. Increases in prison populations, especially African American males (Alexander, 2010), and limited alternatives for placement of dependent children can easily produce a life trajectory of gang involvement and violent crime.

Which outcome turned out to be Mike's fate is unknown to me. If I were to meet him today, I would want to learn from him regarding what we should do as academicians, professionals, and practitioners to reduce the strain created by the many obstacles he and others faced in life. Perhaps it was seeing the life courses and choices of so many minority boys and young men at the District of Columbia Public Defender's Office and my time as a child care worker in Pennsylvania that inspired me to become a community organizer in Texas with the goals of crime prevention and neighborhood elevation.

❖ CONCLUSION

As I reflect on my career in criminology in which I have served on numerous juvenile boards and written several grants, books, and articles on juvenile delinquency and crime prevention, I cannot help but think about John, Mike, and other youth I have come in contact with over the years. All youth in general and minority youth in particular need strong mentors in their lives. The first mentors any child encounters are parents. When the family mentorship is weak or nonexistent, the second layer of mentorship found in the community must be strong. This layer consists of neighbors, teachers, clergy and religious community members, and coaches. For some youth, this second layer may also be weak or nonexistent. Here is where official mentorship programs, such as Big Brothers/Big Sisters, fills a void by providing persons, usually from outside the immediate community, with the opportunity to provide examples of positive lifestyles, social capital, coping strategies, delayed gratification, and social bonding. A youth surrounded by these positive factors has a greater chance of overcoming the risk factors that may be in his or her daily environment.

Being a professor of criminology, I constantly tie together the real world with the theories and research that our discipline produces. By serving on boards, creating prevention programs, mentoring youth, and assisting communities, I have become an advocate for those who may not have the forum or voice to articulate their needs. The responses and solutions to youth delinquency exist within the dozens of journals and other publications our field produces annually. My belief is that a strong tie should exist between the community and the university to implement the most successful methods to reduce violence and crime so that the youth have greater opportunities to be productive law-abiding members of society.

❖ REFERENCES

Alexander, M. (2010). *The new Jim Crow: Mass incarceration in the age of color blindness.* New York: New Press.

American Correctional Association. (1994). *Standards for juvenile community residential facilities* (3rd ed.). Laurel, MD: Author.

Anderson, E. (1994, May). The code of the street. *Atlantic Monthly,* 80–94.

Albanese, J. (1993). *Dealing with delinquency: The future of juvenile justice.* Chicago: Nelson Hall.

Commonwealth v. Fisher, 27 Pa. Super. 175 (January 17, 1905).

DuBois, W. (2002). The spawn of slavery: The convict lease system in the United States. In S. Gabbidon, H. Greene, & V. Young (Eds.), *African American classics in criminology and criminal justice* (pp. 81–88). Thousand Oaks, CA: Sage.

Gottfredson, M. R., & Hirschi, T. (1990). *A general theory of crime.* Stanford, CA: Stanford University Press.

Hirschi, T. (1969). *Causes of delinquency.* Berkeley: University of California Press.

Merton, R. (1938). Social structure and anomie. *American Sociological Review, 3,* 672–682.

Penn, E. (2000). Juvenile residential treatment centers: Organizational structure, treatment standards and success rates (Doctoral dissertation, Indiana University of Pennsylvania, 2000). *Dissertation Abstracts International-A, 61* (05), 2049.

Penn, E. (2006). Black youth: Disproportionality and delinquency. In E. Penn, H. Greene, & S. Gabbidon (Eds.), *Race and juvenile justice* (pp. 47–61). Durham, NC: Carolina Academic Press.

Platt, A. (1969). *The child savers: The intervention of delinquency* (2nd ed.). Chicago: University of Chicago Press.

Shaw, C., & McKay, H. (1942). *Juvenile delinquency and urban areas*. Chicago: University of Chicago Press.

Springer, D., & Roberts, A. (2011). *Juvenile justice and delinquency*. Boston: Jones & Bartlett.

Ward, G. (2001). Color lines of social control: Juvenile justice administration in a racial social system, 1825–2000 (Doctoral dissertation, University of Michigan, 2001). *Dissertation Abstracts International-A, 62* (10), 3582.

❖ RECOMMENDED READINGS

Alexander, M. (2010). *The new Jim Crow: Mass incarceration in the age of color blindness*. New York: New Press.

Anderson, E. (1994, May). The code of the street. *Atlantic Monthly*, 80–94.

Browne-Marshall, G. (2007). *Race, law, and American society: 1607 to present*. New York: Routledge, Taylor & Francis.

Gabbidon, S. (2007). *Criminological perspectives on race and crime*. New York: Routledge.

Penn, E., Greene, H., & Gabbidon, S. (2006). *Race and juvenile justice*. Durham, NC: Carolina Academic Press.

Vankatesh, S. (2006). *Off the books: The underground economy of the urban poor*. Cambridge, MA: Harvard University Press.

DISCUSSION QUESTIONS

1. How does social inequality impact juvenile crime and justice? What are the special challenges in treating minority youth offenders? What kinds of efforts need to be made?

2. In addition to working in corrections, what are some activities one can be involved in to respond to social disadvantage and crime in communities? (Discuss any that you are interested in doing.) Exactly how do these activities help?

3. Should criminologists be expected to become highly involved in crime prevention and intervention efforts, or are they only obligated to study crime? Is "doing something about crime a part of the social science of crime"? Thoroughly explain and/or justify your answer.

15

Working in Corrections and Teaching About the Field

A Short-Term Insider's Perspective

N. Prabha Unnithan

Editor's Introduction: Professor Unnithan worked briefly as a planning specialist for a state correctional system. He believes that his stint in corrections gives him a unique "short-term insider's perspective." Brief insiders gain more direct experience working in specific environments than do "outsiders" but may not have been employed in them long enough to become absorbed into the workplace culture as "true insiders," who may be less inclined to think critically about the organization. He draws from his experiences in generating and

(Continued)

(Continued)

providing information to be used for solving problems and making changes in correctional agencies. Unnithan applies principles derived from organizational sociology to correctional agencies and shows that drawing from employment experiences can help in teaching and learning academic concepts.

My background in corrections began in India where I had, as a master's student in criminology toward the end of the 1970s, conducted research on prison work programs. However, my relatively short (less than a year) stint as a planning specialist for the Ohio Department of Rehabilitation and Correction (ODRC) in the mid-1980s forms the experiential basis for this essay.

After completing my PhD at the University of Nebraska–Lincoln, I worked at the ODRC headquarters in Columbus. I was part of a small unit named the Bureau of Planning and Research (BOPR). This group provided *information* (such as population counts of prisoners and parolees and responses to inquiries from higher administration officials or the legislature about any and all correctional matters), *evaluations* (of a variety of programs being run in Ohio prisons ranging from education to drug and alcohol treatment), and *research analyses* (of various trends and problems such as inmate violence or staff–inmate altercations) to the ODRC. The projects that we worked on resulted in reports that were used for documenting issues and planning the agency's responses to them. As a planning specialist, I worked on a number of projects that were assigned to me by the bureau's director and would help the agency plan for future changes and contingencies. Two took up much of my time there: I researched and recommended a method for forecasting prison intake (i.e., the number of convicted individuals who would show up every year for whom space would have to be found), and I was involved in researching and implementing a new instrument for classifying prisoners and assigning them to the institution that "best" fit their particular combination of risks posed (to society, to others, and to themselves) and needs (for example, education or health care).

I returned to academe shortly after my brief time at ODRC and have remained here since then. The experience gained from India and with the ODRC has "qualified" me to teach corrections at every academic setting in which I have been employed so far. Academically, I use my experience from Ohio in two ways: First, to this day it is a source of examples to enliven all of my courses; and second, it provides a broad organizational perspective on the field of corrections. Within this perspective, I would like students to learn to appreciate three principles. First, the acquisition and proper use of information is crucial to all correctional organizations. Second, correctional organizations and their members can be understood as microcosms of the trends and problems confronted by the larger society within which they operate. Third, the decisions and work products of correctional agencies illustrate the interplay between formal and informal aspects of bureaucratic organizations and their perceived places in society. The operation of these principles may not be as apparent to long-term employees (i.e., insiders) or academic correctional researchers (i.e., outsiders) compared to short-term employee insiders like me. Long-term employees may be too much a part of the organization, too busy dealing with the day-to-day tasks of one's job, to be able to step back and take a broader look at the organization. Academics who do not work for a correctional organization lack the direct contact that helps one understand just what goes on inside the organization and what it does (exactly how these abstract principles more concretely apply to the structure and functioning of the organization). Short-term employee insiders, on the other hand, have worked in an organization long enough to become somewhat familiar with it but not long enough to become absorbed into it.

❖ A BACKDROP: REAL WORLD STORIES IN THE CLASSROOM

The following is a typical scenario in the junior-level Correctional Organizations course that I have taught at Colorado State University every spring semester since moving there in 1987. The time is after 8:00 a.m. on the first day of class. The students eye me warily as I walk into class with a teaching assistant and begin to distribute copies of the syllabus. I clear my throat and discuss the goals of the course, the textbook, what we will cover during the course, my expectations regarding student comportment and decorum, course requirements, and grading policies—the dull but essential details of the next 16 weeks, a portion of which they will be spending with me. Other than a procedural question or two about examinations and assignments, I get very little response to half an hour of talking "at" them and an awkward silence ensues as I wait for more questions. Then, I smile and begin anew, "Let me tell you a little about my background and my interests in the field of corrections." I describe my first master's research project in India on prison work programs (Unnithan, 1986) and other correctional research along the way until a recent series of interviews in Colorado prisons with individuals convicted of violent crimes involving guns (Pogrebin, Stretesky, & Unnithan, 2009). Again, there is not much response. However, downcast eyes become more focused, bored expressions perk up, and an air of interest (even engagement) pervades the classroom as I mention in passing that I worked for the Ohio Department of Rehabilitation and Correction for a brief period of time in the mid-1980s as a planning specialist.

Questions start and continue about my experiences in prisons and around prisoners during that time, which my students appear to feel are more "real" than any of the research concepts and analyses I mentioned: What happens to people after the court sentences them to prison? What is the truth about prison sex? Is prison food the slop that it is shown to be in movies and television? Have I ever witnessed an execution being carried out? When inmates get out of prison, how do they get home? I notice that only a few of the questions were about research that I had conducted before or after my Ohio employment. As I attempt to cope with the rising tide of questions, the teaching assistant looks up at me to indicate that it is the end of the class period. The two of us walk back to the Sociology Department floor, and the teaching assistant offers a parting observation, usually something along the lines of "you should talk more about the time when you worked in the prison system." Then, I think to myself, what just happened or, really, had happened again? Why is it that serving for a short time as a correctional employee rendered what I had to say somehow more credible to students than all of the other decades of research toil in the same field?

All of us who have literally "worked in corrections" for any length of time and either moved on or returned to academe have learned that stories about the time we spent within the system, or our "real world experiences," hold a prominent place in correctional lectures and discussions. I think our stories are only slightly less compelling when compared to those told by the practitioners of "convict criminology" and the "war stories" told by various police officers, prosecutors, defense lawyers, and judges who we invite to our classes as guest speakers. At the same time, they are interesting enough to hold the attention of students as instructors try to sneak in scholarly concepts and academic findings regarding the field of corrections into lectures and class discussions. The challenge for any instructor, of course, is how to do this in a manner in which the student is able to identify the core concept or principle underlying an example without the specific details of the latter overwhelming an informed appreciation of the former. This can be thought of as similar to the familiar pedagogical challenge involved in getting students to perceive the "whole forest" (principle) while they ponder "individual trees" (examples) within it. Below, I offer several illustrations of principles and concepts by integrating stories and examples of my stint as an employee in the corrections sector of the criminal justice system. It should be understood that these illustrations are conveyed to exemplify core concepts or ideas and not just because they happen to be pretty good stories in and of themselves.

Before moving on, I should mention that at every campus where I have been employed, it has fallen on me to teach a corrections course, sometimes the *only* corrections course. While I was generally willing to teach corrections courses, in assigning them to me, department chairs were likely to mention my Ohio experience along with my research interests in the area. I note this to suggest that even academics are not immune to the credibility that appears to accompany real world experience.

❖ PRINCIPLES, APPLICATIONS, AND EXAMPLES

As mentioned earlier, I have taught a course at Colorado State University regularly for the past 2 decades titled Correctional Organizations. It is an upper-level course that students could take after our Introduction to Criminal Justice. However, it is the only one in which students are exposed to correctional issues and therefore functions effectively as an introduction to the field of corrections. After discussing various historical, philosophical, and sentencing topics, I survey institutional (prisons, jails) and noninstitutional (diversion, probation, parole) correctional organizations, their structure and functioning, and discuss the populations served by them as well as their personnel.

At the beginning of the coverage of various correctional agencies, I point out that they are all "formal organizations" that typically operate according to the classic principles of bureaucracies first laid out by sociological pioneer, Max Weber. These principles (see Scott, 1998), which my students are likely to have learned in other social science classes, include the following: hierarchy of authority, impersonality, written rules of conduct, promotion based on achievement, specialized division of labor, and separation of the personal from the official. I first go through these principles using the typical pyramid-shaped organizational chart of a given correctional agency (it really does not matter which one). I mention that with minor reservations (e.g., the personal and the official often tended to mix rather than being clearly separated), I had developed a greater appreciation for Weberian principles while working in the ODRC. I then go on to augment our discussion with three additional principles, which I believe are particularly relevant for correctional organizations. These principles are as follows: (1) The acquisition and use of relevant information is crucial to all correctional organizations, (2) correctional organizations and their members can be understood as microcosms of the trends and problems confronted by the larger society within which they operate, and (3) the decisions and work products of correctional agencies illustrate the interplay between formal and informal aspects of bureaucratic organizations as well as their self-perceived places in society. In the next sections, I explain and illustrate these principles in the context of my Ohio correctional agency experiences. However, the ideas I review are not unique to either the agency I worked for or to me. One or all of these principles may have applicability to other criminal justice agencies and even to how formal organizations operate in general.

Correctional Organizational Principle I:
The Acquisition and Use of Relevant Information
Is Crucial to All Correctional Organizations

There is nothing particularly novel or revolutionary in noting that organizations need information to survive and to meet internal as well as external opportunities and threats. However, in a correctional context, this becomes crucial. The existence of our bureau itself was a function of this organizational necessity. In the past, internal discipline and operations based on information provided by inmates who are trustees have been the norm. This practice presumably endures. However, my points are to be understood in the context of running an entire correctional system. I provide two examples of the use of relevant information in such administrative situations: forecasting prison populations and inmate classification as a management tool.

Forecasting Prison Populations

Generally, when asked in class what correctional agencies would need to operate, students are likely to respond with a litany of answers such as adequate budgets, human resources, proper training, and so on. Some may even mention food and rehabilitation programs. They almost never bring up the need for information acquisition, analysis, and utilization. In this context, I discuss the prison intake forecasting study mentioned earlier in this chapter. The idea behind the project was to develop a way to make bounded predictions of prison admissions (Blumstein, Cohen, & Miller, 1980) for the next planning period, both short and long term. For me, carrying out this project involved learning about population projection methods, especially applications of time series analysis, multiple regression analysis, system modeling (given that the correctional sector serves as the end point of decisions previously made and passed on by the police and the courts) as well as identifying relevant independent variables. This kind of experience provides much needed reinforcement for those who learn and excel in research methods and statistics courses. I note the importance of correctional organizations being able to use information on the number of individuals who will show up at their doors in the future so that planning for everything from food to parole release can be carried out effectively.

Inmate Classification as a Management Tool

When discussing the time devoted and attention that prison systems paid to inmate classification as opposed to indiscriminate warehousing, I bring up a particular event that took place during my Ohio employment. There had been a series of minor disturbances at a medium security prison during that time. As a result, higher administrators in the department decided to move inmates who had been involved in these events to other prisons. The means for doing this was through reclassification of all inmates in that prison using a Federal Bureau of Prisons (FBOP) classification instrument. The instrument had been imported recently into the ODRC, and we had just begun validating it for our prison population. All BOPR staffers were involved in a massive undertaking, and the work of reclassifying the inmates completed quickly. This example not only conveys the importance of inmate classification and timely reclassification (Austin, 1983) but also demonstrates that there are more ways of responding to prison discipline issues beyond the stereotypical show of force or sending troublemakers to solitary confinement. It also illustrates how the policies and practices developed by the FBOP affect state and local correctional agencies.

Correctional Organizational Principle II: Correctional Organizations and Their Members Can Be Understood as Microcosms of the Trends and Problems Confronted by the Larger Society Within Which They Operate

While discussing sociologist Erving Goffman's (1961) influential ideas regarding how total institutions, such as maximum security prisons, encapsulate the lives of one set of members, that is, inmates, I comment that this should not be taken to mean that the outside world does not intrude into the daily lives that are endured and the work that is conducted in these places. Prisons can also be understood as reflecting issues that bedevil and confront society in general. This allows one to see that rather than being places that are isolated and apart from society, prisons also mirror and run parallel to the outside world within which they exist. The following are two illustrations of the interplay between society and prisons: HIV and AIDS and prisoner lawsuits.

HIV and AIDS

I mention to my students that the early 1980s, about the same time as my stint with ODRC, was when AIDS first entered into broad public consciousness. Initially, it was identified with homosexuality and was often referred to as "the gay plague." I also add that the latter term was one that I sometimes heard from prison staff during those years. Ignorance, prejudice, and fear of contracting AIDS through casual means were also rife (Singh, Unnithan, & Jones, 1988). The relationship between HIV and AIDS was, of course, unknown at the time, and no procedures were in place at institutions of confinement for dealing with prevention, management, or treatment of associated complications. Some years after I returned to academe, AIDS had gone on to become a major concern of both society and prisons as inmates with HIV began entering prisons and as those in confinement developed it due to risky sexual behavior (Blumberg, 1989). Correctional organizations along with the rest of society then scrambled to generate policies and procedures for dealing with the problem. This example also provides a good lead-in for a subsequent discussion of health and medical programs in prisons; given the large number of people who are typically confined in close quarters, it is important to make provisions for responding to issues connected to illness before it spreads. In this context, more recent health problems in prisons with regard to multidrug resistant strains of tuberculosis and the fact that American society is seeing resurgence in this evolving form of the disease can also be mentioned.

Prisoner Lawsuits

Perhaps no other topic generates more controversy in my classes than the debate over whether or not inmates should have the right to challenge the conditions of their captivity. Someone is likely to bring up the story of how an inmate sued an institution for being given creamy rather than crunchy peanut butter (or vice versa; the story oscillates between the two choices with each retelling). In some sense, the details do not matter, as students try to outdo each other with tales of what they have heard are some of the ridiculous issues that inmates have either sued or have threatened to sue over. Here, I mention that these lawsuits, while some may indeed be frivolous, cannot all be dismissed as such. Some serve as the impetus for better management practices. During my time in Ohio, one of my office mates was a newly hired nutritionist for the department. Among her responsibilities were planning diets, menus, and meals and providing advice and recommendations to prison officials on nutritional issues. Clearly, our department had either learned from the first wave of lawsuits by prisoners (Nasheri, 1996) in the 1960s and 1970s or anticipated that prison food might be a source of future legal contention. If challenged, the agency was ready to respond with detailed information on systematic arrangements that it had made for providing healthy, nutritious food. Since that time and given the withering of the courts' previous "hands off" doctrine concerning corrections, the issue has received greater media coverage. However, lawsuits that seek damages or improvement for those conditions of confinement are only to be expected in a growingly litigious society, such as the United States. Just as many lawsuits filed by ordinary citizens would be perceived as frivolous by others, so would many lawsuits filed or threatened by inmates.

Correctional Organizational Principle III: The Decisions and Work Products of Correctional Agencies Illustrate the Interplay Between Formal and Informal Aspects of Bureaucratic Organizations as Well as Their Self-Perceived Places in Society

The authors of literature on bureaucracies often note that informal aspects of these organizations not captured by the organizational chart, the formal hierarchy, often affect their functioning (see Baker, Gibbons, & Murphy, 1999) in unanticipated ways. I mention this idea to get students to think of how informal groups such as cliques, friendship groups, and romantic and spousal relationships may affect decisions and organizational functioning and often may serve to subvert and overturn the official line. At the same time, it is difficult for organizational personnel whose work is ignored and devalued by society to be motivated to identify with their occupations, to do better, and "act professional." I illustrate this with two more examples derived from my experiences in Ohio having to do with friendship and bureaucratic errors, and public perceptions and informal interactions.

Friendship and Bureaucratic Errors

On one occasion, a colleague and I walked into a maximum security prison on an official visit to find the place in an uproar. We were told by one of the employees that this was because a prisoner, who I will call by the pseudonym Charles Johnson, had been released by mistake. On further inquiry, it was determined that while a Charles Johnson was scheduled to be released on that day, the wrong one had been let out. There were two prisoners, one white and one black, with the same name, and the white man had been released instead of the black man. The error occurred when a correctional officer (CO), who had developed a friendship with the mistakenly released Johnson, assumed that he was to be let out when he saw the name on the roster of those to be released. The CO asked the man if he was to be released and the prisoner lied and answered in the affirmative. Given their previous friendship, the CO trusted the lying Johnson and sent him on his way. This error was repeated by others in the chain-of-custody-and-release, who failed to check the prisoner's presumed release date, incorrectly believing that earlier colleagues had verified his identity.

This example illustrates that unlike organizations that produce widgets, people processing organizations (Hasenfeld, 1972) interact with those that they are working on, and working with, to classify and dispose properly. Errors and snafus in such situations where the target of the process, a prisoner in this example, can form a relationship, for good or ill, with those doing the processing are understandable and to be expected, though not necessarily excusable. No organizational chart would be able to capture these interactions and their consequences.

Public Perceptions and Informal Interactions

One of my colleagues told me once that correctional agencies were capable of producing only bad news. The only time the media and the public paid attention was when prisoners rioted, killed, or hurt someone else or when staff members were involved in brutality and corruption. To him, this clearly indicated that we were members of a putrid occupation. Although I wanted to, I could not find any counter-arguments or examples at the time. This led me to think about the importance of how correctional staff and administrators presented themselves to the public and how that reflected on the perceived public worth of the organizations they represented. While police officers and their agencies take great pride in presenting a disciplined, professional front and demeanor in their interactions with members of the public, I am afraid the same cannot be said of correctional personnel that I have encountered. In fact, I knew of one of our ODRC employees in our Columbus headquarters whose spouse referred to that individual's job only as "working for the state," without mentioning which department. I bring this issue up not to contest the view that correctional work is often dull and depressing and that success stories are rare, but to try and explain it organizationally. Mentioning the conversation with my colleague allows for an extended class discussion of why those in corrections who perform important residual work that no one else wants but at the same time has to be done are so devalued by the public. I then end the discussion with a final pessimistic note that those whose work and place in society is devalued are unlikely to be motivated to do better and produce success stories through effective custodial discipline or rehabilitation programming.

❖ CONCLUSION

As mentioned before, none of the three correctional principles I have discussed are new or novel. It is the applications and illustrations relevant to the field of corrections mentioned previously that may be unique to my experience. In listing and describing these systematically, I have often wondered if someone else would "see" them in the same way that I had. It appears to me that someone who was an insider to the corrections profession may not agree with the assessments and connections that I have made to the organizational literature. They may rather want to justify and explain why the events unfolded the way they did. On the other hand, someone who is a complete outsider may be automatically suspicious of organizational justifications and explanations. A short-term insider is the term that I have come to see as the best description of my brief employment with the ODRC. The individual in this role is well placed in terms of distance to probe the insider's perspective, while maintaining familiarity and understanding with how such perspective may have developed. The short-term insider also avoids the outsider's trained cynicism while understanding the need for maintaining a healthy skepticism in drawing conclusions about how the objects of study describe and explain themselves. I believe these are all important lessons for students, academics, and practitioners.

❖ REFERENCES

Austin, J. (1983). Assessing the new generation of prison classification models. *Crime and Delinquency, 19*, 561–576.

Baker, G., Gibbons, R., & Murphy, K. J. (1999). Informal authority in organizations. *Journal of Law, Economics and Organization, 15*, 56–73.

Blumberg, M. (1989). Issues and controversies with respect to the management of AIDS in corrections. *Prison Journal, 69*, 1–13.

Blumstein, A., Cohen, J., & Miller, H. G. (1980). Demographic disaggregated projections of prison populations. *Journal of Criminal Justice, 8*, 1–26.

Goffman, E. (1961) *Asylums: Essays on the social situation of mental patients and other inmates.* New York: Doubleday.

Hasenfeld, Y. (1972). People processing organizations: An exchange approach. *American Sociological Review, 37*, 256–263.

Nasheri, H. (1996). Spirit of meanness: Courts, prisons and prisoners. *Cumberland Law Review* 27, 1173–1183.

Pogrebin, M. E., Stretesky, P. B., & Unnithan, N. P. (2009). *Guns, violence and criminal behavior.* Boulder, CO: Lynne Rienner.

Scott, R. W. (1998). *Organizations: Rational, natural and open systems.* Upper Saddle River, NJ: Prentice Hall.

Singh, R. N., Unnithan, N. P., & Jones, J. D. (1988). Behavioral impacts of the fear of AIDS: A sociological model. *Journal of Sociology and Social Welfare, 15*, 29–48.

Unnithan, N. P. (1986). Research in a correctional setting: Constraints and biases. *Journal of Criminal Justice, 14*, 401–441.

❖ RECOMMENDED READINGS

Baker, G., Gibbons, R., & Murphy, K. J. (1999). Informal authority in organizations. *Journal of Law, Economics and Organization, 15*, 56–73.

Blumberg, M. (1989). Issues and controversies with respect to the management of AIDS in corrections. *Prison Journal, 69*, 1–13.

Scott, R. W. (1998). *Organizations: Rational, natural and open systems.* Upper Saddle River, NJ: Prentice Hall.

Singh, R. N., Unnithan, N. P., & Jones, J. D. (1988). Behavioral impacts of the fear of AIDS: A sociological model. *Journal of Sociology and Social Welfare, 15*, 29–48.

DISCUSSION QUESTIONS

1. What are advantages of instructors using personal experiences in the classroom? Which is the most important and why? What are disadvantages of instructors using personal experiences in the classroom? Which is the most important and why?

2. Think of a situation in which you were a "short-term insider"—someone who was a member of some kind of group or organization (work related or otherwise) long enough to get to know it but not long enough to become deeply attached to it. What are some characteristics of the group or organization that you noticed that others (long-term insiders and outsiders) apparently did not?

3. As you think of your prospective career, which organizational-level (not just personal or specific office or department-level) factors, both formal and informal, are you most concerned about and why?

16

Experiencing the Criminal Justice System

Lessons for Later Criminological Understanding

Robert F. Meier and Teresa F. Smith

Editor's Introduction: Professor Meier once worked as a probation officer and has more recently coordinated college student internships. Teresa Smith is a former intern and current practitioner. Their essay is a departure from the others as it deals with the criminal justice internship—a type of work that involves combining academics and practice. They argue that a gap needs to be closed between "vicarious learning"—from others' experiences (i.e., textbooks and lectures)—and "experiential learning"—firsthand through one's own experiences. Meier and Smith identify four benefits of internships: "it's real," observing manipulation and impression management, realizing the importance of social distance, and career preview. Through direct experience, the intern can be prepared to learn more about issues such as the contradictory goals of corrections and recidivism.

❖ INTRODUCTION

This may be a startlingly odd observation, but we have had remarkably few colleagues in criminology who have ever knowingly talked with a criminal. Virtually all of them have acquired their understanding of crime and criminals from the library or a computer program analyzing secondary data. Few have had much experience with people who have lengthy criminal records. This might sound to some as though we are being critical of our colleagues but nothing could be further from the truth. The questions about crime and criminality that most of them have asked could be better answered in the library or in front of a computer monitor rather than asking offenders. The best source of information about the causes and directions of schizophrenia is not a mental patient. The best source of information about the causes and distribution of alcoholism is not necessarily an alcoholic. And, truth be told, the best source of information about the causes and distribution of crime in time and space is not necessarily a criminal. But there are some questions that only criminals can answer, such as, how does it feel to commit a crime, how can one best elude detection from the police, how can one dispose of stolen items and receive money for them, and how many other people do you know who also commit crimes?

Granted, these are not scientific questions and, as a result, criminologists are not inclined to ask them. But there are some disciplines that require contact with clients, such as medicine. It is inconceivable that one could become a physician without having had any contact with a variety of patients as part of one's medical education. Even physicians who decide on a specialty that involves no patient contact (e.g., pathology) should have had experience with patients to help them to understand the larger context of the disease or injury.

It is easy now to criticize—even ridicule—Cesare Lombroso. His ideas have not stood up to the test of time. But, in Lombroso's defense, let us acknowledge that Lombroso changed his mind over time. His "born" criminal, the category that once contained 100% of his sample, fell considerably as his research continued. But, Lombroso knew, met, measured, and analyzed real criminals. It was his empirical experience that made the difference.

In this chapter, we begin by discussing the value of experiential learning in an academic setting as a supplement to classroom learning. Then, we move into a discussion of the impact that our professional experiences in the criminal justice system have had on our perceptions and thinking about crime and justice.

❖ VICARIOUS AND EXPERIENTIAL LEARNING

There are at least two different kinds of learning: vicarious and experiential. Vicarious learning takes place from others who have experienced or trained to do something. It takes the form of lectures, books, media, and so on, where the focal person learns because others have learned, and the focal person is getting the benefit of their learning. Experiential learning, on the other hand, involves firsthand learning by the focal person. By definition, vicarious learning is passive; we receive through some medium the thoughts and experiences of others. Experiential learning is more active since the learner creates and experiences some life situations. Those of us with criminal justice experience learned about the criminal justice system and those who are processed in the system through a combination of vicarious and experiential learning.

We believe that supervised internships can provide students with the kind of knowledge that they would not otherwise get in the classroom. We also believe that internships provide more "context" for classroom information. In a movie titled *Little Man Tate*, one of the characters is the director of a center for intellectually gifted children who evaluates a boy for admission. The child, named Fred, goes through a number of tests while his mother waits nervously in a waiting room. Finally, the director comes out and talks with the mother and informs her that her son has been admitted. The director tells the mother, "It's not what he knows [that impressed her], it's what he understands." Working in the criminal justice system conveys the same sense of understanding that many of our colleagues missed.

❖ THE VALUE OF INTERNSHIPS

Internships are examples of experiential learning opportunities. Here, students can experience firsthand some part of the criminal justice system under supervision from the agency and the university's internship coordinator. In our experience, it is difficult to prepare students for their internship experience. Simply put, one cannot easily duplicate agency experience in a classroom or faculty office. And most students have seen only one side of a "power" relationship; they have been the less powerful person (e.g., as students in school or an employee) although some have experienced the more powerful role in some situations (e.g., babysitting and with younger siblings).

The relationship between correctional officials and correctional clients is based on authority. It is a power relationship unmistakably. This means, among other things, that clients would not be in the relationship, given a choice. Instead, they are ordered to be probationers, inmates, or parolees. No one wants to be on probation, in prison, or on parole (except, of course, inmates). This means the kind of relationships most students have had will not fit the usual kind of relationship between correctional officials and clients. There is no good way to have students anticipate this experience except by throwing them into the field with their agency. Hopefully, the agency will be sensitive to the needs of the students and help them through the process.

There are some benefits of internship experiences that tend to go beyond their immediate internship. Hopefully, the students will learn about crime and criminals in a far more practical sense than in the classroom. But there are other benefits that can be identified.

1. It's real.

Students know in a general way that reading, films, and guest speakers are "real." But these are major sources of vicarious learning. Information obtained this way can be very valuable, if only because one cannot experience everything and because to learn experientially requires some background and preparation.

One student was interning at Federal Probation. When asked what notable event she experienced the previous week, she relayed the following:

> I attended a revocation hearing. The defendant was only several feet away from me and the judge wasn't much further. The judge at the end of the hearing sentenced the probationer to 70 months in federal prison. Then, it struck me: This wasn't a class lecture and I wasn't reading a book about revocation hearings, or watching a TV or movie about revocation. It was real and I was there. (H. S., personal communication, 2010)

This made quite an impression on this student, and this experience is repeated in one form or another by other students in other agencies. This student was prepared; she had taken at least one (but maybe two) corrections course(s).

Another student was interning at the local office of U.S. Postal Inspectors. This sounds, to the uneducated, like a profoundly boring internship, but my students have not found it so. I asked one of my postal inspector students what she experienced in the past week, and she responded:

> Well, another postal inspector and I went to Columbus [a town about 30 minutes from Omaha] to make an arrest. We rehearsed the day before who was going to say what and where to stand. Then we drove to Columbus and made the arrest without incident. It was the first time I had to wear a [bullet resistant] vest and I had no idea how heavy they were. (J. S., personal communication, 2010)

It is notable that the intern referred to "another postal inspector and I" indicating that she saw herself in that role. What she took away from that experience was her participation in the event. It was real.

2. Manipulation and impression management

Probationers, inmates, and parolees are manipulative. They are constantly attempting to make sure you see them in a favorite light. Correctional officials get used to this impression management quickly and understand that there is some element of gamesmanship in interaction with correctional clients.

And this isn't the only context where clients have much at stake in having state officials think of them in a particular way. In the 2009 movie *Precious*, the lead character is an individual who has experienced a lifetime of trauma, mostly from her mother. To her credit, Precious wants to leave her welfare world behind her and views education as the vehicle to complete that journey. But her values are dominated by her past in that she permits (needs?) her grandmother to raise her Down syndrome daughter rather than doing so herself. She steals, she evades, she is an accomplice to her mother's charade before the social worker to keep receiving welfare checks. But it is Precious's mother who attempts to persuade her social worker that she is seeking work (when she wasn't) and attempting to get off welfare (when she wasn't).

One of my correctional interns, who had secured a paid internship with Nebraska Department of Correctional Services, went through a 5-week academy, was issued a uniform and was assigned to be a correctional officer at a state youth facility, and saw the manipulation first hand. At one of our meetings, she remarked, "Inmates are nice to you because they want something from you."

3. The importance of social distance

It is common that new, young probation officers (POs) think that being close to probationers in age is a benefit because the new officer reasons he or she could better understand the probationer. After all, the officer goes through similar life changes at about the same time. But such POs learn quickly that being close in age to a correctional client works against the PO if only because a probation officer–probationer relationship is ultimately built around authority. One of my correctional officer interns found the same thing:

> It is amazing how much the inmates know about staff's personal life. They found out my first name, my age, what I like to do, my relationship status, and my schedule for work. I did not want the prisoners to find out my age because I am only 22 years old and they stay at NCYF (Nebraska Correctional Youth Facility) until they are 21 and 10 months. I think that if they knew my age they would not respect me as much and think of me more as an acquaintance than an authority figure. I was correct. Once they had verification from another staff member that I was 22 I began to get hit on more and more and they started to ask me for favors. (T. S., personal communication, 2009)

An inmate came up to the same intern one day and told her that he had listened to some Jimmy Page music the night before. He then told her that he really enjoyed the music of her (the intern's) generation. The intern didn't know who Jimmy Page was, but she discovered that she felt more comfortable with the increased social distance of different generations. The inmate was 18; the intern was 22. The relationship between correctional officials and correctional clients is never personal. This does not mean that one cannot talk about everyday events, such as sports, with clients. But there are lines that should not be crossed.

4. Career preview

Internships do provide some measure of career preview. One sees exactly what criminal justice professionals do, the kinds of people they deal with, and the mind-set of professionals in approaching and doing their jobs. Interns do not experience everything that correctional professionals do; our probation interns, for example, are not permitted to accompany probation and police officers when they revoke someone's probation and take the probationer into custody. This usually happens both because there are liability issues and agency heads have different degrees of tolerance of student involvement.

A student who was interning at a state youth facility discovered that she did not like her experiences:

The areas out of the textbook that interested me were just that, reading of interest to me. Field work allowed me to observe and experience hands on what is of interest to me. I hated working at the prison. Turns out the best experience of my life was also the worst. (T. S., personal communication, 2009)

It was a good experience because this student discovered while she liked to read about prisons, it was a different matter working in one. Another student discovered the same thing interning in a public defender's office:

When I began my internship, I was in the midst of a decision whether or not I wanted to go to law school. It was what I had planned for the previous four years. . . . My internship confirmed that I did not want to go to law school. I saw the day-to-day tasks of lawyers and they did not really appeal to me. (L. S., personal communication, 2009)

Of course, there are interns who so thoroughly enjoy their intern experiences they continue to aspire to be probation and parole officers, police officers, court administrators, and correctional officers and administrators. One such student who interned at U.S. Probation and U.S. Pretrial Services virtually gushed about the quality of her experience and her continued desire to be a PO." It [the internship] was exactly what I wanted—a preview of what I thought I wanted to do after graduation. I am now more determined than ever."

The Gap Between Vicarious and Experiential Learning

In part because they come from different sources, there are often gaps between what we learn vicariously and what we learn experientially. All vicarious learning, for example, is filtered. Someone who has learned over a period of, say, 7 years about prison riots and the risk factors associated with those events, may not be able to impart every nuance of what she has learned to others. There is only so much one can say within the confines of peer reviewed publications and even technical reports.

The intern at U.S. Probation, mentioned earlier, indicated the following:

My internship in the United States Probation and Pretrial Services offices was a great experience. It was a very challenging four months juggling work, school, and an internship, but all the effort was well worth it. I left my internship experience with knowledge of the United States supervision process that a textbook would have never been able to fully convey. (H. S., personal communication, 2010)

❖ WHAT CAN WE PREPARE INTERNS TO EXPECT

Just as there is a difference between law in books and law in action, so too are there differences in correctional practices. One can see these differences easily by comparing correctional systems in different jurisdictions. The precise movement of cases through the correctional system may be more determined by local custom and tradition than some outline or SOP (standard operating procedure). Instead, practices are determined by understandings and agreements that are informal.

One intern was surprised by the second and third chances some probationers received. One probationer reported for his regular meeting, and the probation officer decided to give him a urinary analysis, which came back positive for methamphetamine. "Drugs completely overtook this man's life," she said,

And he couldn't stop using even if it meant going to prison. . . . I asked [the probation officer] what he does in these situations and depending on the person, he won't go to prison yet! It completely shocked me that they gave him [the probationer] another chance after messing up several times. (S. S., personal communication, 2010)

Just as an individual may keep a schedule or a routine so he is aware of what he has planned for each day, one may try to predict the occurrences at an internship. As any other job, it is important to research the agency or place of employment that you will be interning at. This research allows one to paint a mental picture of what she could expect to occur on a normal day. The real issue is defining a normal day. Normal days are few and far between especially in the criminal justice field.

The only advice we can offer is to expect the unexpected while working in the criminal justice field. As an intern at a state prison describes a normal day for her it becomes obvious that there is no normalness present within the facility:

A normal day at NCYF (Nebraska Correctional Youth Facility) begins in the visiting room inside the prison. After a staff member, inside a central control protected unit, allows the shift workers to enter the secured facility, a heavy and thick stainless steel door slams and locks behind those inside the facility. At this point you realize that you are not free to leave the facility until the next shift arrives to relieve you. If they decide not to arrive then we must remain on staff as there is a minimum for the amount of correctional officers who must be on shift at any given time. The prisoners are not the only persons in prison, so are the employees. It is an eerie feeling to know that if no one shows up to relieve us or if a riot were to occur that we could not freely leave the facility.

At any time a fight could break out, a fire could threaten the security of the facility, an escape could happen, or a staff assault could occur and I may be the first responder. Yes, I was trained but can anyone really be fully prepared to handle these situations. One staff member is placed in a perimeter vehicle and is ordered to shoot a prisoner if they are escaping. Yes, we learn how to shoot accurately and the protocol for the necessary precautions and steps to take in this instance, but I am not ready to shoot a teen-aged offender because they want their freedom back. It is evident that the only normal part of a day in the criminal justice field is how the day will begin; the rest of the day (including the end) is left to chance. (T. S., personal communication, 2009)

As an internship begins, one can accept the changes that come with the tasks at hand. The changes are generally not changes within the facility or agency but changes within the interns. Things that never have surfaced before may become things that begin to weigh on their minds. Interns may discover that they more conservative than liberal when they have always perceived themselves as liberal (and vice versa). Not everyone will be changed by the internship they accept, but all interns will begin to notice different values within themselves. The beauty of an internship is that which we take away from the individualized experience whether that is a new set of values, experience in the criminal justice field, or changes within ourselves.

The value of an internship is the individualized program, goals, and lessons accomplished throughout an experience that is nonreplicable. Nonreplicable refers to the idea that each internship is created and proceeds on an individualized level. This being said, individuals will walk away from a completed internship with a completely different outlook, experience, and feeling than another intern who may have completed the same internship program. Above all, an internship provides individuals with the privilege of exploring themselves and learning new things about themselves as well as the field of criminal justice.

An internship allows one the opportunity to be accepted as an employee at an agency or facility that may have otherwise looked past the resume that a student holds with little experience. In an internship, knowledge and experience are gained at a level that allows the student to work at a different pace. Internships can be a skill builder experience as well as a resume builder. Many opportunities in the future career search may be obtainable due to the experiences earned through a student internship. Internships allow the students to weed out careers in the areas that do not interest them as well as pay close attention to those of significant interest. There is also the possibility that an agency where an internship was successfully completed may create a job so the student can continue on as a permanent employee. Short of that, supervisors at an agency may provide important letters of recommendation.

There are limits to what faculty can do to prepare students to take and benefit from an internship experience. If classroom experience prepared students well for the practical application of classroom concepts, internships would be without value and therefore unnecessary. But they are necessary.

Internships can teach students about the world of work, colleagues, and interpersonal relationships. One student had a tough time during his internship. He reported, after his internship at an adult state prison, that he was often the butt of jokes and pranks. He complained about his differential treatment from other guards, and he complained about a particular supervisor. "He is homophobic," the student wrote, "power tripping, insulting, immature and insensitive. He reeks of immaturity and arrogance" (B. S., personal communication, 2009).

❖ RECOGNIZING THE TRADITIONAL GOALS OF CORRECTIONS

Most students are taught that there are four traditional, and conflicting, goals of corrections: *retribution, incapacitation, rehabilitation,* and *deterrence.* These are usually described as distinct and separate goals designed to placate or appeal to different groups. The goals of deterrence and incapacitation can be coupled to any correctional program, regardless of emphasis, while retribution and rehabilitation are unachievable together because they are contradictory. Presumably, one cannot rehabilitate and punish at the same time.

Presumably, every correctional program wants to achieve these goals at least to some degree. They are as appropriate to probation and parole as they are to institutional programs. As noted earlier, no one wants to be on probation, although probationers accept it because it is less punitive than institutionalization. No one wants to be in prison, even so-called country club prisons. And no one wants to be on parole, except if you are an inmate. There are no waiting lists of people who genuinely want to be a correctional client. Having noted that, let us at once recognize that there are some older inmates who do find a degree of comfort in their imprisonment if only because they are provided for. Most of these have lengthy records of state-run living dating back to their adolescence. The only consistency in these individuals' lives is "three hots and a cot." But this does not accurately describe the vast majority of inmates.

A correctional officer intern was completing her internship at a state prison. She mentioned two times when an inmate was released from prison and thereafter returned either to the same facility or another facility within Nebraska. At her particular prison, there were only 89 inmates, the intern was only employed for 4 months, and she only witnessed 4 inmates being released from prison. This particular intern recalls being surprised after witnessing an inmate's release from the facility:

> It was not at all what I had expected. I always read in text books how unpleasant prison is and how hard some prisoners work to receive parole. But there I was witness to an ex-inmate attempting to re-enter the facility after his release. A Sergeant walked him out and shook his hand after supplying him with some clothes and very little money. The Sergeant pointed the recently free prisoner in the direction of the bus station because no one was there to pick him up. The ex-inmate looked blankly at the Sergeant and attempted to re-enter the facility; he was terrified. The Sergeant had to tell him to leave the grounds and that he could no longer reside at the prison. It was unexpected and somewhat humorous, but the underlying factor is that the young man had no plan, nowhere to go, no way to get there, and no support system. To me, this was a plan for failure. (T. S., personal communication, 2009)

But discussing the goals of corrections in the classroom is not the same as recognizing them in everyday correctional practice. Two of the four goals have external referents: Deterrence and incapacitation, if they are achieved, result in outcomes outside the prison in the form of crimes not committed. Obviously, criminologists have yet to address empirically this issue in any complete manner. We can measure crimes, but we simply do not know how to measure noncrimes. It makes sense, conceptually, that a self-report study might ask respondents, "How many burglaries did you commit in the last 6 months?" But it makes no sense to ask, "How many burglaries did you refrain from in the last 6 months because you feared the legal consequences?" Where would anyone even begin to answer that question? Similarly, it would make no sense to ask an inmate, "How many cars did you not steal because you've been incarcerated?" Basing the recidivism rate off of the offenders who are caught committing a crime does not provide the public eye with an accurate account of how many offenders truly refrain from criminal activities after incarceration.

A correctional officer intern expressed that she felt helpless and that she could not help prisoners break away from the system, legally of course, because she felt they were set up for failure. On paper, the prison systems provide retribution, rehabilitation, incapacitation, and deterrence. Of course, deterrence and incapacitation are goals being achieved due to incarceration, and in reality, there are systems in place whose goal is rehabilitation and retribution. The staff at the prison runs these programs, such as gang resistance and faith building, but even the staff members expressed their hesitation and questioned the effectiveness of the program. If those who advocate and provide support for the prisoners do not believe in their success, then the rest of the population should be skeptical of these unattainable goals.

We would argue that rehabilitation and retribution are goals that have internal referents. The former refers to some personal change because of exposure to a change agent or program, while the latter refers to some degree of punishment. To assess treatment effects, we would need to identify what those efforts consisted of—a program, a strategy, curriculum, or a particular change agent.

The prison experience of one intern raised question about the existence of rehabilitation programs. There were programs, and they were called "rehabilitative," but their intent was otherwise:

> The rehabilitative programs that exist at NCYF are ART (aggression resistance training), gang prevention, parenting classes, K-9 adoption, high school, counseling, parole, and jobs. Some of these may not appear to be rehabilitative programs but the goals of these programs are to teach inmate life skills, responsibility, social skills, and coping mechanisms. (T. S., personal communication, 2009)

Perhaps it is asking too much of correctional programs that they rehabilitate inmates if only because such programs can potentially change only one element in the causal equation: the inmate. When we ask students about the cause or causes of crime, the list of causes is pretty much the same from semester to semester: poverty, neighborhood influences, peer pressure, social inequality, low education levels, economic pressures, and so on. It is but a short step to then ask students which of these prisons control. The answer, of course, is none of them.

❖ THINKING ABOUT RECIDIVISM

One consequence of having worked in the criminal justice system is that one's perceptions are invariably tempered by that experience. Consider the idea of *recidivism*. Recidivism is a common concept in criminology and criminal justice. Usually, it refers to committing a crime again. But beyond this uninformative notion is both the matter of measurement and that of meaning. Let's start with meaning. Here's a quote from a criminology book published about 50 years ago:

> Most criminals are recidivists. One of the first things the police do after apprehending a suspect is to investigate his legal biography. Between 50 and 60 percent of all persons in prisons and reformatories have been imprisoned before. A larger percentage has previously been arrested. (Korn & McKorkle, 1959, p. 24)

The calculation of recidivism rates has been a mainstay of criminologists for decades. It would be a mistake to think that we know what those figures mean. Some think they mean that people who return to crime are "failures" of some correctional program or are criminals who have not been caught and "corrected." We would argue that these conclusions are incorrect.

First, note the generalizations: Recidivism rates are higher from maximum security prisons than from medium, minimum, or camp prisons. And recidivism rates of inmates are higher than those of probationers. This makes sense, of course, since the higher risk offenders are sent to prison. After all, prison is a social networking site where gangs flourish and grow. Gang rivalry is just as prevalent inside the prison walls as it is on "the outs." Also, there are different ways to measure recidivism, and there is no agreed on standard. Finally, it matters on how long you follow up inmates: The longer the follow-up period, the more the recidivism.

Now, check some figures: There have been many studies looking at this issue. Some of them have been from government agencies, some from private sources. We don't have to review many of these since our conclusions will remain largely the same. Let's start with a study from the Federal Bureau of Justice Statistics. One study concluded that 67% of inmates released from state prisons committed at least one serious crime within 3 years of release (Langan & Levin, 2002). There were, to be sure, substantial differences in recidivism among inmates. Car thieves, burglars, and larcenists had the highest recidivism rates (about 70%) while rapists (2.5%) and murderers (1.2%) had the lowest rates. Other studies of either state or federal prisons (e.g., Glaser's pioneering and massive study, 1964) have reported slightly different figures, and it is not our intent to review all pertinent studies to ascertain the "real" recidivism rates. For the sake of argument, let's just agree on the following: At least half of inmates released from prison have a good chance of being considered recidivists.

Working in the criminal justice system is not easy. As a practitioner, for example, one can feel that a particular case is doing well and that the prognosis is very good; but one can be disappointed by negative events the very next day. It does not take too many times for this to happen to affect job satisfaction and morale. There is stress, low pay, and the usual workplace politics. But added to that is extremely high expectations about the effectiveness of correctional programs. To some, rehabilitation and the other goals of corrections are achieved only if a former correctional client never commits another crime. We would argue that such an expectation is too stringent a criterion of effectiveness. Imagine if such a standard were applied to hospitals. Hospitals are effective only if a former patient never gets sick, sees a doctor, or is rehospitalized. That, too, is too stringent.

When I (Meier) was a boy, I seemed to get strep throat over and over again. Each time, I would be taken to our pediatrician and given penicillin. I absolutely hated those shots. Did the penicillin "work"? Yes, I was cured of strep throat. But the penicillin did not prevent the next instance of the disease. Perhaps correctional programs work the same way.

Maybe probation, prison, and parole should be thought about in a similar manner. We see relatively few people who never commit crimes again, particularly after release from prison ("maxing out") and on parole. These are individuals for whom criminality is a deep behavior pattern who are released to the same environment from which they came in the first place. Many will go back to street gangs. Others will struggle with their freedom because they've had little practice being "straight."

Having worked in probation and in a prison, we think that perhaps new criteria should be adopted. Maybe a former correctional client who is committing fewer crimes should be considered a success. Or the former client who is committing the same number of crimes but less serious ones than previously is causing much less damage to the community. Or the former client who is committing the same kinds of crimes as before is doing so over a longer period of time. The concept of recidivism masks these important distinctions.

There are measurement issues that must also be addressed. There is no agreed on measure of recidivism. Conceptually, recidivism means committing another crime, either a repeat of the original offense or a new crime. Since there is no obvious way to measure this reliably, researchers have opted to use one of three measures: rearrest, reconviction, and reinstitutionalization. And depending on which measure is used, different estimates of recidivism will be reported. The rate will be higher with rearrest, intermediate with reconviction, and the least with reinstitutionalization.

Now, consider the same issues with ex-patients from a hospital. Let us now consider parallel measures of getting sick or injured again. We would use whether the person contacted a physician (comparable to rearrest), whether the person was treated as an outpatient (reconvicted), or whether the person was readmitted to a hospital (reinstitutionalization). More former patients will contact their physician again than will those who receive outpatient treatment, and the fewest will be readmitted to the hospital. But does it make sense to evaluate hospitals in this manner? Do such measures really provide us with evidence on the effectiveness of hospitals? These, and similar questions, could be asked about the comparable measures of prison effectiveness.

We've seen probationers who would start their period of probation strong, with substantial motivation to avoid crime. But then, they would experience some setback at home or work. We could arrange for marriage counseling, but we could not guarantee the probationer and the spouse would attend. We could arrange to increase the probationer's work skills, but a quick temper that alienates the boss and those skills are useless. Just as one of our criminal justice interns said:

> I had been talking with her [a probationer] for about a half an hour and I realized that I really didn't know what to say that would keep her off drugs that someone else had already said. I would just be repeating the same old Nancy Reagan line: Just say no! And it just wasn't enough. I really felt helpless. (S. S., personal communication, 2010)

We are well aware of the dangers of comparing prison effectiveness with hospital effectiveness. Patients are mostly in the hospital voluntarily; inmates are not. We are aware that physicians have more problem-specific treatment, while prison officials do not, having more general programs. And we are aware that patients have self-interest in getting better, while probationers, inmates, and paroles may not. Nevertheless, we think it interesting that standards applied to one institution do not seem to apply to another.

❖ CONCLUSION

Experiential learning has the advantage of being direct and personal, while it has the disadvantage of being singular because we cannot have many different experiences. Internships can be an important supplement to vicarious, or classroom, learning if only because they provide a different way to comprehend the world.

Experiential learning also has consequences for how the individual interprets criminal justice events and processes. Learning that there are different objectives of the criminal justice system may not prepare one to actually find mechanisms to accomplish those objectives. There are also consequences for interpreting the meaning of those mechanisms, such as the meaning of recidivism. Although perceptions gained from experience and the degree of interest in a particular field may vary, experiential learning can only benefit an individual as well as enrich and supplement vicarious learning.

❖ REFERENCES

Glaser, D. (1964). *The effectiveness of a prison and parole system*. Indianapolis, IN: Bobbs-Merrill.

Korn, R. R., & McCorkle, L. W. (1959). *Criminology and penology*. New York: Holt, Rinehart & Winston.

Langan, P. A., & Levin, D. J. (2002). *Recidivism of prisoners released in 1994*. Washington, DC: Bureau of Justice Statistics, Office of Justice Programs.

❖ RECOMMENDED READINGS

Gordon, G. R., & McBride, R. B. (2008). *Criminal justice internships: Theory into practice* (6th ed.). Cincinnati, OH: Anderson.

Hassine, V. (2009). *Life without parole: Living in prison today* (4th ed.). New York: Oxford University Press.

Maltz, M. D. (2001). *Recidivism*. (Original work published 1984. Orlando, FL: Academic Press). Available at *http://www.uic.edu/depts/lib/forr/pdf/crimjust/recidivism.pdf*

Packer, H. (1968). *The limits of the criminal sanction*. Stanford, CA: Stanford University Press.

DISCUSSION QUESTIONS

1. What is vicarious learning? What is experiential learning? What is the relative value of each? Do you prefer one type over the other and, if so, which one? Explain your answer.

2. Briefly describe the four benefits of internships identified by the authors. What other benefits can you think of? (Identify at least four.)

3. In which ways have course-related learning and experiential learning taught you conflicting ideas about criminal justice? For example, do books and your teachers "tell you one thing," while personal experiences with criminal justice "tell you another"? How can you resolve these conflicts? (Will you choose one over the other or reconcile the two?) Explain.

17

Conclusion

A Review of the Essays

Lee Michael Johnson

This final chapter provides an overall review of the essays contained in this book. It highlights major points and issues and comments on the significance of each essay. While this book does not provide comprehensive coverage of specific correctional environments, it does offer a useful sampling from the three general types: incarceration, community corrections, and juvenile corrections. More specifically the essays provide glimpses into working in prisons or prison systems, probation and parole, and juvenile corrections (residential and community). This chapter is organized according to these areas.

❖ WORKING IN PRISONS

To begin, in Chapter 7, Professor Chesseman Dial discusses her work overseeing a research program for a state prison system. An administrator in charge of implementing a new systemwide workplace culture program, Cheeseman Dial worked at several prisons across the state. The program was designed to examine staff morale, professionalism, communication, and offender climate for the purpose of designing strategies to improve the prison environment for employees (both supervisors and staff) and prisoners. Implementing the program required gaining the trust and participation of employees and prisoners and getting them to believe in the new program—a difficult mission given the tendency of organizations to resist change. To do so, Cheeseman Dial employed a set of established human resource management strategies (displayed in Table 7.1 of her chapter) predicated on the philosophy "if you take care of your people, they . . . will take care of you." A key part of her approach was using input from supervisors and staff in developing the program and attempting to strengthen the workplace, as opposed to imposing an externally developed model upon them, which fosters an atmosphere of teamwork. This approach is consistent with a Total Quality Management (TQM) administrative management model (see Deming's 14 points in her chapter).

Cheeseman Dial's leadership approach was very clear: Don't just manage but lead, and get employees to change their attitudes and behavior by empowering them. While she encountered difficulties and found that implementation for the program was far from ideal, her experiences, including feedback from many of those with whom she worked, led Chesseman Dial to believe that employing human resource management strategies helped her improve correctional work environments and supervisors and administrators with employee-centered styles to create happier, healthier, more productive work forces. In addition to demonstrating the usefulness of connecting organizational administration scholarship to practice, Professor Cheeseman Dial demonstrates how important it is to learn research methodology; because of her research skills, she was selected for her position from a highly competitive applicant pool.

Professor Ross (Chapter 5) also discusses administrative issues but from the perspective of a former frontline staff employee. As a psychiatric assistant in a prison–psychiatric hospital that provided mental health evaluation and care for pretrial and presentence individuals and prerelease prisoners, Ross experienced what he found to be serious flaws in institutional management and employee supervision. His analysis compares the theory of TQM with actual managerial practices at the hospital. TQM is an administrative model that emphasizes, among other things, workers' well-being and their participation in running organizations. Ross argues that while there are problems with putting TQM into practice, a top-down model of power and decision making that ignores the input of frontline workers is even worse. His narrative shows that disregard for staff harms morale and reduces staff's ability to help achieve the goals of the institution, ultimately leading to increased stress upon supervision and management. In describing the contradictions between ideal and actual institutional functioning, Ross identifies seven specific problems that can be seen as lessons for staff–management relations: (1) Policies and practices must be well conceived, clearly articulated, thoroughly documented, and consistently applied. (2) The qualifications and duties attached to a position should match the professional prestige attached to it. (3) Employees must be of sound mind and character, highly capable of making good decisions. (4) Employees must be provided with adequate training and equipment. (5) Adequate time off must be provided to prevent burnout, or psychological distress. (6) Frontline staff need to be equally involved—not just symbolically—in running "the milieu," the presumably therapeutic day-to-day interactions between staff and residents taking place in the unit. (7) And academic research must reflect a thorough understanding of corrections and mental health practice.

Some, administrators and supervisors, for example, may find what Ross has to say about his employment experience to be rather harsh, but to dismiss his views would be to ignore his useful insights. Like other authors, he struggled to "make a difference"—improve the organization, work environment, and ultimately the clients—against several obstacles and constraints. He points out important sources of employee stress—regimented work environment, routine, lack of autonomy, frustration, boredom—as well as some "not so helpful" coping responses such as substance use, reducing care and effort in one's work, and passive-aggressive acts against authority. However, Professor Ross's role as shop steward shows how a dissatisfied employee can use legitimate means to effectively improve the quality of the workplace, in contrast to resorting to antagonistic behavior that hurts workplace quality and organizational functioning.

Other authors in this book (Durán, Penn, and Johnson) also write from frontline staff experience. A frontline perspective is an important, useful view to take into account in corrections. Because staff members are immersed in the day-to-day interaction with persons under correctional supervision in specific environments, they are responsible for carrying out the goals of corrections in very tangible ways, and they can report on problems and successes not immediately visible to administrators and supervisors. However, because staff members tend not to know "the world" of administration and for a variety of other reasons, higher authorities may be hesitant to base decisions on staff input. The extremes of frontline employee participation should be avoided: allowing them to make major decisions without scrutiny and giving them no say at all. At times, staff input may not be helpful due to lack of knowledge, human error, or even dishonesty or selfish motives. Staff criticism may often stem from an organizational subculture of complaint characterized by low staff morale. However, if this is the case, then there may be something wrong with an agency's organizational structure and/or managerial strategy. (If the problem is simply bad employees, then the agency would need to seriously reconsider its hiring practices.) It is in management's interest to pay attention to frequent unconstructive feedback by staff, not to take it as directives but as symptoms of deeper problems. Staff empowerment does not necessarily mean giving employees equal power in major administrative decision making (it does not mean that the supervisor or administrator is not the boss), and taking staff members' input seriously does not mean giving in to all of their demands. Rather, staff empowerment means drawing from the frontline knowledge and abilities that are needed to achieve institutional goals. Ultimately, staff and management need each other, so conflict between the two, arising from management's disregard for staff or staff's disregard for management, harms staff, management, and the organization as a whole.

In contrast to an administrator or staff member view, Professor Polizzi (Chapter 6) provides the perspective of a clinician. Approaching the subject of prisoner mental health, he discusses the challenges of providing therapy to incarcerated clients, particularly by applying humanistic psychology. Polizzi's insights are especially important for persons interested in providing treatment in corrections. His experiences illustrate the conflict that often exists within corrections between factions with different goals, concerns, and backgrounds. Polizzi identifies the need of the individual and the institution to somehow reconcile psychotherapists' pursuit of treatment with officers' pursuit of security. Psychotherapists and others concerned primarily with helping prisoners are often viewed with suspicion, perhaps seen as outsiders, and may face interference from staff and other professionals. This may be especially true for those working from client-centered theoretical and professional perspectives, such as humanistic psychology. There may be a prevailing assumption that anyone working in the prison regardless of what they do should be primarily loyal to the institution. This situation puts pressure on helping professionals to adopt the dominant correctional subculture, which would seem to compromise their efforts to help clients.

One of the problems that treatment professionals face is the widely held belief that offenders manipulate therapists, counselors, and social workers in their efforts to fake transformation and gain early release or other advantages. Although this belief may to some extent be justified, Polizzi identifies prisoners who had no apparent possibility of gaining early release but nonetheless became actively involved in therapy and showed evidence of undergoing true change. Thus, Professor Polizzi demonstrates that despite facing obstacles and widespread pessimism, one can be successful in providing treatment in a correctional setting and applying academic knowledge to practice.

Professor Furst (Chapter 8) also tried to help prisoners by advocating for their rights. A self-labeled outsider, she worked for an agency that oversees and monitors a state prison system. As she points out, individuals working on behalf of "criminals" are widely viewed with skepticism by corrections employees and the public. Many may lack compassion for people who have broken the law and presumably hurt others. However, prisoner advocacy is an important part of making the criminal justice system work properly in a civil society because it helps guard against institutional and individual misconduct, human rights violations, and "cruel and unusual punishment." Like Polizzi, Furst faced many obstacles in carrying out her work, including interference or lack of cooperation from other corrections workers. In her many visits to prisons, Furst found several problems with prison environments and practices, such as using intentionally bad tasting food as punishment and failure to properly respond to mental illnesses. She attempted to do something about these problems by recommending changes to authorities.

In her conclusion, Furst reveals how difficult it is to make a desirable impact while working in corrections. She reports that her recommendations had no impact on prison administration. As she points out, prisons are bureaucratic systems that by nature are resistant to change. Because her work did not appear to result in improving people's lives, she decided to leave her job. Her essay should not suggest that one should give up or not try to improve corrections, however, but sometimes, a person has to decide if there are other ways in which she or he can make a difference. Her work at least had a beneficial impact on her. She notes that she appreciates having had the opportunity to work in corrections and learned very much from her experiences. Furst decided to work toward change by becoming a professor and educating future leaders in corrections.

While touring prisons, Furst personally observed the racial and ethnic disparities indicated by statistics—that despite making up a smaller portion of the U.S. population, minorities—primarily African Americans and Latinos—constitute the majority of the country's jail and prison population, while whites make up the majority of those who run and work in correctional facilities. Furst sensed the racial tensions existing in prison. While she recognizes that prison is a tough environment for women as well as men, she did notice major gender differences. There may be less violence in women's prisons, but female prisoners face different struggles, such as the loss of their children and experiencing different kinds of emotional distress. Thus, as Furst points out, *prisonization*—a socialization process in which a person adapts and conforms to prison life—is different for women. Professor Furst also had a chance to view the experiences of elderly prisoners. Life and long-term sentences combined with an increasing prison population and the aging of the population in general mean that elderly issues are becoming more significant in corrections. One of these issues is medical costs, which are higher inside prisons—a problem that may lead lawmakers and other authorities to reconsider the necessity of mandatory sentences and stiff penalties decided on seemingly arbitrary criteria like "three strikes."

Professor Lombardo (Chapter 9) taught prisoners at the historically significant Auburn Prison in New York. He gives a bit of a corrections history lesson as well as a window into what it may have been like to work in prison during the "pendulum swing" from the emphasis on rehabilitation during the 1960s to the emphasis on punishment during the 1970s. Lombardo makes important connections between his experiences and scholarship while offering lessons to another generation of corrections workers faced with navigating major social changes. He wanted to help prisoners improve their lives by educating them, which he found difficult to do against institutional pressure to put more of a security emphasis on his position. Conscientious correctional workers usually experience conflict between their ideologically driven desire to help people and the reality of restrictions and obstacles built into a failing "system." Many feel compelled to somehow steer through these barriers to achieve noble goals, and some become inspired to engage in activism intended to change the system. Professor Lombardo implicates a dominant way of thinking among correctional authorities as the source of many institutional shortcomings. He recommends that authorities think with new perspectives, including those from academia, and maintain human beings as the focus of problem-solving strategies.

Like some of the other authors, Professor Unnithan (Chapter 15) worked for a state correctional system, not a particular prison, illustrating that there are a variety of jobs in corrections in addition to prison and juvenile center administrators, counselors and therapists, correctional officers, and probation and parole officers. As a specialist in a planning and research bureau, Unnithan participated in conducting program evaluations and research projects and in providing other information that his state department of corrections and rehabilitation used to respond to problems and make organizational changes. His application of sociological principles of organizations to the structure and functioning of correctional organizations shows that employment experience can make academic concepts more interesting in addition to understandable and relevant.

The essays in this book present a variety of perspectives such as frontline (Ross, for example), administrative (Cheeseman Dial), clinical (Polizzi), and outsider (Furst). Professor Unnithan introduces yet another one—a "brief insider's perspective." Unlike pure outsiders, brief insiders have direct experience working in specific environments and are thus potentially more responsive to the challenges of the job. At the same time, brief insiders have not worked in an environment long enough to become absorbed into the workplace culture and thus may be more inclined to think critically and sociologically about the organizations for which they work. Because of this sort of limbo, a brief insider may "see things" that others do not. Another lesson the essays offer is that opinions regarding the purposes and functioning of an organization or larger system depend largely on the perspective used to evaluate it and that one's perspective depends significantly on one's position relative to the organization or system (outsider or insider, brief or long-term employee, administrator or supervisor or frontline staff, etc.). This should explain in part why practitioners and scholars in corrections do not "see eye-to-eye" on several matters.

❖ WORKING IN PROBATION AND PAROLE

Professor Fuller (Chapter 2) was both a probation and parole officer during a time when community corrections, a type of corrections intended to be more rehabilitative, also was affected by the 1970s conservative shift back to an emphasis on punishment. Like Lombardo, Fuller experienced role conflict while trying to be a rehabilitator in a correctional system and political climate geared more toward punishment and security. He offers a frank and honest account of the pressures of his job and the problems that occurred while trying to help his clients. His experiences illustrate how things can go wrong with external circumstances (such as bureaucracy, politics, and lack of resources) as well as one's own efforts. In addition to policies and programs (intensive supervision, for example), individual efforts can have consequences opposite to those which are intended. Actions taken to help clients can sometimes be used to facilitate deviance, as when clients use group therapy to build criminal networks.

In applying academics to practice, Fuller specifically draws from established theories of crime causation and counseling. Although he finds working in corrections without a theoretical basis to be problematic, he also shows that applying social science is not easy and will not always yield desirable results. It is very disappointing when one comes up with good ideas and thinks that he or she is really doing something to help people only to find out that this is not the case. This is especially true when the corrections worker "gets burned"—deceived or betrayed by those he or she is trying to help. Even when taking an intellectual approach, achieving noble goals in corrections work will be very difficult, though not impossible.

To continue working toward making a difference, persons entering employment corrections will likely have to account for their naïveté. It will take more than a good heart and good ideas to help people—for example, the wisdom, not to be confused with pessimism and defeatism, that can come with experience. Professor Fuller warns that burnout is an occupational hazard of corrections, not to discourage people from working in corrections but to prepare them to deal with the challenges of the profession and thus find more success in achieving their goals. It is important to note that his experiences also show how helpful probation and parole officers can be, as when they help their clients find or maintain employment, which is crucial to keeping ex-offenders tied to the community and out of trouble.

Professor Strobl (Chapter 3) worked as a federal presentence officer, a type of probation officer who works for the federal government investigating cases involving persons accused of breaking *federal* laws (most probation officers work at the state level). Many of the defendants in Strobl's caseload were poor women from different countries who worked as "drug mules," or more technically, "drug couriers." Couriers are referred to as mules because they tend to be used and mistreated, exploited really, in the illegal drug trade. Couriers do the "dirty work" of transporting drugs on their person, possibly risking more detection and punishment compared to the higher level drug traffickers for whom they work. A courier can be an impoverished, desperate person lured by money, which presents a challenge to criminal justice processes. Strobl's account shows that it can be tough to cope with cases in which persons are as much victims as offenders, especially when they face punitive sentencing without consideration of mitigating circumstances connected to socioeconomic status. Strobl identifies narrow sentencing guidelines, a reflection of corrections' emphasis on punishment and control that continued into and throughout the 1990s, that ignore factors such as the detected person's culpability in the crime. Importantly, she places local corrections work in its proper global context, recognizing the part that political-economic globalization and global inequality plays in making women in low-income countries vulnerable to criminal exploitation.

Like other essays, Strobl's identifies monotony as a threat to work satisfaction as well as the conflict one experiences between idealistic expectations of being able to do something good for society and working in a position, organization, and broader social institution or "system" that seems to be designed to benefit only a few special interests (economic, political, and of the correctional organizations themselves) at the expense of the rest of society. Though she, like many who have worked in corrections and social services, became disenchanted with her profession, Professor Strobl's experiences showed how meaningful her prior studies of social theory, globalization, and inequality were to the "real world" of criminal justice. Also, she ends on an optimistic note. Recent U.S. Supreme Court decisions seem to be giving federal courts more discretion in deciding drug sentences that should make the information that presentence investigators gather about defendants' circumstances more important and thus the job a little more appealing to conscientious probation officers.

Social inequality is one of the most important issues currently facing criminal justice practice and scholarship. It is up to scholars and practitioners alike to understand the part that social inequality plays in crime and justice and to eliminate biases in justice processes that are based on social statuses, such as race and ethnicity, sex and gender, and social class. Social inequality is a major focus in essays such as Professor Barfield-Cottledge's (Chapter 10). As a state parole officer, she was charged with, among other duties, helping ex-prisoners reenter the community after long periods of incarceration. Incarceration results in lost resources and ties to the outside community, which makes transitioning back to society difficult. Thus, released prisoners have needs—education, employment, housing, counseling, health care, and prosocial relationships, for example—that must be met for successful reentry. Prisoner reentry period is a critical period; failure to successfully integrate into the community can lead to re-offending. Barfield-Cottledge offers insights into the challenges of helping parolees overcome obstacles in reestablishing their lives outside bars.

Having worked with a diverse population, Barfield-Cottledge discusses the additional reentry challenges faced by women and racial and ethnic minorities in her caseload as well as the difficulties she faced in responding to their particular needs. She found that for female parolees, reentry often also meant solving problems associated with abuse victimization, pregnancy, children, and other family issues. Also, racial and ethnic minorities made up the majority of her parolees, which presented her with additional challenges in helping them with reentry. Citing research, she points out that while all ex-prisoners face limited educational, employment, housing, and health care opportunities, minority ex-prisoners are subject to additional strain due to racial and ethnic discrimination and socially disorganized neighborhoods. Barfield-Cottledge also discusses another current major issue: working with sex offenders. While drug offenders made up the majority of her caseload, she also worked with a significant number of serious violent and sexual offenders. Since she was responsible for helping everyone in her caseload with reentry, she had to be concerned not only with the supervision of sex offenders but also with problems they faced such as restrictions on where to live and work as well as potential retaliation by members of the community. Professor Barfield-Cottledge underscores the importance of having resources that offset the social strain ex-prisoners face during reentry, suggesting that one solution to the problem of recidivism lies in providing ex-prisoners with the assistance needed to overcome their educational, economic, and social deficits when attempting to fit into the community.

Professor Wodahl (Chapter 4) worked as an intensive supervision program (ISP) agent, another type of community corrections officer. As the name suggests, intensive supervision is a more restrictive type of control placed on community sanctioned individuals, mostly those on probation or parole, who are at higher risk of re-offending. Intensive supervision can involve measures such as electronic monitoring (ankle devices) and random drug testing but is characterized more by increased contact with officers with smaller caseloads and deeper involvement in treatment programs. Relatively new, ISPs are intended to improve rehabilitation and save money by keeping offenders in the community instead of prison, while the increased intensity of supervision responds to the need for public safety. Although his position placed more emphasis on supervision, Wodahl, like traditional probation and parole officers, provided a variety of services to persons in his caseload; ISP agents too are charged with attempting to simultaneously help clients while protecting society from them.

Wodahl uses his personal experiences to assess how effective ISP was at achieving its (often conflicting) goals, which he identifies as reducing prison overcrowding, saving money, providing more appropriate punishment, improving public safety, and improving rehabilitation. He focused on more than just whether or not his clients were rearrested, and because his caseload was so diverse, he devised an interesting and provocative client typology by which to judge the impact of the program: the Good—less serious but usually chronic offenders who presented the lowest risk to public safety; the Bad—more serious offenders who presented a more substantial risk to public safety; and the Ugly— typically violent and sexual offenders who presented the greatest risk to public safety. Professor Wodahl found the ISP to be successful in achieving many of its goals but that this success depended on the interaction between the type of offender and the characteristics of the ISP; for some goals, ISP worked for some types but not others. His analysis not only illustrates the importance of accounting for several contingencies when judging program effectiveness, but also gives reasons to be optimistic about the potential of community corrections.

❖ WORKING IN JUVENILE CORRECTIONS

Professor Durán (Chapter 11) discusses two jobs that he held: a youth worker at a private residential treatment facility and a youth security officer at a state juvenile correctional facility. Residential treatment facilities or centers, usually operated by nonprofit social service agencies, typically house low to moderate risk offenders or more serious offenders given a "last chance" before being sent to a secure juvenile correctional facility. Their residents often also have victimization, family disruption, mental health, and intellectual functioning issues determining their placement. Secure juvenile correctional facilities house serious juvenile offenders whose criminal offending becomes the focal point of placement. They are the type of juvenile correctional setting that most resembles adult prison, although they too are supposed to be treatment based. Durán experienced what most corrections workers encounter: a disproportionate number of racial and ethnic minorities, primarily Latinos and African Americans, sanctioned by the juvenile and adult criminal justice systems (*disproportionate* here meaning that minorities' percentage of people under correctional supervision is significantly larger than their percentage of the local or national population). His essay has three general areas of importance: He discusses racial and ethnic inequality in juvenile justice from his perspective as a minority youth worker, student, and scholar who wanted to put more social justice in juvenile justice.

While he looks back fondly on his experiences, identifies favorable aspects of juvenile corrections, and appears to have met several good people, Durán also encountered instances of discrimination against minority youth. Societal-level inequality is manifested in interpersonal relationships in particular environmental settings, including corrections. Inspired by his studies in sociology, Durán thought it important to employ the sociological imagination and knowledge of the dynamics of social inequality in his work. As he learned, it is difficult to put knowledge derived from sociology into practice because it often implies changing social structures and the way other people behave, not just adjusting one's own behavior. His experiences show that working toward social change from within a social system, though not impossible, can be very limiting. However, as Professor Durán points out, correctional employees have the power to avoid actively replicating the racial and ethnic biases existing across the wider society. Countering racism in corrections work is not just a matter of proper moral behavior; it is essential to rehabilitation and the prevention of re-offending. System-involved persons have presumably harmed others with their behavior—treated them unfairly. Can a corrections professional expect a juvenile or adult offender to treat others justly when one does not act justly him- or herself? As many youth workers know, hypocrisy is very detrimental to treatment.

Professor Johnson (Chapter 12) draws from his experience as a youth worker in a residential treatment facility to provide another frontline perspective. Johnson argues that by helping youth pursue their personal interests, such as art, staff members can significantly contribute to treatment and make their jobs better in the process. He found consistencies between his experiences in supporting artistic activities and the educational, therapeutic, socially integrative, and managerial benefits of art in corrections identified in the literature, which could explain why he was able to have enjoyable experiences working with youth with serious offending and victimization issues. He believes that by helping youth to pursue their interests, he was able to establish rapport and build productive relationships with youth, manage behavior, and improve the workplace environment. Also, Professor Johnson offers another possible strategy for reducing job stress: use creative and recreational activities to counteract stressors (the sources of stress), such as interpersonal conflict, boredom, violence and aggression, and visually unappealing surroundings.

Professor Reyes (Chapter 13) held multiple positions in juvenile and adult probation and parole. Thus, she is in a unique position to compare juvenile and adult community corrections. Probation and parole officers provide a wide variety of important public services, and Reyes appears to have "done it all" in probation and parole work. These officers are not just community agents of control and punishment; they also provide services intended to meet clients' needs as a part of preventing criminality. This involves having a variety of personal and social skills to be used in several types of close interactions with clients and important people around them. Perhaps the purpose of probation and parole officers is to help offenders, and consequently the community, more than punish them.

Reyes identifies important safety issues that future and current probation and parole officers should be concerned with, and she recognizes that some of the factors and processes identified in differential association and social learning theories were evident during her interactions with probationers and parolees and their families. Further, her positions illustrate how knowing a second language can benefit a career in corrections. Professor Reyes's analysis of her experiences seems to offer some general principles useful in any potentially dangerous helping profession: cooperate with clients and those with whom they have close relationships as much as possible, establish rapport and earn the respect of clients and others, always be aware of potential danger, try to diffuse not just react to dangerous situations, and remember wisdom not bravado makes a corrections worker safer and more effective.

Like Professor Durán, Penn (Chapter 14) discusses racial and ethnic inequality in juvenile justice. Among other valuable experiences in criminal justice and community building, Penn worked as a child care worker in a residential treatment facility for youth offenders. He paints a detailed picture of a residential treatment facility that, again, is intended to resemble a homelike environment instead of an "institution." Penn makes a profound connection between scholarship and practice by describing how his practical experiences, ranging from volunteer work to creating programs, has gone hand-in-hand with his scholarly studies as both a student and a professor. It appears that Penn finds academic knowledge to be very useful to practice as he has been intertwining the two for quite some time now.

Like the justice system as a whole, the juvenile facility in which Penn worked held a disproportionately higher number of racial and ethnic minorities, primarily blacks and Latinos. He was exposed to the socioeconomic disadvantages of minority youth as well as the violent subcultures to which many were exposed and in his essay uses two of the minority youth with whom he worked as interesting illustrations.

However, Penn argues that the current state of disproportionate minority confinement (DMC) is not incidental or just a result of current social circumstances. He addresses the social and historical context in which DMC developed, which was shaped within the development of the very concept of adolescence, the perception of juvenile offenders as children in need of help, and the juvenile justice system. Penn points out that in early U.S. history, the concept of adolescence does not appear to have been developed with minority children in mind. Slave children, for example, were not raised to be autonomous adults and thus were not provided with a preadulthood socialization stage. Even after the end of slavery, the belief that adolescents are not as responsible for their behavior as adults and can still be molded into good people was not equally applied to African American youth. Professor Penn raises an important concern for criminal justice scholarship and practice: the possibility that race and ethnicity are being included as indicators of corrigibility (the potential to be rehabilitated) in justice processes. Intentional or not, this type of discrimination interferes with civil rights, reduces treatment effectiveness, and serves to replicate social inequality.

❖ CONCLUSION

Discussing the last essay by Meier and Smith (Chapter 16) is a good way to conclude as it helps place the book in a larger educational-professional context. Their piece is a departure from the others. It deals with a type of criminal justice work that is a hybrid of academics and practice thereby directly confronting the issue of connecting scholarship and practice: the supervised internship. Professor Meier, a one-time probation officer, has coordinated internships, and Teresa Smith is a former intern and current practitioner. They argue that crime and justice studies can be not only a matter of "vicarious learning" from others (from textbooks, videos, and lectures, for example) but also a matter of "experiential learning"—learning firsthand through direct experience with subjects being studied (such as internships and practicum). The authors in this book have benefited from the combination of experiential and vicarious learning in corrections. Through internships, practicum, and other experiential learning strategies, students too can benefit from this combination.

Generally, through direct contact, criminal justice internships teach students more about offenders and how criminal justice systems work. For example, interns can see the problems that occur when correctional agencies try to achieve the often conflicting goals of retribution, incapacitation, rehabilitation, and deterrence, and they can witness the many variations in recidivism (re-offending)—an often oversimplified concept. Meier and Smith identify four specific benefits that help make internships valuable. First, the concrete reality makes a heavy impression upon learners. Second, one can become more aware of the manipulative and impression management behaviors often used by offenders. Reducing naïveté without becoming jaded is good preparation for entering the field. Third, one can see the importance of social distance between corrections workers and sanctioned persons. Rapport does not mean establishing a personal relationship. Fourth, the intern gets a preview of a prospective career—a more concrete impression of what it would be like to work in a position—so that one can decide if he or she really wants to work in it.

While internships and other experiential learning activities offer opportunities to illuminate concepts taught in courses and even learn things not taught in courses, they have an important limitation to recognize: One cannot make generalizations on the basis of individual experience. A corrections internship, for example, does not teach the intern "how corrections work." This is where vicarious learning can help out—information communicated from others can help one get a bigger picture of what is going on across the field. As pointed out in the introductory chapter, making connections between academic knowledge taught in courses (acquired through vicarious learning) and what is discovered in a field setting (through experiential learning) during internships and other field experiences is very difficult. This is a challenge not only for students but also for academic and site supervisors and coordinators. The importance of Professor Meier and Teresa Smith's essay is that they offer some direction in meeting this challenge.

Today, academic scholars continue to be seen by many as out of touch with the real world, tucked away in their secluded colleges and universities, and what they publish and teach is widely thought to have no use in daily life. After beginning with a strong desire to apply their education but later struggling to find the relevance between academics and practice, students may also come to hold this perception. Practitioners are often resistant to academics; scholars frequently threaten deeply held beliefs and values and suggest changes that interfere with special interest agendas. Although the perception of academics as impractical is undeserved, there is not a large amount of research and publication focused on connecting academics and practice, and like other professionals, scholars may become preoccupied with the immediate demands of their positions that steer them toward a kind of isolation. However, there does not have to be a gulf between academia and practice. Many scholars, practitioners, and students believe that the two can and should be brought together. Together, all parties can engage in teaching and learning activities that close the gap between vicarious and experiential learning in the study and practice of criminal justice, including corrections.

Working in corrections is very challenging and may not be for everyone, but it can also be rewarding. There are many career opportunities in corrections and people interested in the field should be encouraged to explore it. Academics can potentially improve corrections and help make working in it more rewarding. Indeed, most crime and justice scholarship—whether it is research, theory, or policy analysis—is very concerned with helping practice. However, there need to be ways to transport the usefulness of academic knowledge to practice and the usefulness of practical knowledge back to academics. The educated individual is a powerful vehicle for transporting feedback between academics and practice. The collection of essays in this book is offered to help individuals develop their abilities to connect academics and practice and, in doing so, increase their power to improve practice and make corrections work more rewarding.

❖ RECOMMENDED READINGS

Cornelius, G. (2001). *Art of the con: Avoiding offender manipulation.* Lanham, MD: American Correctional Association.

Dilulio, J., Jr. (1990). *Governing prisons: A comparative study of correctional management.* New York: Free Press.

Pollock, J. M. (2004). *Prisons and prison life: Costs and consequences.* Los Angeles: Roxbury.

Ross, J. I. (2008). *Special problems in corrections.* Upper Saddle River, NJ: Pearson.

Ross, J. I., & Richards, S. C. (Eds.) (2003). *Convict criminology.* Belmont, CA: Wadsworth.

DISCUSSION QUESTIONS

1. What do *you* think are the most important points made in this book? Which ideas, issues, problems, solutions, and so on would or do you plan to focus on in corrections or other criminal justice work?

2. In which ways has this book changed your mind about your perceptions of corrections? In which ways has it confirmed or disconfirmed your perceptions of corrections?

3. If you could change one thing in corrections, what would it be and why? Please be elaborate.

Index

About the Editor

Lee Michael Johnson is an assistant professor of criminology at the University of West Georgia. He earned a PhD in Sociology from Iowa State University, and his background includes work with behavior-disordered and delinquent youth in residential treatment. His research and writing interests are in juvenile delinquency, victimology, and criminal justice policy and practice, and he has published articles in journals such as *Youth and Society, Journal of Social Psychology, Czech Sociological Review, Southwest Journal of Criminal Justice,* and the *International Journal of Criminal Justice Sciences.* Dr. Johnson regularly teaches juvenile delinquency, victimology, family violence, race and crime, and research methods courses.

About the Contributors

Tiffiney Barfield-Cottledge is an assistant professor in the Department of Criminal Justice at the University of North Texas at Dallas. She received a BS degree in Criminal Justice and a MA and PhD from Prairie View A&M University. Dr. Barfield-Cottledge has worked in various positions in the criminal justice field, such as a state parole officer, child support officer, and researcher, and she has over 12 years' experience as a counselor. In 2003, she worked with the Arrestee Drug Abuse Monitoring (ADAM) project researching drug use and abuse among recently arrested males in Harris County, Texas. Dr. Barfield-Cottledge is published in the *Criminal Justice Review* and has an upcoming article in the *Encyclopedia of Race and Crime*. She has presented various papers at regional and national conferences, and her current research interests involve juvenile justice and delinquency, female gangs and delinquency, criminological theory, juvenile sex offenders, drug use and abuse, and racial conflict. Dr. Barfield-Cottledge regularly teaches courses on judicial and legal issues, offender behavior, criminology, and juvenile delinquency.

Kelly Cheeseman Dial is an associate professor of criminal justice at Messiah College. She received her PhD from Sam Houston State University. Her current research interests include female offenders, prison deviance, correctional officer stress and job satisfaction, institutional corrections, the death penalty, ethics, and sexually deviant behavior. Dr. Cheeseman Dial has published articles in journals such as the *Journal of Criminal Justice, Journal of Criminal Justice Education, American Journal of Criminal Justice*, and *Deviant Behavior*. She has also coauthored a book on the death penalty.

Robert J. Durán is an assistant professor of criminal justice at New Mexico State University. He received his PhD in Sociology at the University of Colorado–Boulder in 2006 with an emphasis in criminology and race. His research interests include gangs, aggressive law enforcement, border enforcement, and disproportionate minority contact with the juvenile justice system. Articles can be found in *Aztlán: A Journal of Chicano Studies*, *Journal of Contemporary Ethnography*, *Latino Studies*, and *Social Justice: A Journal of Crime, Conflict, and World Order*.

John Randolph Fuller is a professor of criminology at the University of West Georgia where he has taught for over 28 years. He has experience in the criminal justice system as a probation and parole officer as well as a criminal justice planner. His research interests are in critical criminology, especially peacemaking criminology. He teaches a wide range of courses at both the undergraduate and graduate levels and maintains an active writing agenda. In addition to numerous articles, book chapters, encyclopedia entries, and book reviews, Dr. Fuller has published five books. His most recent book is *Criminal Justice: Mainstream and Cross Currents*, second edition.

Gennifer Furst is an assistant professor in the Sociology Department at William Paterson University of New Jersey. She holds a doctorate in Criminal Justice from City University of New York (CUNY) John Jay College/CUNY Graduate Center. Her research interests include the use of animals in the criminal justice system, drug policy, and the death penalty. Her book, *Animal Programs in Prison: A Comprehensive Assessment*, features the first national survey of prison-based animal programs in the country.

Lucien X. Lombardo started his career in criminal justice as a teacher in the Osborne School at Auburn Correctional Facility from 1969 to 1977, where he taught English and Spanish to students who lived in the maximum-security prison. Dr. Lombardo is a professor of sociology and criminal justice at Old Dominion University, where he has taught since 1977. He received his doctorate from the School of Criminal Justice, State University of New York, Albany in 1978. He also earned an MA in Criminal Justice in 1974, an MA in Latin American Studies from the University of Wisconsin–Madison in 1969, and a BA in Spanish Linguistics from the University of Rochester in 1967. Dr. Lombardo has authored numerous articles and professional presentations in his areas of expertise. Lombardo received Choice Magazine's Outstanding Academic Books in Sociology Award for *Guards Imprisoned: Correctional Officers at Work* (1st and 2nd updated editions). He is coeditor of the second edition of *Prison Violence in America* and coeditor with Dr. Karen Polonko of a volume of the journal *Global Bioethics: Children in a*

Changing World. Dr. Lombardo serves as a board member of End Physical Punishment of Children (EPOCH-USA) working to end corporal punishment of children and a Fellow of the Society for Values in Higher Education.

Robert F. Meier is a professor of criminology and criminal justice at the University of Nebraska at Omaha. He was an intern at a federal prison in Kentucky as an undergraduate and a probation officer in Wisconsin for 3 years before getting his graduate degrees.

Everette B. Penn is an associate professor of criminology and division chair of Behavioral and Social Sciences at the University of Houston–Clear Lake. He is the author of several books and articles on juvenile justice, crime prevention, and homeland security.

David Polizzi is currently an assistant professor with the Department of Criminology and Criminal Justice at Indiana State University and the editor of the e-publication the *Journal of Theoretical and Philosophical Criminology* (jtpcrim.org). He is the contributing coeditor of *Transforming Corrections: Humanistic Approaches in Corrections* and *Offender Treatment and Surviving Your Clinical Placement: Reflections, Suggestions and Unsolicited Advice.* He has also published a variety of journal articles and book chapters related to offender psychotherapy, the social construction of crime and race, and restorative justice as well as the phenomenology of general strain theory and deviance. Prior to his current academic position, he worked for nearly 18 years in a variety of community mental health and penitentiary settings providing psychotherapeutic services to inmate and parole and probation clients as well as individuals diagnosed with a variety of co-occurring disorders. Dr. Polizzi is currently credentialed by the State of Indiana as a Licensed Clinical Addictions Counselor.

Cassandra L. Reyes is an assistant professor of criminal justice at West Chester University of Pennsylvania. Her teaching and research interests include the relationship between animal cruelty and other forms of delinquency and criminality, juvenile delinquency and aggression, violence and victimology, and corrections. She has published in the *Journal of Offender Rehabilitation* and *International Criminal Justice Review.* Additionally, in March 2010, she published a book titled *Of Fists and Fangs: An Exploration of the Degree to Which the Graduation Hypothesis Predicts Adolescent Delinquency and Aggression.* Prior to starting her career in academia, she worked as a probation and parole officer-bilingual for approximately 10 years and briefly as a county correctional officer.

Jeffrey Ian Ross, PhD, is an associate professor in the School of Criminal Justice, College of Public Affairs, and a Fellow of the Center for International and Comparative Law at the University of Baltimore. He has researched, written, and lectured on national security, political violence, political crime, violent crime, corrections, and policing for over 2 decades. Ross's work has appeared in many academic journals and books, as well as popular outlets. He is the author, coauthor, editor, or coeditor of 16 books including *Behind Bars: Surviving Prison, Convict Criminology, Special Problems in Corrections*, and *Beyond Bars: Rejoining Society After Prison*. Ross has performed consulting services for Westat, Comprehensive School Reform (CSR) program; U.S. Department of Defense; Office of Juvenile Justice and Delinquency Prevention, U.S. Department of Justice (USDOJ); the National Institute of Justice, USDOJ; U.S. Department of Homeland Security; and Intel Science Talent Search. From 1995 to 1998, Ross was a Social Science Analyst with the National Institute of Justice, a division of the U.S. Department of Justice. In 2003, he was awarded the University of Baltimore's Distinguished Chair in Research Award. In 2005 and 2006, Ross was a member of the Prisoner Advocate Liaison Group for the Institute of Medicine (part of the National Academy of Sciences). Also, Dr. Ross worked nearly 4 years in a correctional institution. His website is www.jeffreyianross.com.

Teresa F. Smith is a graduate of the University of Nebraska at Omaha where she experienced an internship at the Nebraska Department of Correctional Services in the summer of 2009. She was a correctional officer at the Nebraska Youth Services Facility in Omaha. She is presently an In Home Family Consultant at Boystown.

Staci Strobl is an assistant professor in the Department of Law, Police Science and Criminal Justice Administration at John Jay College of Criminal Justice and the 2009 winner of the British Journal of Criminology's Radzinowicz Memorial Prize for her work on the criminalization of domestic workers in Bahrain. Her areas of specialization are women in policing in the Arabian Gulf, multiethnic policing in Eastern Europe, and comic book portrayals of crime in the United States. Earlier in her career, she worked as a U.S. Probation Officer and a crime journalist. Dr. Strobl completed her doctorate in Criminal Justice at the City University of New York's Graduate Center, received her MA in Criminal Justice at John Jay, and her BA in Near Eastern Studies at Cornell University.

N. Prabha Unnithan completed his bachelor's and master's degrees in Criminology in India before receiving his PhD in Sociology from the

University of Nebraska–Lincoln. He then worked as a planning specialist for the Ohio Department of Rehabilitation and Correction before returning to academe. He has been a sociology faculty member at Colorado State University in Fort Collins since 1987 and currently serves there as the director of the Center for the Study of Crime and Justice. His research and teaching focus on violence, corrections, policy analysis, and evaluation. He has coauthored three books, *The Currents of Lethal Violence: An Integrated Model of Suicide and Homicide, Guns, Violence and Criminal Behavior: The Offender's Perspective,* and *Policing and Society: A Global Approach.* Dr. Unnithan edited the *Journal of Criminal Justice Education* between 1999 and 2002 and currently edits the *Social Science Journal.*

Eric J. Wodahl is an assistant professor of criminal justice at the University of Wyoming. He received his PhD from the School of Criminology and Criminal Justices at the University of Nebraska at Omaha. Wodahl has over 8 years of professional experience in the corrections field working with both juvenile and adult offenders, including 4 years as an intensive supervision program agent. His research interests include alternatives to revocation for noncompliant offenders, prisoner reentry, and rural issues in the criminal justice field. Dr. Wodahl's research has appeared in numerous publications such as *Crime and Delinquency,* the *Prison Journal,* and *Criminal Justice Policy Review.*

SAGE Research Methods Online

The essential tool for researchers

Sign up now at www.sagepub.com/srmo for more information.

An expert research tool

- An **expertly designed taxonomy** with more than 1,400 unique terms for social and behavioral science research methods

- **Visual and hierarchical search tools** to help you discover material and link to related methods

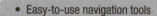

- Easy-to-use navigation tools
- Content organized by complexity
- Tools for citing, printing, and downloading content with ease
- Regularly updated content and features

A wealth of essential content

- The most comprehensive picture of quantitative, qualitative, and mixed methods available today

- More than **100,000 pages of SAGE book and reference material** on research methods as well as editorially selected material from SAGE journals

- More than **600 books** available in their entirety online

Launching 2011!

⑤SAGE research methods online